Final Hours in the Pacific

ALSO BY DONALD J. YOUNG

The Battle of Bataan: A Complete History, 2d ed. (2009)

The Battle of Bataan: A History of the 90 Day Siege and Eventual Surrender of 75,000 Filipino and United States Troops to the Japanese in World War II (1992)

Final Hours in the Pacific

*The Allied Surrenders of
Wake Island, Bataan, Corregidor,
Hong Kong, and Singapore*

Donald J. Young

McFarland & Company, Inc., Publishers
Jefferson, North Carolina, and London

An earlier form of this book was published as
*The Bitter End: The Final 24 Hours of Wake Island,
Hong Kong, Singapore, Bataan and Corregidor*
(ISBN 0-974-0532-0-1) by Pacific War Study Group in 2003.

LIBRARY OF CONGRESS CATALOGUING-IN-PUBLICATION DATA

Young, Donald J., 1930–
Final hours in the Pacific : the Allied surrenders of Wake Island, Bataan, Corregidor, Hong Kong and Singapore / Donald J. Young.
p.   cm.
Includes bibliographical references and index.

ISBN 978-0-7864-5938-4
softcover : 50# alkaline paper ∞

1. World War, 1939–1945 — Campaigns — Pacific Area.   2. Capitulations, Military — Pacific Area — History — 20th century.   3. Wake Island, Battle of, Wake Island, 1941.   4. Bataan, Battle of, Philippines, 1942.   5. World War, 1939–1945 — Campaigns — Philippines — Corregidor Island.   6. Hong Kong (China) — History — Siege, 1941.   7. Singapore — History — Siege, 1942.   I. Title.
D767.Y68   2011   940.54′25 — dc22   2010045482

British Library cataloguing data are available

© 2011 Donald J. Young. All rights reserved

*No part of this book may be reproduced or transmitted in any form
or by any means, electronic or mechanical, including photocopying
or recording, or by any information storage and retrieval system,
without permission in writing from the publisher.*

Front cover image: Corregidor Island, May 6, 1942 (AP Photo)

Manufactured in the United States of America

*McFarland & Company, Inc., Publishers
Box 611, Jefferson, North Carolina 28640
www.mcfarlandpub.com*

Dedicated to those men who,
with absolutely no hope of victory,
continued to fight on until the bitter end.

Table of Contents

Introduction   1

One. Wake Island's Final Hours   3
Two. Bataan's Final Hours   43
Three. Corregidor's Final Hours   87
Four. Hong Kong's Final Hours   129
Five. Singapore's Final Hours   145

Chapter Notes   175
Bibliography   177
Index   179

Introduction

This work covers the final days and hours of those places in the distant Far East that, with no hope of holding out against the Japanese, fought on to the bitter end. This poem, as a final epitaph to the hopelessness of their struggles, was written by one of the thousands of men who, though their lives were fraught with unknowns, kept fighting on:

> I see no gleam of victory alluring
> No chance of splendid booty or of gain
> If I endure — I must go on enduring
> And my reward for bearing pain is pain
> Yet, though the thrill ... the hope are gone
> Something within me keeps me fighting on.
>
> Lt. Henry G. Lee
Bataan 1942

From December 7, 1941, until the battle of Midway in June 1942, the war with Japan was a losing one. It became the darkest period of the entire three-year, nine-month-long Pacific war. Of those days, none were darker than the final hours for those embattled men trapped on Wake Island, Bataan, Corregidor, Hong Kong, and Singapore.

Although the Japanese had to fight to take Wake Island and Hong Kong, their fate was actually sealed even before the first shots were fired. The first to go was Wake, which held out for 16 days before surrendering on December 23. Two days later on Christmas Day 1941, Hong Kong fell.

In Malaya and the Philippines, there were standing armies that would take a major effort by the Japanese to overcome. Following the staggering loss of Malaya, however, Singapore, after just eight days of fighting, gave up on February 15.

The loss of vaunted Fortress Singapore and the capitulation of over 100,000 men to a Japanese army of less than a third of its size shocked not only the British Empire, but the entire free world as well. In the Philippines, the key to holding the islands was the Bataan Peninsula and the island fortress of Corregidor, which, in combination, blocked the Japanese from securing Manila Bay and claiming victory there. The Americans and Filipinos held out on Bataan for three months before surrendering as much to starvation and disease as to the Japanese.

Corregidor, whose fate once Bataan fell was a foregone conclusion, hung on another month, surrendering on May 6, 1942.

This book about the bitter end to their ordeals covers the crucial days and final hours that led to their surrender. As the end neared, it was by then, of course, no surprise to any of those involved. The only question was how it would come: would it be like the Alamo — a knock-down, drag-out fight to the death on the last day, or would it be a peaceful surrender to avoid a last stand ending and possible massacre? The defenders of Wake and Corregidor, despite facing the inevitable, courageously chose to fight it out to the end rather than concede to the obvious. Hong Kong, Singapore, and Bataan, on the other hand, whose troops, unlike those at Wake and Corregidor, were exhausted and close to collapse, chose to surrender peacefully rather than fight to the bitter end.

Once the capitulations were accepted, however, the most crucial and delicate task, that of laying out the surrender terms, had to be negotiated. None were easy or without threats made by the Japanese. As might be expected, few conditional requests made by the vanquished British and Americans were granted, whereas little or no choice was given them as to accepting their captors' terms and demands.

As the end grew near for those on the front lines, thoughts of surrendering to an enemy already known for their atrocities and mistreatment of prisoners filled most with anxiety and trepidation as to what might be in store for them when the end came. Sadly, it was a feeling that for tens of thousands was well-founded.

This book is a revised and expanded version of my 2003 book *The Bitter End: The Final 24 Hours of Wake Island, Hong Kong, Singapore, Bataan and Corregidor*, which was never sold commercially. Continued research unearthed additional information that made this expansion possible.

CHAPTER 1

Wake Island's Final Hours

The fate of the 439 U.S. Marines of the First Defense Battalion, 77 sailors, 6 army personnel and 1,146 construction workers on tiny Wake Atoll following the Japanese attacks throughout the Western Pacific on December 7 and 8, 1941, was not, until its final 24 hours, a foregone conclusion.

Despite the results of the devastating Japanese air attacks on December 8 — where nine of Marine Fighter Squadron 211's twelve Grumman F4F fighters were destroyed and 11 civilians and 23 Marines killed — and despite air attacks on December 9, 10, 11, 12, 14, 16, 17, 18, 20, and 22 involving approximately 350 enemy sorties and the loss of the last F4F on December 22, there was still hope that Wake could be saved.

Up to the last 24 hours, Wake had more than held its own against the Japanese. Along with shooting down ten enemy planes and counting close to a dozen probables by fighter and anti-aircraft action, on December 11 the defenders had frustrated a Japanese invasion attempt by sinking two and damaging seven enemy ships, taking the lives of an estimated 700 men in the process.

When the enemy invasion force, composed of the heavy cruiser *Yubari*, two light cruisers, six destroyers, four troop transports, and two submarines, was spotted, it was anticipated that the Japanese could pound the tiny atoll into submission, after which the 450-man landing force could walk ashore.

At 3:00 A.M. on December 11, the overall commander on Wake, Navy Commander W. Scott Cunningham, asleep at his quarters at Camp Two, was awakened by a phone call. It was from the battalion command post on Wake.

A few minutes earlier, Marine lookouts had spotted what they said was "some sort of movement" off the southern coast of the island, at which point they contacted the Marine commander on the island, Major James Devereux. After seeing for himself, Devereux notified Cunningham, and the two agreed that the only chance they had was to passively wait until the Japanese got well within range of their 5-inch guns before returning fire. Hopefully, if the damage inflicted by the enemy guns remained minimal, the non-response from Wake would draw them well within range. Perhaps the greatest ploy of World War II, it worked.

By the time Devereux's commence fire order came at 6:10 A.M., the *Yubari* had turned and was running broadside to Battery A on Peacock Point, two and a half miles out — point-blank range for the battery's two 5-inchers. Before the big cruiser escaped, it was severely damaged from the five hits it took from the two guns.

Over on Wilkes, not to be outdone, shells from Battery L made a direct hit on the unsuspecting destroyer *Hayate*, which had also crept to within 4,500 yards of the island.

Both shells from the battery's third salvo hit the ship, and the ensuing explosion caused it to break in two and sink within minutes.

Accurate fire from Battery B at Toki Point on Peale then forced three unsuspecting destroyers, behind a hastily laid smokescreen, to turn and high-tail it out of range.

It was now VMF-211's turn. Somehow they were able to get four patched-up F4Fs into the sky as soon as the 5-inch guns opened up. The four planes, led by squadron commander Major Paul Putnam, caught up to the fleeing enemy ships in time to attack with 100-pound bombs off of improvised bomb racks and liberally strafe every ship in sight. Twice more the planes returned to attack, the last time only two of the four making the run.

The ensuing damage inflicted by the four planes, in what would be their biggest day of the 16 days of Wake Island, amounted to sinking the destroyer *Kisaragi*, damaging both light cruisers and two troop transports.

The victory was not without a price, however. The fuel line on Captain Hank Elrod's plane was hit on the second attack, forcing him to nurse the sputtering, crippled fighter back to Wake. With everyone holding their breaths as he approached the island barely over the waves, he crash-landed on the beach. Although the plane was a total loss, as he was being helped unscratched out of the cockpit by a relieved Putnam, he apologized. "Sorry as hell about the plane, Skipper," he said.

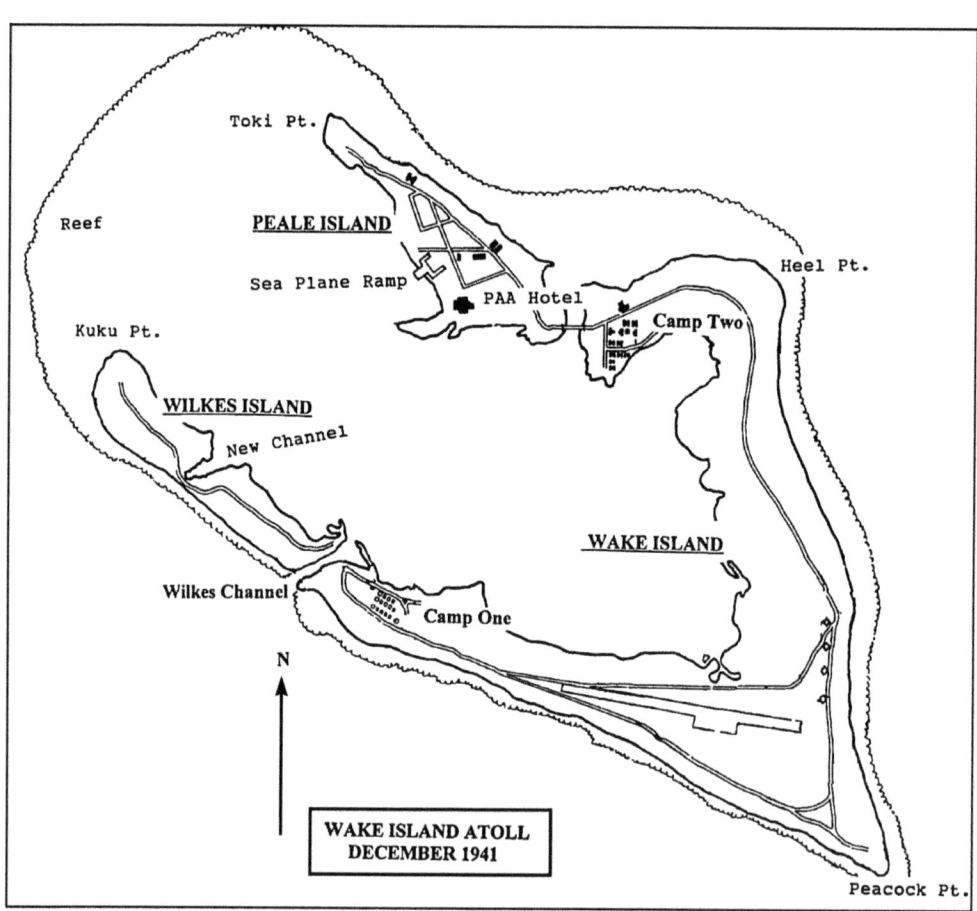

On the same run, Herbert Fueler's Wildcat was also shot up so badly that, although he was able to nurse it back to the airfield, it had to be totally written off.

Although down to only two planes, the day was still not over for VMF-211. The daily routine air patrol of the air approaches to the island would still have to be flown. Two anxious second lieutenants, Carl Davidson and John Kinney, who, although disappointed that they had missed their chance against the ships of the foiled Japanese invasion, would end up feeling more than compensated for that lost opportunity.

On the northeast leg of their patrol, they spotted 30 Japanese bombers heading for the tiny atoll, which they ripped into with all guns blazing. Two enemy bombers were shot down on the first pass, and a third, trailing heavy smoke and losing altitude, broke away from the formation and headed for home.[1]

For years controversy would accompany Japanese first-day success in the Pacific against Pearl Harbor, the Philippines, and Malaya. Although not involving the first day of the war or enemy success, controversy would not escape the story of Wake Island. It actually began on Tuesday, December 9 (10 at Wake), in Pearl Harbor.

Working from an amended war plan from Washington, Pacific Fleet commander Admiral Husband Kimmel and his staff put together a plan to reinforce both the air and ground forces at Wake.

Fearful of weakening Hawaii's ability to defend itself against a possible Japanese invasion and of weakening the already decimated Pacific fleet, only 200 Marines and 18 obsolete Brewster Buffalo fighters were allotted for the relief force to fight its way, if necessary, through to Wake.

The bulk of what was called Task Force 14 was made up of 13 combat ships, including the carrier *Saratoga,* heavy cruisers *Minneapolis* and *San Francisco,* and nine destroyers. The oiler *Neches* was to accompany the force to refuel the destroyers, along with the seaplane tender *Tangier,* to carry the Marines.

The next day, December 10, as the Marines of the 4th Defense Battalion eagerly awaited their orders to get under way, the expedition was halted. Although temporary, sadly it would mark the first of many decisions involving orders for the task force to go or not to go.[2]

The first inkling Wake got that help might be on the way came on December 12, when CINCPAC (Commander-in-Chief Pacific) inquired, as Commander Cunningham remembered, "on the status of aviation material for maintaining planes" and for "a report on the ammunition situation."

Eight days later, on December 20, the question of reinforcements was positively answered when a PBY came in from Pearl with sealed orders containing information on the relief expedition.

"We were to prepare to receive another fighter ... squadron," said Cunningham. "Ground troop reinforcements were on the way (and) all but 350 civilians were to be evacuated." Although the "estimated date of arrival ... was not indicated ... it was enough to send our spirits soaring."

The reason the date of arrival was not indicated, Cunningham guessed, because it was impossible to predict.[3]

The 15-ship task force got under way on December 15. Seven days later, on December 21, they were 625 miles from Wake. Fourteen of the fifteen ships had been forced to a 12-knot speed because of the only ship they could not leave behind—the oiler *Neches.*

At that point, Admiral Frank Jack Fletcher, in command of the task force, was faced with a dilemma. To push on to Wake without refueling his destroyers, he felt, could jeopardize their ability to maneuver in case of a running sea battle with the Japanese. By the time he decided that caution was the better part of valor, the weather had deteriorated to the point where it took all day on the twenty-second to refuel just four ships.

Two days earlier on December 19, another task force was also 625 miles from Wake, only this one included two carriers, nine cruisers, 15 destroyers, a mine layer, five transports, and a seaplane tender. That day the 31 Japanese ships left their base at Roi-Namur in the Marshall Islands for Wake, except this force was not only two days ahead of Task Force 14, but also would not be held up by refueling situations or a command racked with indecision and doubt.

Relative to the latter, while Task Force 14 was fighting the stormy seas to finish refueling the last four destroyers on the 22nd, events were taking place back at Pearl that, magnified by the refueling problems, would lead to the cancellation of the entire operation.[4]

On December 17, ten days after the attack on Pearl Harbor, Admiral Kimmel was relieved as CINCPAC commander. Although Admiral Chester Nimitz was appointed to replace him, he wouldn't be in Pearl until December 25. In the interim, Vice Admiral William Pye was given the job — and with it the unenviable position of having to make the difficult decisions regarding Task Force 14.

Throughout the 22nd, as the Americans pushed on toward Wake, the day was rife with orders from Pearl.

The first, influenced by a 9:00 A.M. message from Commander Cunningham that Wake had just been attacked by carrier planes, brought Pye to order the *Saratoga* to steam full speed to within striking range of the Japanese, and launch her 18 Buffaloes. Before the order could be carried out, however, it was countermanded.

Because the *Saratoga* was deemed too valuable to expose to attacks by Japanese carrier planes, Admiral Fletcher was then ordered to send the *Tangier* on ahead to evacuate everyone from the island. But that too, was rescinded.

As the Japanese landing force moved into position in the early morning darkness of December 23, the American task force, although some 20 hours sailing time from Wake, was still not giving up hope.[5]

On Wake itself, in anticipation of the Japanese invasion, whenever it came, Major Devereux had gambled that the southern shoreline between Peacock Point on Wake and Kuku Point on Wilkes would be the location of the main assault. Along with it being the leeward side of the island, it was the only side of the tiny atoll where the surrounding reef was close enough to allow enemy landing craft reasonable access to the beach.

Protecting the four-and-a-half-mile-long area between the two 5-inch batteries on Peacock and Kuku points were a scattering of 13 beach defense guns. These included seven .50 and five .30 caliber machine guns and one 3-inch gun on Wake that could be brought to bear on the beach.

The nearly 3-mile stretch of shoreline along Wake's south-facing beach, the most logical objective for the Japanese, as Devereux had guessed, was particularly lightly defended.

Outside of the 3-inch gun that was located near the beach about halfway down the runway, there were only three .50 caliber machine guns available to cover the highly exposed mile-and-a-quarter area fronting the airstrip. Between there and four .30 caliber machine guns located opposite abandoned Camp One, the three-quarters of a mile of open beach between the two was totally undefended.

1. Wake Island's Final Hours

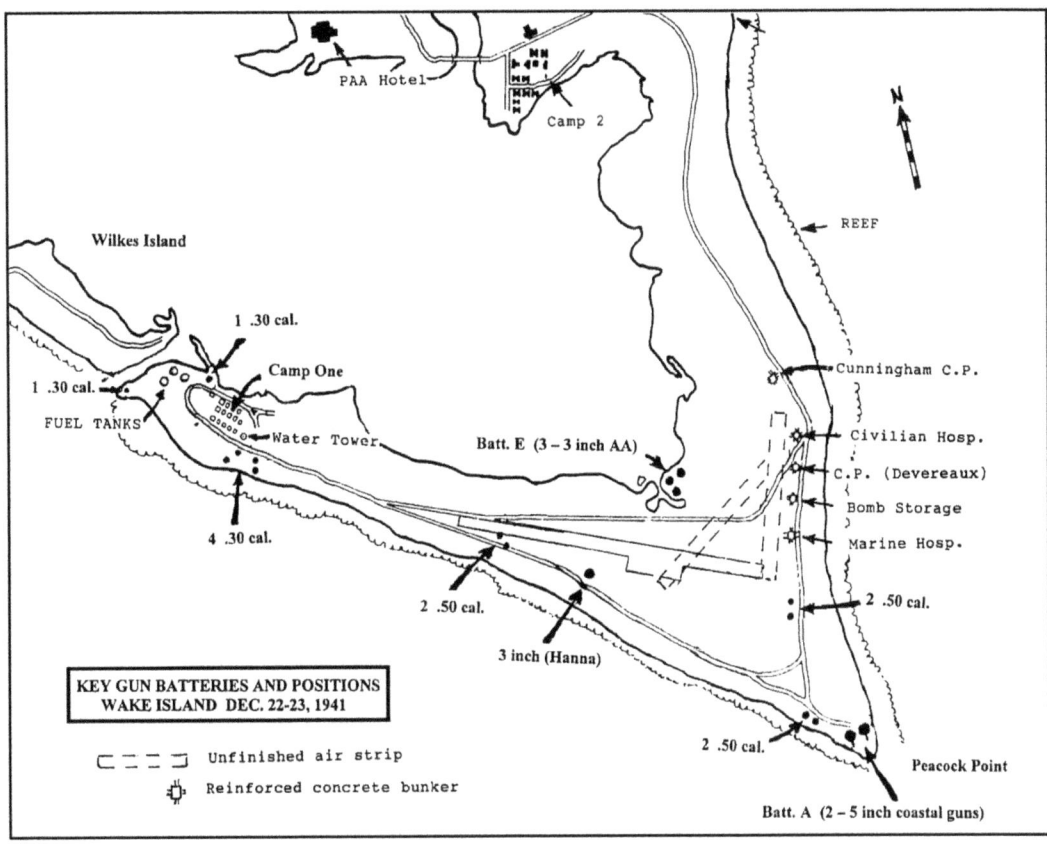

To cover the entire area between Peacock and Wilkes Channel, Devereux assigned, as he said, "85 Marines and a handful of volunteers." Despite being convinced that the invasion would be launched against the southern shore, "[It]" he said, "was the best I could do to defend our front door without leaving a back door wide open for the Japs to walk in."[6]

On the nearly isolated western end of Wilkes, a mile from the western tip of Wake, Captain Wesley Platt had four .50 and two .30 caliber machine guns and a contingent of 70 Marines—a much better ratio of men and guns per yard of beach than on Wake.

A not-so-obscure factor in the final battle was what is variously referred to as the dense undergrowth, scrub, bush, or brush that dominated close to 80 percent of the Wake atoll. It would play a role that both aided and hindered both sides.

Looking at his chances, Devereux said the obvious: "We were in for a bad time unless reinforcements arrived before the Japs did, and every man on the island knew it."

Since the air attacks on Wake by Japanese carrier planes on December 21 and 22, there was little doubt in anyone's mind that a second invasion attempt would be coming within 24 hours.

The first indication that Japanese ships were present came late on the night of the twenty-second, when a series of strange flashes far to the northwest was seen by practically everyone on the island. That they were from the approaching enemy invasion fleet there was little doubt. Other than that and alerting the Wake defenders that the anticipated wouldn't be long in coming, no one knew what caused it.

Actually, the flashes were from gunfire from the Japanese cruisers *Tenryu* and *Tatsuta*, which had been assigned to circle north of the atoll and bombard Peale in hopes of drawing U.S. attention away from the planned landing on the island's southern shore. They had somehow lost their bearings and fired at an empty stretch of sea far to the northwest of the island.

Commander Cunningham, reacting to what he called the "report of lights," at 1:45 A.M. messaged Pearl Harbor, "Gunfire Between Ships to Northwest of Island."

"[With] no definite conclusion as to their meaning," he said, "I went back inside my command post and was about to try for a little more sleep when the first blow fell."[7]

It came when Gunner John Hammas from Devereux's command post notified him that Captain Platt on Wilkes had just reported "ships on the horizon."

Unknown to Cunningham, a few minutes earlier a message had also awakened Major Devereux with news that the Japanese were landing.

Corporal Robert Brown, half awake with the phone to his ear, heard a voice on the other end say, "There are enemy ships off Toki Point." Brown reached over and shook Devereux. "The enemy is reported off Toki Point, sir!" he said in an anxious voice.

"Any confirmation?" he asked.

"No sir."

Devereux quickly called Lt. Woodrow Kessler, commander of the 5-inch gun battery at Toki Point. "Any boats beached?"

Kessler told him that there were lights but no landing yet, but one of his observers spotted "bobbing lights" and small boats off the north shore. "I'm ordering beach defenses manned," he said.

At that point, Devereux got Captain Platt on Wilkes again, telling him of Kessler's report. Platt, in turn, instructed his Battery L commander, Lt. John McAlister, to send 30 men from one of his gun sections to the north side of the island as a precaution against an attempt to invade from the lagoon side.

Despite this, Devereux was still sold on the probability that the Japanese would land on Wake's southern shore, particularly after Kessler called back a few minutes later informing him that, aside from "plenty of lights out there," there was still no enemy landing.

"I passed the word that the Toki Point landing was a false alarm," said the Marine commander, and that "he had not yet made his move."

Unfortunately for the Marines, it was a rainy, windy, stormy night, so black that, as Devereux put it, "no matter how alert a man may be ... he can't see through a wall—and the darkness around the island was a wall."

Wall of darkness or no, soon reports of "movement off shore" and "some kind of craft close in" began coming in from all along the southern shore.

Wesley Platt from Wilkes reported what looked like a destroyer 4,600 yards off Kuku Point and requested permission to use his searchlight. "I notified Devereux, who asked Cunningham for permission," remembered Gunner Hammas. The island commander, until he was absolutely sure the ships were not part of the U.S. relief force, ordered him "not to use searchlights or open fire until further notice."

Moments later, when the Japanese opened fire on the island, Devereux had John Hammas contact Cunningham for permission to fire back. "What are we waiting for, John?" said Cunningham. "Open fire. Must be Jap ships all right. Open fire!

A few minutes later, Cunningham messaged CINCPAC, "Island Under Gunfire X

APPARENTLY LANDING." Remembering that the *Triton*, one of the two submarines that had been operating in the waters around Wake, was still in the vicinity, Cunningham yelled to the radio operator, "Send a message in plain English directing the *Triton*, if it [hears] us, to attack enemy ships to the south!"[8]

The Japanese, meanwhile, anticipating trouble with the reef fronting Wake's southern shoreline, had decided to sacrifice two old destroyers that had been converted to transports for the operation, by running them full-speed up onto the reef. The two ships, officially Patrol Boats 32 and 33, carrying approximately 140 men each, both would hit the reef opposite the east end of the airstrip.

It was 2:35 A.M., Tuesday, December 23, 1941, and the battle for Wake Island was about to begin — a battle whose outcome was dictated by two elements: darkness and, for the Americans, the deciding and most damaging factor, confusion caused by the total loss of communications, which came just minutes into the fight.

Because of this and the total lack of coordination it brought to the isolated units scattered along the four-and-a-half mile-southern shoreline, the stories of the eleven-hour battle that both started and ended on Wilkes are written without reference to each other.

For the first few minutes it was darkness that led to the confusion. Over on Wilkes, Gunner Clarence McKinstry, commander of the 3-inch battery on the island, was the first to detect a motor noise over the incessant roar of the waves pounding on the reef. He called Captain Platt at his command post in the center of the island.

"Are you sure it's a motor, Mac?" asked Platt.

"Yes!"

"Then open fire!"

Seconds later, a stream of tracer bullets from the nearest .50 caliber machine gun that cut loose at the motor sound momentarily illuminated a large enemy landing craft a few yards off the reef.

At that point, Lt. John McAlister, commander of Battery L, who had moved eight men from his battery range section into position behind and just east of McKinstry's 3-inch gun, yelled to Platoon Sergeant Henry Bedell to "send two men to grenade that boat."

"Yes, sir," said Bedell, who, picking himself as one of the men, shoved a handful of grenades into the arms of 19-year-old PFC William Buehler, and said, "Come along."

Moments later, the two men broke out of the scrub onto the beach, throwing grenades as they advanced toward the faint outline of the enemy landing craft. Although none of their tosses came close to the boat, the grenades momentarily stopped the Japanese at the water's edge. Then Bedell, as he threw his last grenade, was shot dead. Buehler, seeing his comrade fall to the ground, was also hit, but was able to scramble back to McAlister.

"Sir, they got Bedell. He's dead," he said, not mentioning that he had been hit in the foot.[9]

Reacting to the sound of gunfire, Platt quickly called Devereux, asking permission to turn on the searchlight.

"Permission granted," replied the Marine commander.

The truck-mounted searchlight, which had been damaged in the December 10 bombing and had not worked well since, stayed on for about 60 seconds before flickering out, long enough, however, to illuminate the enemy barge and momentarily transfix the advancing Japanese.

"Cut the fuses to zero," McKinstry shouted to his largely civilian crewmen, while he quickly bore-sighted one of the guns before the light went out. Despite the adjustment, the guns, located on the edge of a steep slope above the beach, could not be depressed enough for direct fire. Realizing this, the Japanese were quick to work their way around the battery, where they began lobbing grenades into the gun pits.

Recognizing that they were in an untenable position, McKinstry had his men remove the breech blocks from the guns then fall back to the road. As they pulled back, they were joined by Sergeant Edwin Hassig and his squad of searchlight operators, together numbering 15 riflemen plus several civilian volunteers.

Although McAlister was initially unaware of McKinstry's presence, they soon linked up forming the semblance of a line running from the New Channel some 300 yards west to a position on the road above the battery.

The Japanese in the meantime wasted no time in going after McKinstry but were stopped and forced to fall back into the 3-inch battery area by fire from both his and McAlister's men. Although unable to get a visual fix on the enemy because of the darkness and the stormy conditions, McAlister told his men to "fire at the muzzle flashes."

Once their position in the 3-inch gun pits had been secured, Japanese commander Ensign Toyoji Takano dispatched a patrol to attack Battery L's 5-inch guns near Kuku Point.

Standing in its way was a single .50 caliber machine gun manned by PFC Sanford Ray.

Located some 75 yards west of the 3-inch guns, it was the tracer fire from Ray's gun that first illuminated the Japanese landing craft.

If there was a key to holding Wilkes against the 100 Japanese of the Special Naval Land-

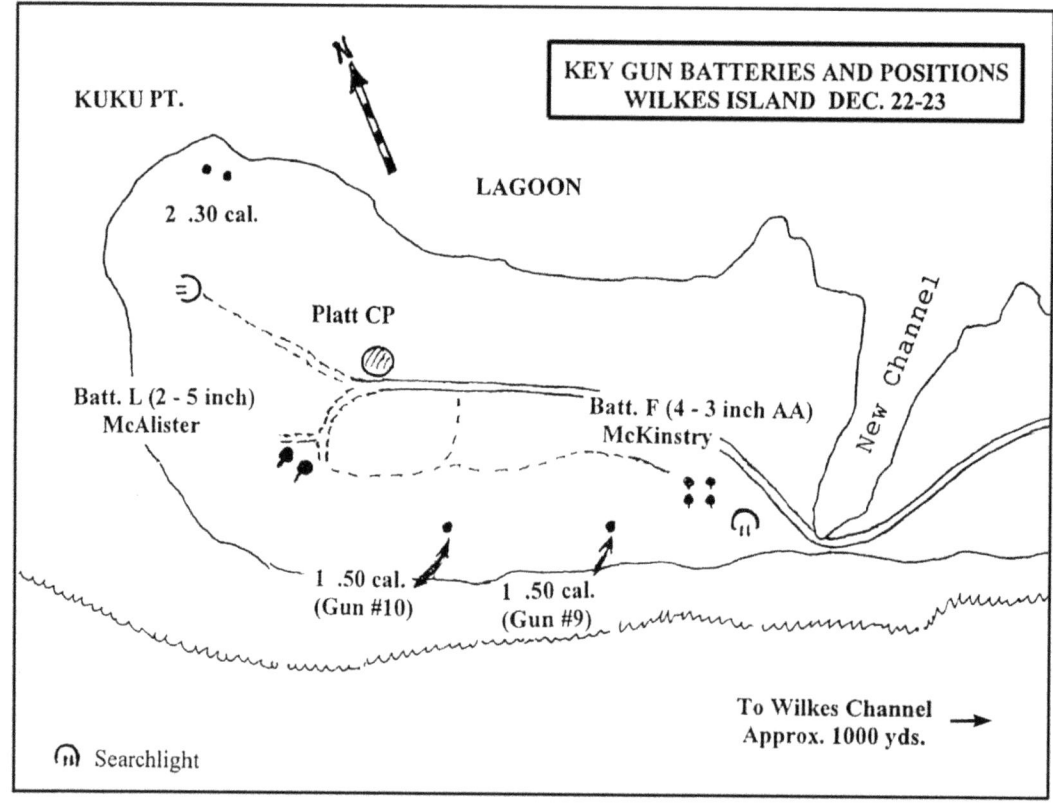

ing Force (SNLF) — a rough equivalent to a U.S. Marine assault force — it was the defense put up by Ray and his gun crew throughout the early morning.

Despite several rushes by the enemy, from his well-camouflaged position Ray single-handedly was able to keep the enemy from moving any closer than 40 yards from his gun.

He was so effective, in fact, that outside of harassing fire from a handful of the enemy whom he had forced into the brush along the beach, he forced the Japanese into giving up trying to capture Battery L altogether.

Around 3:00 A.M., approximately 25 minutes after the main Japanese landing on Wake, all lines of communication between Major Devereux's command post and every Marine unit that either was or would soon be involved with the enemy went dead, severed no doubt by the invader.

On Wilkes, not only did Captain Platt lose contact with Devereux, but with both McKinstry and McAlister as well.

The only line open was to PFC Ray's .50 caliber position, but for a moment it seemed that even it was in jeopardy.

It happened when Ray called Platt to tell him that he was in trouble.

"Sir," he said, "they're all around me."

Could he hang on? Platt asked.

"We can try, sir."

An eruption of gunfire, punctuated by the unmistaken sound of Ray's .50 caliber, was followed by silence. Then Platt's phone rang. "We're still here, sir," said Ray.[10]

Frustrated by the loss of communications, around 4:00 A.M. Platt decided he had to find out for himself what was happening. With the continuing sound of small arms fire

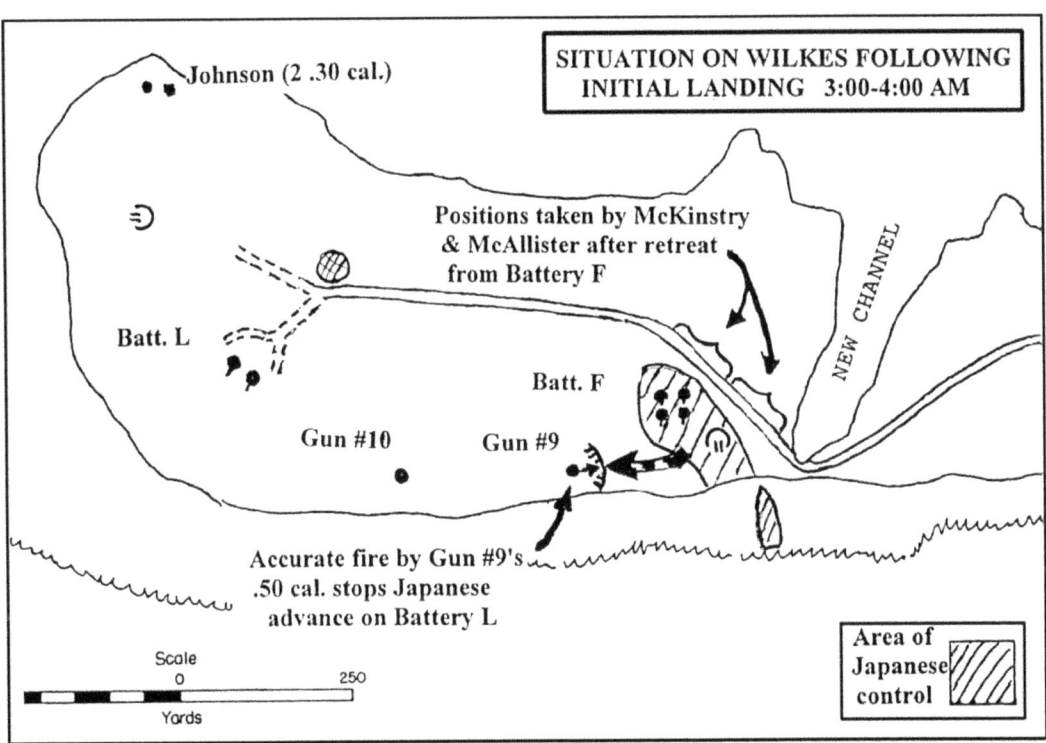

coming from the 3-inch gun position and still able to communicate with PFC Ray, he knew his Marines were making a fight of it, but that was all.

At 4:30 he set off toward the sound of gunfire, cautiously darting in and out of the thick brush and coral outcroppings along the beach until he reached Gun 10, some 350 yards from the 3-inch position. From that point he crawled along the beach to a point where, in the early morning light, he saw something that he could not believe. The Japanese, so concerned on what was happening to their front, had, as Platt said, "no security to their rear."

Scrambling back to Gun 10, out of breath he told Sergeant Raymond Coulson, commander of the .50 caliber gun platoon on Wilkes, to hustle across the island and bring back the two .30 caliber machine guns from Kuku Point, along with the second searchlight crew and anyone else he could find.

An hour later Coulson returned with eight Marines from the searchlight but no one else.

Unknown to Platt and Coulson, Corporal John S. Johnson, in command of the two .30 calibers, realizing the threat of an enemy landing from the lagoon side of Wilkes was a false alarm, had already pulled out his two guns and their crews and headed for the sound of PFC Ray's Gun 9s .50 caliber.

His crew, made up of a single Marine and six civilians carrying the two .30s, tripods and all, with belts of ammunition in case they ran into trouble, looked, remembered Johnson, "like a combination of pack animals and Mexican bandits."

Nearing PFC Ray's position, they were fired on as they moved into the brush. Pinpointing the enemy position, Johnson quickly devised a plan of attack. With covering fire provided by one machine gun, the crews of the second gun, tripod and all, would sprint forward a few yards, set up its gun and cover the first as it leapfrogged past them.

The process would be repeated until return fire from the enemy position stopped. It worked. Johnson found the bodies of seven Japanese in the scrub just off the beach.

By the time Johnson had pulled his men back to Gun 9, Captain Platt appeared with Sergeant Coulson and the eight Marines. At that point, Platt formed his makeshift group into a skirmish line, anchored on each end with a .30 caliber machine gun and a single rifleman. Filling the 30-yard space between were two lines of three riflemen.

Platt's plan was to advance as close as possible to the unsuspecting enemy's rear, then open fire when they were spotted. Because he was unaware of the situation with McAlister and McKinstry, he ordered his men on the machine guns to "shoot short, well-aimed bursts" and "only at targets identified as Japanese."

With Platt in position behind the beachside .30 caliber, the 11 Marines and six ammunition-carrying civilians advanced some 40 yards before they were spotted by the surprised Japanese.

Meanwhile, McAlister and McKinstry, who had joined forces but were still totally unaware of Platt's assault, had begun a move to recapture the 3-inch gun position. It was decided that McAlister would push in against the enemy's right flank from the beach. McKinstry would lead his fifteen Marines and six civilians against the Japanese center. A third force of Marines, probably from Battery L, who had initially been ordered to the lagoon side of the island and led by Corporal Alvey Reed, would attack out of the bush from the right.

Before McAlister and McKinstry split up, they ran into a three-man Japanese patrol moving east along the beach.

1. Wake Island's Final Hours

Although they killed one of the enemy soldiers, the other two scampered behind a coral boulder, at which McKinstry started forward to clean them out. He was stopped by McAlister, who told him, "No—detail a man for that job."

"I got it, Gunner," replied Corporal William "Whitey" Halstead, who moved forward to a spot overlooking the crouching enemy. From his position behind a large rock, he threw two grenades down on the surprised Japanese, then quickly "finished them off" with his rifle.

With six-foot-three McKinstry in the lead and diminutive Corporal Halstead close behind, the two men led the charge out of the bush against Japanese holed up and dug in around the 3-inch battery.

Following close to keep everyone supplied with grenades were civilians "Chuck" Smith, Forrest Read, John Schultz, and three other construction workers who had initially volunteered to work as ammunition handlers for McKinstry's 3-inch gun.

It was quite a show—civilians feeding grenades to McKinstry and other Marines who, in turn, threw them at the Japanese.

Unknown to McAlister and McKinstry as they fought toward the 3-inch emplacement, the assault by Platt on the enemy's rear had forced Takano to reduce his forward defense by at least 30 percent. Nevertheless, the Japanese did not make it easy. With the bulk of his men positioned around the four 3-inch guns, the Japanese commander placed riflemen and machine guns around the outside of the battery to cover the flanks.

As the Marines worked their way toward the gun pit, they witnessed something the Japanese would come to be known for in the three-and-a-half years of Pacific war to come—playing dead.

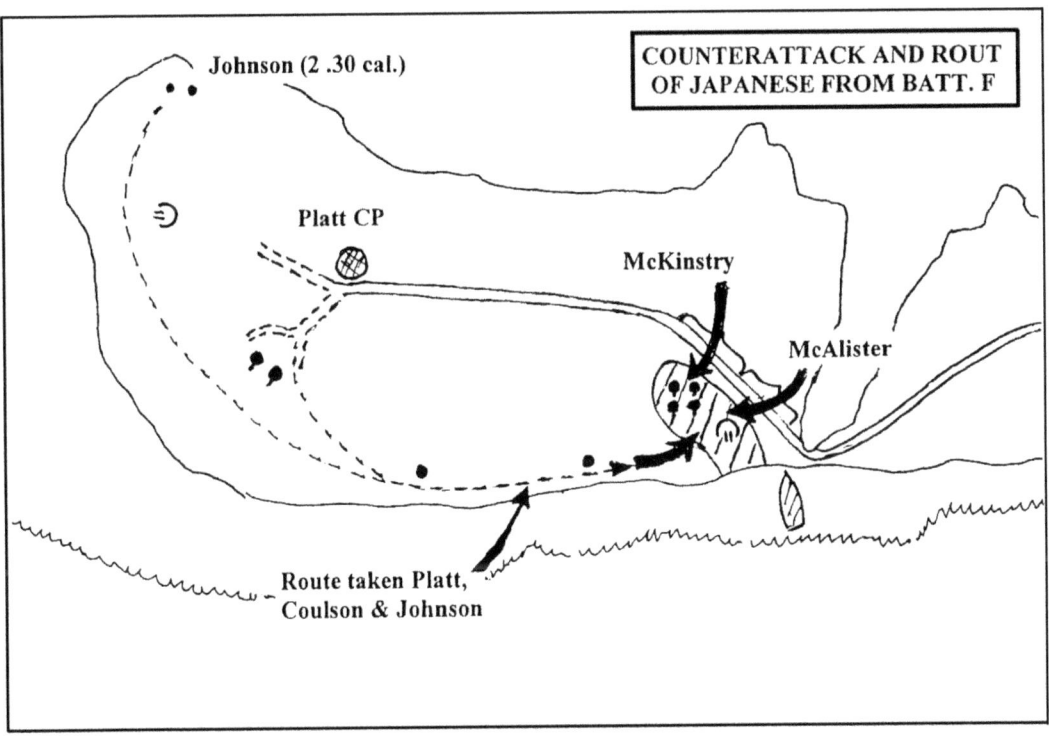

It happened when the Marine in front of McKinstry passed an apparently dead enemy soldier, who suddenly rose up and attempted to bayonet him in the back. He was quickly shot and killed, bringing McKinstry to yell, "Be sure the dead ones are dead!"

As they began to close in on the Japanese, the big Marine seemed to be everywhere, throwing grenades, directing fire, yelling at his men.

An enemy machine gun had pinned down one of his men, PFC Wiley Sloman, behind a coral rock. Spotting three Marines crouched in a nearby shell hole, he yelled for them to go after the gun. "Come on," he said. "Move forward! Move ... or I'll shoot you in the ass!"

Unknown to McKinstry, Sloman mistakenly thought he was yelling at him. "Look, you S.O.B.," he said to himself, "I can't walk into that machine gun. Give me some time before you start shooting at me."[11]

When the Japanese turned their fire toward the three advancing Marines, Sloman also started forward but was shot in the head, falling to the ground. Although left for dead, he was found alive on December 25, two days after the surrender.

As he worked his way closer to the emplacement, McKinstry spotted several Japanese in one of the 3-inch shell storage bunkers that had been dug into the hillside. With Corporal Halstead as his side, the two men threw grenades, then rushed the position.

Although the grenades did the job on the Japanese in the bunker, Halstead was hit square in the chest by automatic weapon fire. He fell dead at McKinstry's feet.

As the Marines moved in on the emplacement itself, five Japanese scampered up the bank and disappeared into the brush. As Corporal Robert E. Lee, cautiously checking the area for live enemy soldiers, came around the base of one of the 3-inch guns, he found himself face to face with a bayonet-wielding supposedly dead Japanese that he had nearly stepped on moments before. Facing each other with fixed bayonets, they both lunged, missed, then lunged again. This time neither missed, the two men fatally impaling each other.[12]

As McKinstry, who had seen the five Japanese escape into the brush, started after them, he saw someone in a Marine uniform move up from the beach. It was Wesley Platt, who, grinning, said, "Mac, that ugly voice of yours sounded like an angel's when [I heard it]."

McKinstry waved, then continued up the bank. "Bring back one alive, Mac!" shouted Platt.

The Japanese McKinstry was after were not the only ones who escaped, or rather that attempted to escape. Thirty enemy soldiers who were flushed out of the battery foolishly took refuge under the searchlight truck.

They were quickly spotted by marines searching the area for stragglers. Unresponsive to attempts to coax them into surrendering, marine riflemen and Corporal John Johnson's .30 caliber machine gun made quick work of them.

"I kept the trigger on the machine gun depressed and watched the bullets going where I wanted them to go," said Johnson. "[With] every fourth bullet a tracer, I realized how severe the gun fire was as shrieks and screams came from the Japanese.... [When] the machine gun quit ... our riflemen leaped up and charged forward with fixed bayonets."[13]

As soon as the battery was secured, Platt assigned Lt. McAlister and 10 men to reconnoiter the area around the 3-inch position for wounded and possum-playing enemy soldiers, and to "get [him] a count of the dead ones." He then led a handful of men on a sweep of the island, finding only one man, a dead Japanese officer whose body was found on the lagoon-side beach.

It was 7:30 A.M., and the fighting on Wilkes was over.

All totaled, the count of enemy dead, including the five dispatched by McKinstry, came to four officers, including Ensign Takano, and 90 enlisted men. Two wounded possum-playing enemy soldiers were captured. Four Japanese, if the number of invaders was an even 100, were never found.

U.S. losses were eleven killed — nine Marines and two civilians. Four Marines and a civilian were wounded.

The battle for Wilkes, which took place on the westernmost half of the island, was over a mile away from the nearest fighting on Wake. The combination of both isolation and loss of communications not only made the victory over the Japanese on Wilkes meaningless in the long run, so was it the same for the fighting on the western end of Wake itself.

When Major Devereux was awakened earlier that morning with word that lights had been seen off Toki Point on Peale, the conversation was overheard over the warning net by Second Lieutenant Arthur Poindexter.

Even before Devereux got off the phone with Toki, Poindexter left a message that he was loading up his mobile reserve and on his way.

Located at Camp One, the unit, officially designated as Defense Force Mobile Reserve, was made up, as he said, of the "spare parts" of the detachment, including "remnants of my machine gun battery [two sections of .30 caliber machine guns under Sergeant Q.T. Wade] and all of the special-duty personnel [including] cooks, truck drivers, ordnance mechanics, supply clerks, and a searchlight crew — 20 Marines in all. Also assigned," he continued, "was a detachment of about 18 very young sailors under Boatswain's Mate 2nd Class James Barnes and a dozen more civilians. We were dubbed 'mobile' because we were provided with a couple two-and-a-half ton trucks to transport [us] to where the enemy might attempt to land.

"Sergeant Wade already had his machine gun crews and a couple of squads of riflemen loaded into our trucks," said Poindexter, who, jumping on the running board of the lead vehicle, ordered the driver to proceed to the command post.

By the time the young second lieutenant entered the CP, Devereux had received enough information to have him stand by until the situation was clarified. It was cleared up a couple minutes later when Lt. Kessler at Toki Point called Devereux back to tell him that his report of landing boats off Peale was a false alarm.

"With reports coming swiftly from all along the southern beach of movement off shore," said Devereux, "I ordered Poindexter to take his mobile reserve to the most lightly held sector of the southern beach between the airfield and Camp One."

"I dashed back to the trucks and we sped back toward the airfield," said Poindexter. "Within 15 minutes we reached a point west of the runway, where two roads converged in a 'Y' to form a junction. I ... emplaced two machine guns on each side of the road, facing east toward the airfield. The guns ... on the right had a clear field of fire along the roadway and down the beach."[14]

By the time they had set up their machine guns, the two Japanese converted destroyers, Patrol Crafts 32 and 33, had already scraped bottom on the reef a few yards off the beach. Their presence was supported by defensive fire from the 3-inch gun halfway down the runway.

While the belts of .30 caliber ammunition were being loaded into the machine guns, Poindexter, hoping for advance warning of possible enemy infiltration from the airfield, ordered Sergeant Gerald Carr to send a man to challenge anyone coming down the road toward them.

Carr detailed anxious civilian volunteer John Valov, who, with an '03 Springfield rifle in hand, took off down the road into the black, stormy night.

A few yards down the road, he spotted several dim figures moving across in front of him. "Who goes there?" he yelled. Not only was there no response, but the figures suddenly disappeared into the bush.

Valov fired one shot then turned and ran back toward the position, calling for Carr to open fire, that the enemy had landed.[15]

"Both machine guns opened fire," said Poindexter, "[but] by the time we were in action, several hundred [enemy] troops had already worked their way ashore.

"Flares then illuminated [their] assembly area [a pre-arranged signal indicating the landing had been accomplished], and my gunners and riflemen [did] great work interdicting their movement and discouraging them from fanning out toward [us].

"At about this time I heard several machine guns open up to our rear," said Poindexter. "They were our machine guns manned by the bluejackets [behind us] near Camp One."

Concerned that the inexperienced young sailors might be "firing at shadows or imaginary targets," Poindexter, leaving Sergeant Wade in command, jumped into a truck and was driven a quarter mile down the road to where they were dug in.

Unable to see anything because of the muzzle flashes from the two guns, Poindexter yelled at one of the gunners, "You goddamn sailors are firing at shadows!"

"I chewed them out in the most emphatic terms for wasting ammunition, until, when they ceased firing and I was able to move forward a few yards, I made out the silhouette of two large landing craft maneuvering up to the reef."

Dashing back to the gun, as he said "like a striped-ass baboon," he grabbed one of the guns and began firing, "laying a stream of tracers on one of the craft."

Unable to beach themselves on the steep edge of the reef, the two boats backed up and moved parallel to the shoreline for a few yards, then headed in again.

"While they continued this," he said, "we peppered them with machine gun fire from all four guns, the tracer fire [however] ricocheted harmlessly off the sides of the craft."

At that point, Poindexter decided that his only option was to attack them with grenades. "Boatswain's Mate Barnes agreed to join me," said the young Marine, "and we moved cautiously toward the water's edge. [It] was difficult to judge distance as we crept toward the nearest landing barge. When we thought we were within range, we heaved the grenades. Each of us threw two, but ... they fell short."[16]

Unaffected by the two men's efforts, the Japanese continued to probe the shoreline for an opening in the reef.

With the enemy soldiers in the landing craft unable to offer a threat until they landed, Poindexter and Barnes, joined by Sergeant Carr and a civilian World War I veteran named Raymond Rutledge, decided to have another try.

With each man carrying four grenades, they waded out near the coral heads of the reef to get close enough to lob them into the boats. Barnes, holding his grenades until one of the barges ground ashore, hurled all four of his at the boat then scampered back with the rest.

"After our second attack, I was satisfied we had neutralized the landing craft," said Poindexter, "and, worried more about the Japanese landing near the airfield, I returned to the position at the (road junction)."[17]

Unknown to the game young lieutenant, he had overestimated the effectiveness of his grenade attack. Although two or three may have exploded in the barges, once beached solidly on the reef, an unknown number of enemy soldiers, aided by the dark, rainy night, were able to cross the beach and work their way into the heavy underbrush between Camp One and Mobile's position back at the "Y."

One of the first indicators of Japanese presence in the area came when the two Navy lookouts on the water tower at Camp One were sniped at, forcing them to quickly abandon the position.

The only other pre-daylight incident involved another sailor, who was bayoneted in the rump by one of the Japanese who had infiltrated Camp One. A Marine, alerted by screams from the bluejacket, shot and killed the brave but foolish enemy soldier.

When Poindexter arrived back at the Mobile Reserve position, Sergeant Wade, with panic in his voice, said, "[The Japs] are all around us, sir! They're on our left flank and maybe our rear!"

"I knew it was high time to evacuate the area before they turned our flank and surrounded us with our backs to the ocean," said Poindexter.

Before pulling back he called Devereux on the warning net to fill him in on what was happening. Poindexter told him that he was being flanked and was being pushed back toward the [Wilkes] channel. Then, as what happened on Wilkes and to virtually every unit engaged with the Japanese on the island's south shore at that moment, the line went dead.[18]

Poindexter directed Wade to pull the left machine gun section back 150 yards then cover the beach-side section as it fell back. "We repeated this tactic throughout the night as we withdrew toward Camp One," he said. "The enemy's difficulty in moving through the dense scrub on the inshore side of the atoll saved us from annihilation."

It did. In fact, by using the scrub to conceal their presence and movements, the Japanese, despite outnumbering the Mobile Reserve by at least three to one, found it virtually impossible to coordinate or sustain any offensive action.

Poindexter, on the other hand, when his small force reached the "flat, cleared ground of the Camp One area, with clear visibility all the way across the island," decided it was a good place to set up a line of defense.

As soon as the withdrawal was completed, Poindexter sent two men into the Camp One area to scout up as many men and guns as they could. Platoon Sergeant Dave Rush returned with six machine guns that he found in the camp gun shed, bringing Mobile's number to ten.

PFC Jim Rasor, who was given the job of having all the Camp One special duty personnel fallout with rifles, found his order met with reluctance. Checking the camp bomb shelter first, he found 20 men sitting in its dark confines.

"The lieutenant says for everyone to grab a rifle and move up to the line on the other side of the water tower."

His order was met with silence, that is until Corporal Cyrus Fisher, a slight, bespectacled quartermaster clerk, stood up, grabbed a rifle, and said, "Well, what are we sitting on our asses for?"

The courage displayed by the least likely among them apparently shamed the rest of the truck drivers, supply personnel, and others into joining Fish. "With their arrival I now had a small force of fifty-five to sixty [Marines]," said Poindexter.[19]

It was now close to 7:00 A.M. Anticipating an attack by the Japanese facing the Camp One area, the young officer spread out his ten machine guns, each supported by riflemen and ammunition-carrying civilians, all the way the way across the open area.

"All the guns were 'laid in' with interlocking fields of fire extending across the entire width of the island," said Poindexter. "I then organized three squads of riflemen to bolster any part of the line that might require reinforcements."

Hampered by the dense undergrowth from which they were forced to attack, all Japanese attempts against the line were piecemeal and easily beaten off.

Around eight o'clock, Poindexter, with the steady sound of gun fire coming from Peacock Point, decided he'd had enough: "With the enemy only probing and delivering sporadic small arms fire [against us], I decided to use my support squads to mount a counterattack. The Marine Corps," he said, "had taught me that the only way to accomplish anything is to take the offensive."

His plan was to use the three 10-man squads of Marine riflemen he had put together as reinforcements against a Japanese breakthrough. With one in support, two would alternately leapfrog forward down the beach road. "The support squad would follow to protect the exposed left flank," he said. "Sergeant Wade would have a section of machine guns ready to move up on my order. Sergeant Rush would remain in the rear echelon command post to provide a supporting fire from the left."

With Poindexter and his runner, PFC Pershing Bryan, at the head of the support squad, the counterattack began. Success was immediate. Within 30 minutes, they had reclaimed close to 500 yards of ground.

"We advanced by bounds, right and left," said the young lieutenant. "The squad on the right moved rapidly, clearing the enemy from bomb craters on the beach that they were using for foxholes. Tangled brush slowed the squad on the left, but we made progress.... Sgt. Wade complied promptly when I passed the word for him to move forward with his machine guns. He also brought more hand grenades to distribute to the assault riflemen. I then directed him to emplace his guns to protect our exposed left flank because my line of skirmishers extended into the brush for only about 50 yards." Not wanting to worry about how many enemy troops they bypassed as they moved forward, he said, "When we detected any movement on the flank, we tossed grenades in that general direction or let loose a few bursts of machine gun fire and kept advancing.

"At our rate of advance, we soon would be able to link up with whatever Marines were still holding out at the airfield, and perhaps ... we could effect a juncture with Marines who might be moving toward us from Peacock Point."[20]

By 11:15 A.M., some eight-and-a-half hours since Arthur Poindexter's Mobile Reserve had originally taken position at the "Y," they had fought their way back to the same spot.

This time, however, the young lieutenant's mind was on attacking rather than defending from the position.

Five hundred yards east of his position at the junction of the two roads was the end of the airstrip. Following the devastating air attack on December 8, Major Paul Putnam, believing that enemy bombers had purposely avoided hitting the runway so it could be used to fly in troops when the invasion came, decided to blow it up before that happened.

Dynamite charges, placed along the edge of the runway at 150-foot intervals, were wired to a small gasoline generator that was located in a sandbagged position on the south side of the strip, 300 yards east of the end of the runway.

On the afternoon of December 22, following the loss of VMF-211's last plane and its pilot, Lieutenant Carl Davidson, Putnam and his entire squadron reported to Major Devereux for infantry duty.

1. Wake Island's Final Hours 19

Maps drawn from memory by Arthur Poindexter

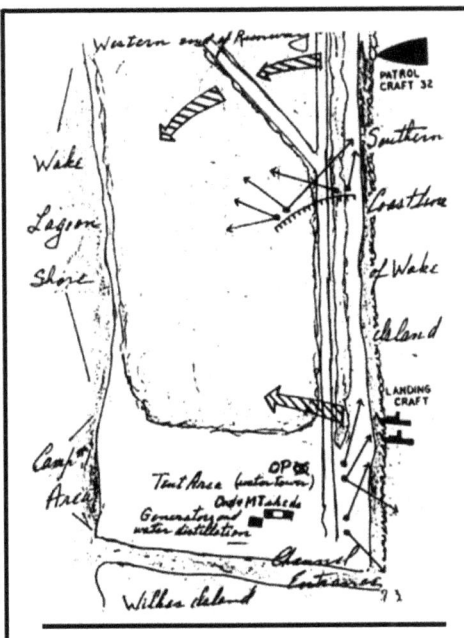

Map No. 1 - Mobile Reserve's position at "Y" and Japanese landings and penetration - 3:00-4:00 AM 12/23/41

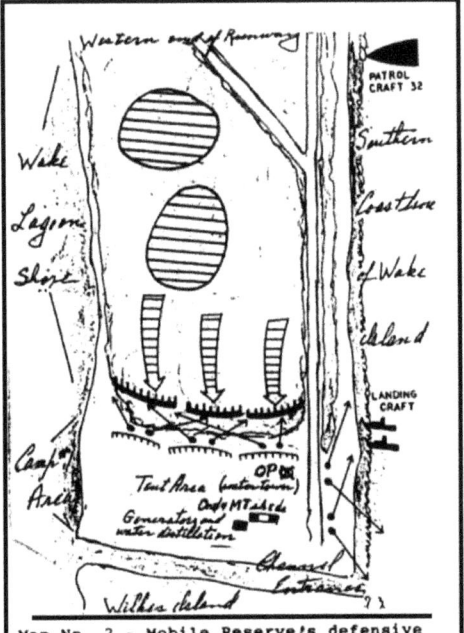

Map No. 2 - Mobile Reserve's defensive position at edge of Camp One clearing, approx. 6:30 AM.

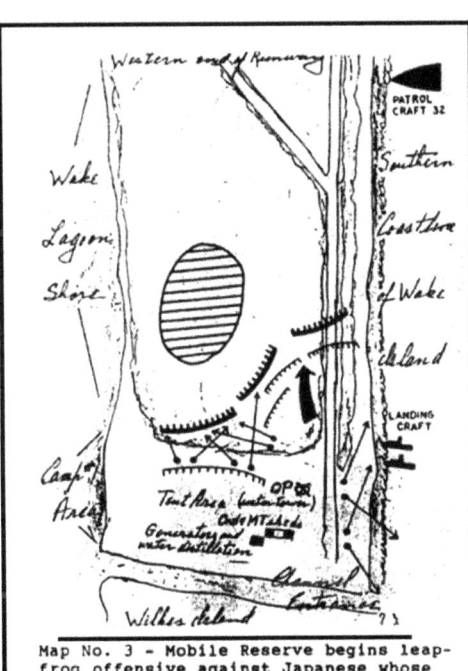

Map No. 3 - Mobile Reserve begins leap-frog offensive against Japanese whose attacks are subdued by dense scrub.

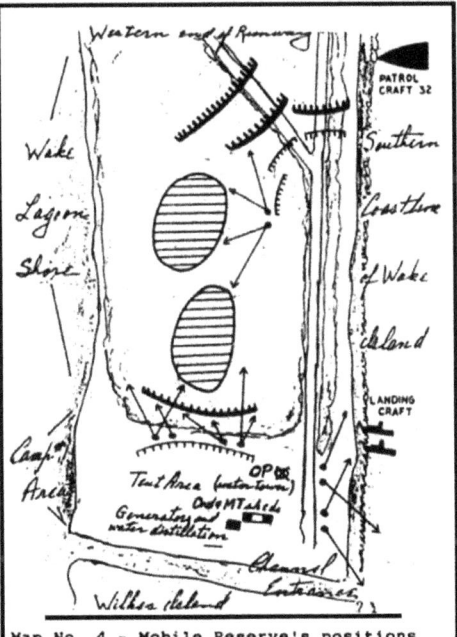

Map No. 4 - Mobile Reserve's positions at "Y" and Camp One at time of surrender, approx. 12:30 PM.

Early the next morning when the Japanese began landing on the south shore, Putnam ordered Second Lieutenant David Kliewer and three veteran Marine aviation NCOs, Staff Sergeant John Blandy and Sergeants Robert Bourquin and Carroll Trego, to the generator with instructions to blow up the airfield upon orders from the Marine commander.

The four men were armed with two Thompson sub-machine guns, two boxes of grenades, and three .45 pistols.

Ironically, by the time the four VMF boys reached the generator, Japanese Patrol Crafts 32 and 33 had hit the reef.

Obscured by the rain-driven wall of darkness and therefore unknown to Kliewer, Patrol Craft 33 was getting ready to disgorge 140 Japanese Special Naval Landing Force troops directly in front of his position — obscured, that is, until shots from the 3-inch gun, located some 500 yards east, caused it to literally blow up.

Although the burning ship was 400 yards in front of Kliewer's position and well out of range of their Tommy guns, they could see Japanese troops stagger out of the surf, the bulk of them moving east toward the 3-inch gun.

It is not known when the Japanese discovered the four Americans. What is known is in the all-night battle against infiltrating and occasional wildly charging enemy troops, they fended off everything thrown at them.[21]

By daylight, it appeared that scenario would be played out. Throughout the night, all of the enemy attacks against the four men had come from the east. In the darkness, however, several Japanese had crossed the runway and gathered in the heavy undergrowth northwest of the field.

It was from this position at dawn that they rushed Kliewer's position. Unknown to the Japanese, however, one of the two .50 caliber machine gun positions Major Devereux had set up along the south shore was dug in at the end of the runway, some 150 yards west of the four Marines.

When the Japanese came charging out of the brush and across the runway toward

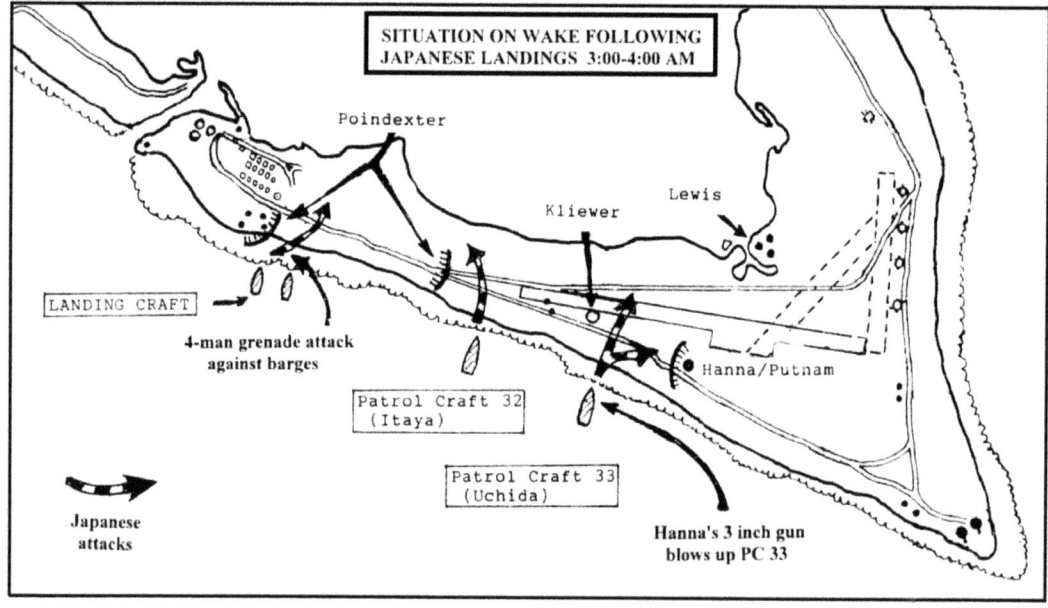

Kliewer, two .50s were quickly swung toward the unsuspecting enemy. Their devastating fire and the sub-machine guns and grenades of the four men broke up the attack.

As things quieted down, Kliewer got a chance to look around. What he saw presented a discouraging picture — Japanese flags planted all along the beach in both directions. As had happened to everyone else, communications with the Command Post had been lost at 3:00 A.M. The decision to blow up the airfield was now his and his alone. Although sporadic gunfire could still be heard, he decided it was time.

"We'll set her off and then retreat to that .50 caliber position behind us," he said.

Unfortunately, the rain that had fallen throughout most of the night had dampened the ignition. Try as they might, they could not get the stubborn generator to start. For over an hour the four men, despite being interrupted several times by infiltrating Japanese and another attack from the airfield, cussed and struggled unsuccessfully to get it started.[22]

About 20 minutes before Patrol Craft 33 hit the reef in front of Lt. Kliewer's position, it was spotted by Second Lieutenant Robert Hanna, officer in charge of the .30 and .50-caliber machine gun sections protecting the two and a half miles of southern beach from Peacock Point to Camp One.

Hanna quickly contacted Major Devereux, who, in turn, relayed the information to Battery A on Peacock Point. By the time Lieutenant Clarence Barninger had readied one of his 5-inch guns to fire, the ship had disappeared behind a small sand hill west of his position. Unable to elevate the gun because of the near point-blank range, the disgusted battery commander told Devereux he was unable to fire on the ship.

Following the Japanese attack on December 8, it was decided that the 3-inch anti-aircraft batteries, the island's primary defense against air attack, would have to be moved periodically to avoid the enemy from zeroing in on them in future raids.

Despite the moves, which proved successful, one of the four guns of Battery E, originally located on Peacock Point, had its control mechanism shattered in one of the raids, making it useless as an anti-aircraft weapon.

In line with Devereux's belief that the Japanese invasion would be launched against the island's southern shore, he had the damaged gun dug in on a slight rise between the shore road and VMF 211's parking stand for use as an anti-boat weapon.

Unfortunately, using it to defend against an enemy landing would be difficult, as none of the army's 3-inch AA guns came equipped with sights for direct fire, nor had a crew been trained or assigned to use it.

As the officer in charge of defending against an enemy invasion, Hanna, who earlier had been assigned to Battery D's 3-inch antiaircraft battery on Peale, asked Devereux for permission to man it himself. His request was granted.

Grabbing Corporal Ralph Holewinski, in charge of one of his .50 caliber machine gun sections, and three civilian volunteers, Bob Bryan, Paul Gay, and Eric Lehtola, Hanna and the four men took off running for the 3-inch position.

Even though no one had been assigned to crew the gun, several rounds of high-explosive ammunition had been stored nearby in anticipation of it having to be used.

In the several minutes they had before Patrol Craft 33 was spotted on the reef, Hanna quickly refamiliarized himself with the operation of the gun. He assigned Holewinski to work the traverse wheels and for the three civilians to keep the ammunition coming. With no sight, it had to be aimed by opening the breech and sighting through the bore until the target came into view.

With all five men straining to spot the enemy ship through the black, rain-swept night, PC-33 hit the reef some 500 yards away.

Suddenly, as Hanna remembered, someone on the ship hung what appeared to be a lantern over the side near the bridge. Opening the breech he peered down the bore as Holewinski traversed the gun until the target came into view. At that point he raised his hand to stop, shoved a 3-inch shell into the breech, locked it and pulled the lanyard.[23]

In the excitement, no one knew if it was the first or second round that hit the enemy ship. All everyone knew was that it appeared to hit amidship near the bridge. Unknown to the excited Americans, the shot killed two Japanese sailors outright and wounded seven, including the ship's captain and navigator.

With only minor adjustments needed between rounds, a dozen more high-explosive shells were rapidly pumped into the enemy ship.

A Japanese in the PC-33 landing party, recalling those first moments, said,

> With a loud crunching sound, the ship rode up onto the shore.... As we started to rise to our feet, the enemy opened fire all at once. Out of the darkness in front of us, shells came shrieking like a thousand demons let loose.... Several men fell where they stood. Clambering down ladders and ropes, we disembarked in great haste. But we were still not on land, as our ship had gone on a reef. The water was so deep we could hardly walk. Rifle in hand, we desperately fought our way forward.... The resisting fire of the enemy grew to a mad intensity. Lying flat on our faces on the beach at the edge of the sea, we could not wiggle an inch. The enemy's position seemed no farther than fifty yards away.... Bullets began to pass close to our backs, but we could not move an inch.... We could not maintain this for much longer. It was either death or a charge at the enemy. An inch at a time we crept [forward] ... twenty yards before the enemy we charged.... Huge shadows which shouted something unintelligible were [heard] one after another.[24]

One of the last shells fired at the ship evidently hit the powder magazine, the explosion causing it to burst into flames. For the Marine defenders, totally in the dark up to then because of the stormy conditions, the burning ship lit up the entire beach in front of the airstrip like it had been illuminated by searchlights. Arthur Poindexter, when he saw it, noted that "[the] tremendous blaze illuminated the beach for several hundred yards."

Seven hundred yards west of PC-33, the explosion had exposed the second enemy landing craft.

"We spotted PC-32 when PC-33 lit up with the fireworks display," said Hanna. "As soon as I determined that our first target was a goner, I switched to the new one. Like PC-33, it too was point-blank shooting, maybe 1,200 yards. Every round of the 24 or 26 we fired hit one of the two ships."[25]

Although hit several times, it did not blow up or catch fire. What his accurate fire against the two ships did, however, was force the crews of both, amounting to close to 100 men, to abandon the boats and join the invading troops on the island.

The moment Robert Hanna opened fire on PC-33, unofficially announcing that the enemy landing was underway, Major Devereux called Paul Putnam at the airfield. Realizing that Hanna's position would become the focal point of the Japanese assault, "I ordered [him] to place his aviation personnel as infantry between the 3-inch gun and the beach to protect Hanna while he fired," he said. "Major Putnam had Hank Elrod, David Kliewer, Captain Tharin, and perhaps twenty enlisted men."

With no telephone communications between his command post and Hanna or Putnam, Devereux, like with Platt and Poindexter, would remain totally in the dark as to their tactical situation until the end.

After sending Lt. Kliewer and the three men to the generator with orders to blow up the airfield if and when all seemed lost, Putnam the two officers, and ten aviation Marines started across the airfield for Hanna's position.

A few steps underway, Putnam halted his little band, turned, and walked back toward the end of the file.

Because of the heavy losses suffered by VMF-211 on December 8, that same night 22 civilian construction workers volunteered to fill in for the 23 squadron men who were killed that day.

Where the majority of the civilians had done little but sit in shelters or hide in the brush after the attack, it is estimated that close to 300 of the 1,146 on the island participated in some military-related capacity during Wake's sixteen days.

Because of the actions of the loyal 22 civilians, Putnam walked back to speak to them. It seemed that they had decided to accompany their adopted squadron into battle.

"You can't go with us," he said. "If you're captured in combat, your chances are mighty poor."

At that point, John P. "Pete" Sorenson, acknowledged leader of the group, stepped forward and, towering over Putnam, said, "Major, do you really think you're big enough to make us stay behind?"

Putnam, ignoring Sorenson, said, "I'm proud of you. I'd be glad to have you as Marines. But take off. Join the other civilians." He then turned, and at a fast pace led his men toward the steady sound of Hanna's gun.

Putnam's orders having fallen on deaf ears, all 22 civilians, loaded down with all the ammunition they could carry, fell in behind the line of Marines, both soon disappearing into the dark, forbidding night.[26]

By the time the VMF boys reached the 3-inch gun, PC-33 was burning brightly enough for them to see, as predicted, that it had become the enemy's main objective.

Ralph Holewinski remembered that after they fired twenty or so rounds at the two ships, "bullets from small arms began to hit the brush around us, and when a few hit the gun barrel, Hanna told us to get down off the gun platform."[27]

Establishing a line some 30 yards in front of the gun, Putnam initially spread his twelve men facing west on both sides of the beach road. Unknown to him, however, a large group of Japanese had crossed the road and worked their way around to his right, taking position in the brush and dug-up area around the unfinished aircraft revetments on the south side of the field. It would be from here that most of the trouble would come from.

As the first faint light of day began to show across the eastern horizon, the Japanese opened up with several rounds from their Type 89 grenade launchers, called knee mortars by the Americans. This was followed a few minutes later by an all-out attack against Putnam's line.

On the left side of the Marine position, the Japanese SNLF sailor who earlier had described the effects of Hanna's 3-inch gun on PC-33, said that they had steadily crept forward "an inch at a time. Twenty meters before the enemy," he said, "we prepared to charge. 'Charge!' the commander's voice rang out.

"We jumped to our feet and charged.... One large figure appeared before us to blaze away with a machine gun from his hip as they do in American gangster films."

The "large figure" referred to was probably Aviation Machinist's Mate First Class James Hesson, who courageously jumped up from his position and "blaze[d] away" with his Thompson sub-machine gun, killing several Japanese in the process.

One of those killed may have been Lt. Kinishi Uchida, commander of the 140 SNLF troops from PC-33. In fact, his shout to "charge" was no doubt the last word he ever said, as no sooner had he stood up and yelled than he was shot in the head.[28]

Not far from Hesson's position, fire from another automatic weapon was also heard. It was from Frank Tharin, who had yanked a machine gun out of the hands of a dead Japanese and used it, as he said, "successfully and effectively against its former owners."

A few yards to the right of Hesson and Tharin, two Japanese, who had silently crawled to within a few feet of Paul Putnam, suddenly jumped up. The startled major, who had been lying on his stomach under a bush, quickly rolled over and emptied his .45 into the two men, killing both; one fell nearly on top of him and their helmets collided. In the midst of the close quarter battle that ensued, Putnam saw Pete Sorenson get hit. The big man was standing up throwing rocks at the Japanese when he was cut down.

Defending the right flank of Putnam's line was Captain Hank Elrod, three or four Marines, and a few civilians.

Because of the dense scrub into which he had been forced to establish his position, defending against the enemy assault was particularly difficult.

When the Japanese came charging out of the bushes, Elrod, with sub-machine gun in hand, jumped up and yelled, "Kill the sons of bitches!" at which he raked the attacking enemy with fire. Together with his Marines and three or four of the civilians firing discarded rifles, the enemy assault was momentarily stopped.[29]

Results against what had become scattered although uncoordinated Japanese attacks against Putnam's line soon began to take its toll. Of the three officers, Hank Elrod was the first to go down. Witnesses said he was shot, as he prepared to throw a grenade, by a Japanese lying among the bodies of several of his own dead.

The courage and leadership the young captain showed in the brief encounter that morning, coupled with his record as an F4F pilot, earned him the Medal of Honor—the only one given in the battle for Wake Island.

Relative to his contributions that morning, the citation reads:

> Captain Elrod assumed command of one flank of the line ... and conducting a brilliant defense, enabled his men to hold their position and repulse determined Japanese attacks, repeatedly proceeding through intense hostile fusillades to provide covering fire for unarmed ammunition carriers. Capturing an automatic weapon during one enemy rush ... he gave his own firearm to one of his men and fought on vigorously against the Japanese. Responsible in a large measure for the strength of his sector's resistance ... [he] led his men with bold aggressiveness until he fell mortally wounded.[30]

Elrod's death, coupled with building enemy pressure against his right flank, forced Putnam to order what was left of his battered group to pull back all the way to the 3-inch gun, forming them in a north-facing horseshoe-like position with their unguarded backs to the sea. As he moved his men back, he yelled, "This is as far as we go!" It was.[31]

Putnam, who took position under the gun platform next to Hanna, was shot by an infiltrating Japanese. After disposing of the sniper with his .45, Hanna tended to 211's commander. "He was shot in the face," said Hanna. "He was bleeding and tried to stop it with his bandage pack. When it became soaked with blood he asked me for mine, which I gave him. It wasn't until daylight that we discovered that the bullet had hit his jawbone, making an ugly wound. It then hit his throat a glancing blow which left a bruise but somehow didn't break the skin. Ironically, the bruise on his neck was where he felt the most pain and not where he was bleeding. Between the jaw blow and loss of blood, he passed out from time to time."[32]

Perhaps unknown to the Marine flyer, by reducing his perimeter around the gun it gave his men, whose numbers, including civilians, amounted to perhaps two dozen, their best chance against a far superior number of Japanese.

With its ammunition expended, the 3-inch gun ceased to exist as an effective weapon. Finding themselves, like Putnam's men, in a life or death struggle with the Japanese, Holewinski and the three civilians, Gay, Bryan, and Eric Lehtola, had taken position on the east side of the gun platform, where, throughout the early morning hours, they battled the enemy with grenades, rifles, and a single .45 automatic that was shared by Gay and Bryant. Holewinski later wrote:

> One of the civilians took a box of grenades that were left by the 3-inch gun. He used up the whole box by himself. A lot of grenades were thrown at us, but many didn't go off. We were at very close quarters. The Japs were brave or stupid, as they would crawl toward us in the brush then get up on their knees to take aim. It was easy to get them first. One got so close, I could see the blood come out of his forehead when I shot him. Two more came up to see what had happened. I didn't wait for them to get that close to our gun.[33]

Around 8:30, Japanese carrier-based planes were launched over the island, one of their focal points being the stubbornly held area around the highly visible 3-inch gun. On the first strafing run by one of the fighters, Gay and Bryan were both killed. Holewinski took a bullet in both legs on the first pass, and two more on the next. Ironically, all four wounds were from bullets that penetrated the perforated steel gun platform under which he had managed to conceal that part of his body.

Although not hit in the strafing, Hanna too, was wounded. "The perforations in the gun platform really didn't afford us that much protection. I had several lead fragments in my left leg from grenades and bullets that hit the pedestal of the gun and ricocheted. I really didn't feel the bullet that hit and lodged in my right knee."[34]

One of the lines of communication that remained open to the command post during the battle was to the 5-inch gun battery on Peale. Immediately after dispatching Major Putnam to Hanna's aid, Devereux called Captain Bryghte (Dan) Godbold, commander of Battery D, ordering him to send one of his two 9-man gun squads to the command post. They were needed, he told him, to reinforce Major Putnam's defensive position around the 3-inch battery.

The squad, under the command of Corporal Leon Graves, arrived 15 minutes later in a contractor's vehicle driven by a civilian. Devereux's orders were to drive down the shore road about a mile to where it turned west, disembark at that point, and work their way as quickly as possible to the 3-inch gun.

Less than an hour later, Corporal Graves was back at the command post. Soaking wet and out of breath, he told Major George Potter, Devereux's executive officer, that they had been stopped from reaching Hanna's position by what he thought might have been friendly fire, but because of the dark night they could not verify exactly who it was.

Potter, after Graves described what happened, judged that because of the short time he'd been gone, they'd been dropped off several hundred yards short of the road junction.

"Owing to the blackness of the night, the absence of land marks, and relative unfamiliarity with [the] vicinity," said Potter, "[I doubt] that ... Graves ... had more than an approximate idea of his own location."

In their conversation, Graves told him that he lost "Hezzie" Picket, a Marine private known to everyone on the island from Devereux on down. The story was that the nickname "Hezzie" had come from the numerous times he had "hesitated" to make PFC. Picket, who Devereux classified as "a good man for morale," had been up for PFC "three or four times before ... Wake, but each time he celebrated his impending promotion so enthusiastically that he always lost his stripe before he actually got it."[35]

With no Marines in the area where Picket had been killed, Potter concluded that the Japanese had penetrated what was called the Peacock triangle—an unconnected V-shaped area anchored by Peacock Point and lines following the coastline west and north a mile or so in both directions.

More confirmation came when both Battery E at the inside elbow of the triangle and Battery A on Peacock notified Devereux that they were taking machine gun and mortar fire.

At that point, Lieutenant Wally Lewis, commander of Battery E, who had located where the flash from the enemy machine gun had come from, bore-sighted one of his 3-inch guns at the spot. With the fuse set at two seconds, a single shot silenced the Japanese gun. He then ordered Sergeant Raymon Gragg to take a 10-man patrol and work his way west down the road north of the runway toward where the enemy fire had come from.

No sooner had Gragg's patrol disappeared into the darkness than they ran into heavy enemy small arms fire, forcing them to disperse into the dense brush on the north side of the road. Although pinned down, their defensive presence kept the Japanese from attacking Battery E from that direction.

Meanwhile, Lt. Clarence Barninger at Peacock, responding to the enemy fire on his position, ordered the men in his range section to grab a weapon and dig in on a sand hill behind the battery.

"Barninger reported he was placing his range section with machine guns to hold the higher ground commanding his position," said Devereux. "Then the line went dead. By this time, we had lost communications with all forward positions except Lewis' battery [E] and a .50 caliber machine gun position just east of the airstrip."

The .50 caliber position he referred to was under the command of Corporal Winford McAnally. With him were six Marines and three civilian volunteers. His two guns were located in the brush off the end of the runway, some 750 yards south of the command post.

McAnally, who had become the eyes and ears for Devereux relating to enemy activity in that area, reported that he was coming under attack by Japanese moving towards him from the vicinity of the south shore road.

Help against the Japanese movement came from a second .50 caliber position located just east of Peacock Point, and with whom McAnally was in communication. By coordinating bursts from the two positions to avoid shooting at each other, they soon forced the confused enemy troops off the road and into the bushes.

Although slowing their advance northward, the Japanese use of the cover provided by the brush into which they had been chased enabled them to discover McAnally's position, which, by the first light of dawn, they had nearly surrounded.

At least six different times the Japanese tactic of infiltrate then charge in an attempt to overwhelm the young corporal's band of ten was beaten off with staggering losses to the enemy.

Following one of the failed attempts, one of the Marines, pointing to a dead Japanese, said, "What the hell's that?"

McAnally took a look. There were two of them, both were wearing goggles and had tanks strapped on their backs.

"Look like men from Mars," he said.

"The 'men from Mars' were Japanese ... armed with flamethrowers," said Devereux when he got word of the two unusually uniformed men. "They had been sent to burn out the position still holding up their advance."[36]

A few minutes later McAnally contacted Devereux. "Sir," he said, "we've got to have some help if we're going to hold."

Devereux told him he had no reinforcements and to pull back if he had to.

The young corporal, looking at his men, not one of which had even been wounded, thought for a second and said, "Well, I reckon we can make out a little bit longer."

Realizing after their conversation that it was just a matter of time before his tiny force would be overrun and that there was nothing behind him to stop the Japanese from reaching the command post, Devereux told Major Potter to round up everyone he could find, including Corporal Graves' squad, and set up a defense line across the shore road 100 yards south of the command post.

Including headquarters, supply, and service personnel, by about 6:00 A.M., Potter had close to 40 men spread out across the road. Once the line was established, McAnally, sadly forced to leave his two dug-in, water-cooled, .50 caliber anti-aircraft machine guns behind, was ordered to pull back and link up with the new position.

In the meantime, Devereux called Dan Godbold on Peale and ordered him, outside of his communications section, to bring everyone from his Battery D and the two nearby .50 caliber machine gun sections over by truck to the command post.

While the Marine commander awaited the arrival of the last reinforcements available on the island, he still clung to the distant chance that the relief force would still come through and save them.

In his partially completed, doorless, concrete command post a half mile to the north, island commander Scott Cunningham, because of continuous radio contact with CINCPAC, was already aware that there would be no help from the outside.

Following his 2:50 A.M. message to the 14th Naval District at Pearl Harbor, "ISLAND UNDER GUN FIRE X APPARENT LANDING," he, it will be remembered, told his radio operator to message the submarine *Triton*, which he assumed was still in nearby waters, to "attack enemy ships to the south."

Unknown to him, CINCPAC had overheard the message and responded a half hour later, "TASK UNITS SEVEN TWO FOUR AND SEVEN TWO THREE [Subs *Triton* And *Tambor*] ARE RETURNING PEARL X NO FRIENDLY VESSELS SHOULD BE IN YOUR IMMEDIATE VICINITY TODAY X KEEP ME INFORMED X PYE."

"At 3:19 [the] chilling reply came," said Cunningham.

"It was not from *Triton*, but from Admiral Pye's headquarters." Reading between the lines, he knew that the anticipated relief expedition had, as he said, "been called off. ... We were on our own."[37]

Although the decision to call off the expedition was the right one given the circumstances, it was not easy or without controversy.

Unknown to Cunningham, of the messages he sent to Pearl that fateful morning, it was his 2:50 "APPARENT LANDING" one that triggered the decision to recall the task force.

With the expedition still some 20 hours' sailing time out from Wake, upon receipt of the message, Admiral Pye sat down with his chief of staff and operations officer in an effort to decide what to do.

The two primary questions were: Could Wake hold out until the task force arrived, which meant at least another 24 hours; and second, whether it did or not, could they risk a battle with an enemy force of unknown strength, which could result in the loss of the carrier *Saratoga,* or worse?

The question was answered at 7:30 A.M. [5:00 A.M. Wake time], when Pye was handed a second message from Cunningham: "ENEMY ON ISLAND X ISSUE IN DOUBT."

With the main reason for the entire operation — the relief or rescue of the Wake garrison — apparently gone, Pye decided to recall the task force. His justification was supported by a dispatch from the Chief of Naval Operations in Washington that he received a half hour earlier. It read, in part, "General considerations and recent developments emphasize that Wake is now and will continue to be a liability."

The liability he referred to related directly to the possible loss of American ships should the expedition continue.

With the loss of the island to the Japanese now all but confirmed, Pye considered the CNO's message an indirect order to call off the expedition.

Elaborating further on its message in his meeting to decide on the fate of the expedition, Pye said, "The time of enemy attacks by carrier planes the last two days followed by landing operations indicates the enemy has estimated closely the time at which our relief expedition might arrive. They may," he said, "be waiting in force."

After notifying Admiral Fletcher that the operation had been canceled, Pye sent the following reply to Washington:

"The use of offensive action to relieve Wake had been my intention and desire. But when the enemy had once landed ... the general strategic situation took precedence and the consideration of our naval forces became the first consideration. I ordered the retirement with extreme regret."

On board the cruiser *Astoria,* Frank Jack Fletcher, after receiving Pye's message, angrily exclaimed, "We're called back to Pearl Harbor!" after which he yanked off his cap and flung it to the deck in disappointment and disgust.

Needless to say, the reaction was the same throughout the entire task force. On board the *Saratoga,* the ship's captain was urged to contact Fletcher and request permission to launch an air attack on Wake the next morning. It was denied.

Disappointment later turned to controversy, as many claimed Fletcher's decision to refuel his destroyers caused an unnecessary delay that, in the end, took away the task force's chance to save Wake.[38]

At 10:22, Hawaii received its last message from the beleaguered island. Sent at 7:52 A.M., it read, "ENEMY ON ISLAND X SEVERAL SHIPS PLUS TRANSPORTS MOVING IN X TWO DD [destroyer] AGROUND."[39]

In the nearly 3 hours between "ISSUE IN DOUBT" and the final message, the battle for Wake Island went from one of cautious optimism for some to despair for others.

While Devereux was waiting for Captain Godbold to arrive, Corporal Robert Brown, listening on the warning net at the command post, heard someone whisper, "There are Japanese in the bushes."

"Who is this?" said Brown. "Where are you?"

"There are Japanese in the bushes," came the reply again.

"For Christ's sake, where are you?"

Again, "There are Japanese in the bushes."

Devereux, who overheard the conversation, recalled that "it was like hearing a dead man talk.... He could not even know that anyone was hearing his message. He could only whisper into a telephone ... trying to warn us before they got him ... to warn us before he died. [Then] there was a blast of sound, then silence."

"I guess they got him," said Brown.[40]

About 15 minutes after Devereux's call to Godbold, the first of two Battery D trucks arrived with 20 men. Under the command of Second Lieutenant Robert Greeley, they were immediately double-timed down the road to the line Potter had hastily thrown up.

Some 450 yards in length, it ran from the island's eastern shoreline, across two roads to the unfinished western edge of what was laid out as a northwest-facing airstrip.

It was close to seven o'clock when Godbold arrived in the second truck. Counting his men — a few civilians, McAnally's ten, the eight from Graves, and twenty with Potter — there were close to 80 officers and men available to occupy the line. Although at least 60 were Marines, their automatic weapons amounted to no more than one or two .30 caliber machine guns and a few BARs.

Among the men that came over with Godbold were 16 civilians who had volunteered to assist Sergeant Walter Bowsher on one of Battery D's 3-inch guns. All but two brought weapons they had scrounged up from the wrecked Pan American Hotel. Among them were two .22s, several hunting rifles of various calibers, and shotguns.

Devereux, by ordering Major Potter to establish his line where he did across an area almost totally void of cover, unknowingly took away any chance of holding out. Had there been more natural cover and had he been able to link up with Battery E, some 300 yards of brush-covered terrain east, a stand may have been possible. As it was, the line with its dangling right flank, occupied by no more than a rifle platoon in number, had no chance.

Just outside the command post itself, Gunner Harold Borth, set up what could be called a last-stand position, anchored by two .30 caliber machine guns, their crews, and a few headquarters Marines.

By daylight, if it wasn't already obvious, all one had to do was look out to sea to know it was over. The Japanese fleet "lay in a vast circle around the island," said Devereux, "surrounding us, but far out of range of any gun we had." Not that it made any difference in the long run. The count of enemy ships varied from sixteen light and heavy cruisers to twenty-seven ships of all kinds. Lt. Kessler reported that at least four of the ships were battleships.[41]

Ironically, no sooner had Devereux made his out-of-range comment than came the unmistakable sound of several 5-inch artillery rounds fired from the vicinity of Toki Point on Peale. That they were from Kessler's Battery B, there was no doubt. What was not known was that the nearest of three Japanese destroyers, the *Mutsuki*, had been hit in the eight-shot salvo, seriously enough for it to veer out of formation and head for the open sea. By the time Kessler shifted his fire to the other two ships, both had turned away and were out of range.[42]

What everyone was to soon find out was that Battery B's fire on the three enemy ships brought the Japanese to launch close to 60 bombers, dive bombers, and fighters from the carriers *Soryu* and *Hiryu* against the island.

The immediate target was, of course, Battery B, which took a fatal pounding. That is not to say that Battery E or any of the remaining fixed position guns were overlooked, nor were troops caught hopelessly out in the open.

Particularly hard hit were the men manning Potter's line, the constant threat of strafing from Japanese planes making it virtually impossible for them to move about or sustain any organized resistance against the enemy.

A few minutes before eight o'clock, Devereux called Commander Cunningham to, as he said, "report ... the way the situation looked from my CP." Earlier he had received a call from Kessler on Peale, saying he'd seen several Japanese flags on Wilkes from his position across the lagoon.

"We had no communication with Wilkes ... or any other forward positions," he said, and that "it looked as though the Japs had secured Wilkes, Camp One ... and probably Barninger's position, and was eating his way into the island and Potter's line as the next bite. [Also], Lt. Kliewer's detail should have blown up the airstrip ... but there had been no explosion, and now the enemy was well past [his] position."

"Isn't any help coming?" he then asked Cunningham.

"No, there are no friendly ships within 24 hours."

"Not even submarines?"

"Not even them."

"I told him I needed riflemen desperately, but [he] didn't have any to send," said the Marine commander. "The only riflemen guarding the CP were the five army communications men I had armed when the war began. Five men would not have helped much."[43]

After Cunningham hung up the phone, he wrote out his final dispatch to CINCPAC, reporting that the two destroyers had run aground and that the enemy fleet was moving in. "Then I had all codes, ciphers, and secret orders destroyed, and ordered the ... transmitter antenna hauled down," he said. "It would be too easy for the Japanese dive bombers to spot. Besides, I had no more messages to send."[44]

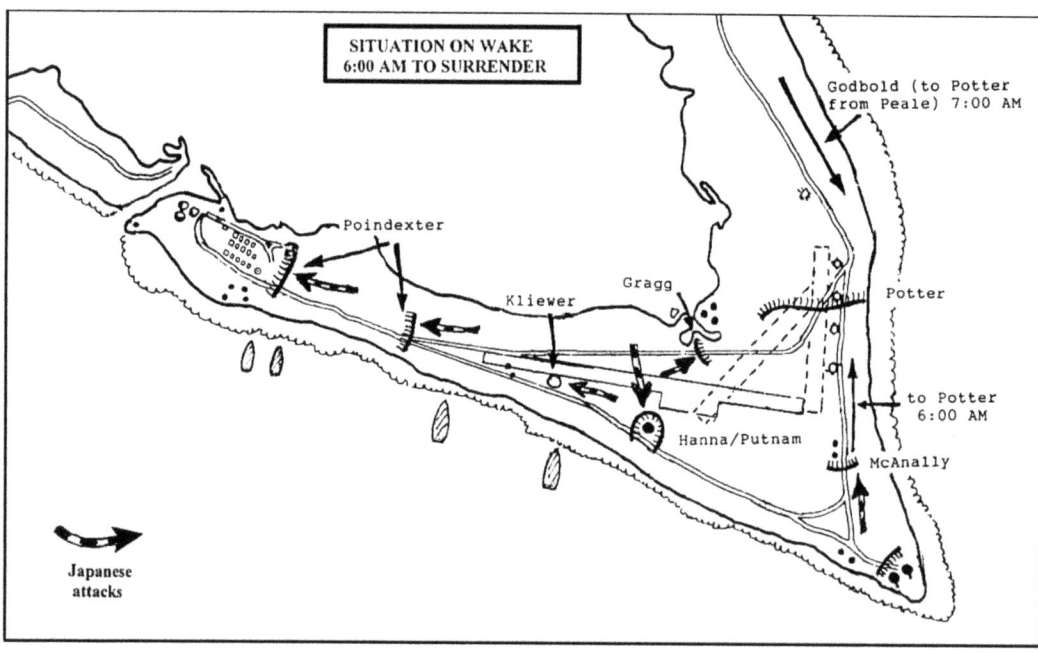

A few minutes later Devereux called back asking if he had reached the Japanese commander by radio.

"I told him that I had not," remembered the island commander, "then asked if I would be justified in surrendering in order to prevent further and useless loss of life."

Unknown to the two men, the rest of the conversation was overheard by the Air Station commander, Commander Campbell Keene; he and Dan Teeters, superintendent of civilian construction on Wake, were in his dugout on Peale.

"I picked up the telephone and found both Commander Cunningham and Major Devereux on the wire," said Keene. "During the conversation Major Devereux said he did not feel he should make the decision to surrender, that [it] should be made only by the commanding officer. After a short pause, Cunningham informed Devereux that he authorized the surrender of the island and for him to take the necessary steps to effect it."[45]

At that point Devereux said that he was not certain of his ability to contact the Japanese commander and asked Cunningham to also attempt to make contact, to which he said he would see what he could do.

But it was too late.

"Before I could do anything," said Cunningham, "it was over.... I became aware that the surrender had begun when someone reported that bed sheets could be seen flying above the civilian hospital near [the] command post."

At the command post Devereux said that he had "just got up to do what [he] had to do when Gunner Hammas came in. He reported that the last of Godbold's men had arrived on the line, then asked 'What [are] my orders now?'"

"It's too late, John. Commander Cunningham has ordered us to surrender. Fix a white flag and pass the word to cease fire."

"Yes, sir," he said with a dismayed look on his face, then turned walked out.

From the doorway Devereux heard him shout, "Major's orders! We're surrendering ... major's orders!"

"I stepped to the entrance and yelled at him, 'It's not my order, Goddamn it!'"[46]

And so, despite who initiated it, the wheels of surrender were put into motion. But it would be slow and it wouldn't be easy, particularly since there were four positions totally out of contact with each other and the command post.

The easy part, if there was one, involved those positions still in phone communications with the CP, or, in Major Potter's case, through direct command.

While preparing to get word to batteries A, E, and B on Peale, whose lines were hopefully still connected with the command post, a call came through from Lt. Barninger on Peacock Point. "They had managed to repair the line at last," said Devereux. "They still held their position, ready for attack."

"Cease fire," said the Marine commander. "Destroy all weapons. The island is being surrendered!"

There was silence on the other end, then, "It's over. We're surrendering."

The reaction was pretty much the same with Wally Lewis at Battery E, who immediately sent a messenger to have Sergeant Gragg pull his men back.

Over on Peale, cupping the mouthpiece with his hand, Lt. Kessler's telephone operator told him, "Sir, they say to stop firing the 5-inch guns—we are surrendering the island."

Kessler told him to have them repeat the message.

"Same answer, sir."

In disbelief, Kessler rang up the command post himself, but could not get through. Failing this, he contacted Lt. Barninger at Peacock, who confirmed the surrender order.

At the three batteries men began destroying everything of possible use to the Japanese. Nothing on any of the guns escaped being smashed, bent, or taken off and thrown away.

Grenades were dropped down the bores. Breech-blocks were removed and buried, tossed into the sea, or wrecked beyond use. Fire-control telescopes and gunsight lenses were smashed, telephones destroyed, and cables cut.

Lt. Lewis and Sergeant Robert Cox pumped several rounds from their .45s into the sensitive parts of the only remaining height-finder on the island. Unfortunately, Cox was hit by a ricocheting bullet from his own gun. Even more frustrating to the Marine veteran, he was the only man in Battery E to be wounded in the battle.

At Peacock Point, Lt. Barninger's runner, PFC Jesse Nowlin, was knocked unconscious when a ricocheting enemy bullet put a substantial dent in the side of his helmet.

Barninger, meanwhile, guessing that feeding his men would not be high on the enemy's priority list, opened up the food stores and told them to eat all they could while waiting for the Japanese.

It was the same with Lt. Kessler, who passed out everything that was left in the battery mess, including candy bars.

About 40 minutes after the order to surrender had been given, Lt. Lewis marched his men under a makeshift white flag to the command post. Reporting to Devereux, he said, "Sir, the guns and fire control equipment of Battery E have been destroyed."

Devereux looked over at his men. "[They] stood staring at the white flag over the CP — a bedsheet nailed to a timber — and there was bewilderment and resentment in their faces." This, no doubt, was because they could still hear firing somewhere on the island, and, said their commander, "that they had just been ordered to lay down their arms and surrender."[47]

Back on December 9, following the devastating air attack of the day before, Commander Cunningham decided to convert two of the four ammunition storage magazines on the edge of the north-south road on Wake into underground hospitals. "Their reinforced concrete and steel would protect our wounded more effectively than a cross painted on a building," he said. "Each had room for 21 beds. Gasoline-driven generators provided electricity for lights and refrigeration."

The southernmost of the four magazines became the military hospital. The northernmost was set up for civilian use. On December 14, Major Devereux moved his command post into the third bomb-proof, 400 yards north of the hospital.

The Marine commander, realizing after the surrender decision that it was well within the area of enemy control, had Cpl. Brown call the hospital.

"I called Dr. [Mason] Kahn, the Navy doctor, to raise a white flag and give word of the surrender to a Jap officer, if he could manage to contact one," said Devereux.

Brown told him that the hospital didn't answer.

Stepping outside, Devereux said to the group of men who had gathered around the command post that he needed a volunteer to rig a white flag and accompany him to the hospital.

"Sergeant Donald Malleck volunteered," he said, "and tied a white rag on a swab handle, and the two of us started walking down the road toward the enemy."

Unknown to the two men as they apprehensively moved past Major Potter's thin line, the call to the hospital announcing the surrender may have got through after all.

Several patients remembered the call coming in.

Sheltered from the sounds and impact of the battle because of the tightly shut steel door, no one inside the magazine was aware of what was going on outside. Nor did the Japanese know or suspect that behind the big door they would find a room full of wounded Americans.

Faced with the difficult question of how to surrender the hospital, Dr. Kahn had an orderly tie a bedsheet to the end of a broom handle, then open the door just wide enough to push the flag through.

Lieutenant John Kinney, one of Paul Putnam's pilots, who had reluctantly gone to the hospital the day before suffering from, as Dr. Kahn wrote on his chart, "severe diarrhea and complete physical exhaustion," remembered hearing "Japanese soldiers banging on the door with their rifle butts."

"Dr. Kahn opened the door," he said, "and all of us who were able ... raised our hands above our heads.... We did not want them to think that they had stumbled into a fighting bunker and come in shooting."

The first man through the door was a pistol-wielding Japanese officer, followed by four or five more of his men, all holding their rifles in the ready position.

At that point, for whatever reason, the officer fired his pistol into the domed ceiling, the bullet ricocheting wildly around the room, eventually hitting and killing a wounded civilian. Another man was also hit.

Needless to say, the situation was wrought with anxiety. What was next? wondered Kinney. Was it true that the Japanese killed all prisoners? Ironically, the three pilots, Tharin, Elrod, and Kinney, had asked themselves that very question the night before.

"Apparently satisfied with ... establishing their authority over us," said a relieved young fighter pilot, "[they] made it known that we were to move out onto the road where prisoners from other parts of the island were assembling." Doctor Kahn was allowed to remain in the hospital with the half a dozen patients who were unable to walk.[48]

Meanwhile, about 250 yards north of the hospital, Major Devereux and Donald Malleck, who had walked unchallenged up to that point, had been halted by a Japanese of no recognizable rank.

"We stopped ... and Sergeant Malleck held up the white flag," said Devereux. "The Jap came toward us with slow caution, covering us with his rifle.... He stopped a few feet from us, his fixed bayonet ready to lunge, and peered at us."

Making the two men remove their helmets and pistol belts, he stepped aside and gestured with his bayonet for them to move toward the enemy lines.

"We had gone only a few steps," continued Devereux, "when we saw a second Jap waiting in the road. As we approached him, a rifle cracked (from) the brush. The Jap fell on his face."

Obviously startled and frightful of the possible repercussions, Devereux turned and yelled in the direction from where the shot had come from, "The order has been given to cease firing, and damn it, you'll obey that order!"

He then turned and, fearing the worst, was motioned by the guard to walk over to the fallen man.

"He stopped and rolled over the body," said the apprehensive Marine commander. "He saw the man was dead but ... show[ing] neither pity nor anger ... simply motioned us to move on."[49]

As the three men, with Malleck holding the white flag high above his head, continued on toward the hospital, the American walking-wounded who had been herded outside had found their captors completely indifferent to their situation.

After making them strip down to their shorts, "they prodded us onto the road with the points of their bayonets," said John Kinney. "While some ... kept their rifles turned on us, others rummaged around and came back with pieces of communication wire to truss us up."

Forcing Kinney and the rest of the men, about 24 in number, to cross their hands behind their backs, they wrapped them together then looped a second strand around each man's neck and attached it to their wrists.

It was torturous. "If I relaxed my arms to relieve the growing discomfort in my shoulders," remembered Kinney, "it would pull down against the wire around my neck and I would strangle myself. After they tied us all up, [they] ordered us on our knees, and we spent the next several hours in that uncomfortable position."[50]

By the time Devereux arrived, the wiring-up of the wounded men had been finished. He was shocked by what he saw: "stripped down to their skivvies ... they sat in four rows behind the road with eight machine guns at their back."

In fear of why so many machine guns were aimed at the helpless, tied-up group of wounded Americans, as difficult as it was, Devereux restrained himself from showing any anger toward his captors lest he trigger a massacre.

Still looking for his first Japanese officer, he spotted one standing near the hospital door. "[He] was wearing a sword, so I knew he was an officer. I asked him, 'Do you speak English?'"

"Yes," he said, "a little."

"Well, we are surrendering.

"His face lit up. He said something to his men and then gave me a cigarette," said Devereux.

"Where did you learn English?"

The officer, a navy lieutenant junior grade, told him he had studied English at school and that he had been at the World's Fair in San Francisco in 1939.

There was some excitement behind them. Devereux turned in time to see several Japanese soldiers, with guns lowered, stop a battleship-gray truck with U.S. Navy painted on the door. It was Commander Cunningham.

"He got out and walked toward us," said Devereux. "I was surprised to see he had changed to his formal blue uniform."[51]

It had been over a half an hour since the two men had talked. Cunningham, after the decision to surrender was made, said that, in sort of a daze, he'd walked out of his bunker, tossed his .45 into a nearby latrine, climbed into his truck and drove away.

"Instead of going south toward the enemy," he said, "I drove north to the cottage I had occupied in the early days of the defense. It was battered and badly damaged, but, moving ... through the debris, I took off [my] dirty old khakis ... shaved and washed my face, and put on a clean blue uniform.

Then I got back into the truck, drove down the road, and surrendered."[52]

The Japanese officer standing next to Devereux looked at Cunningham, then turned and asked, "Who Number One?"

Devereux pointed to Cunningham, then walked over to him and said, "While you arrange the formal surrender, I'll go around the island with Malleck to be sure that everybody gets the word."

At that point, the two men were escorted back to the command post by the man Devereux called "World's Fair jg," and 20 men. There, after making sure everyone in the vicinity was disarmed, they took out across the airstrip toward Hanna and Putnam.

As they were crossing the airfield, they met another Japanese naval officer, Lieutenant Yakichi Itaya, commander of Patrol Craft 32. Devereux noticed that his hand was bandaged.

Asking him if he spoke English, the officer shook his head, then handed him a pencil and paper.

Remembering that many Japanese could read but not speak English, he wrote, "I will stop the fighting," made a casual salute and started again for the 3-inch gun.

As they got under way, a second Japanese officer joined them. Devereux, noticing that he had unsheathed his sword, turned and asked, "Do you speak English?"

"No. I do not speak English," he said in a disparaging tone. "Do you speak Japanese?"

It was 9:30 A.M.—seven hours since communications had been lost with the forward units. Thus far, the wheels of surrender had turned smoothly. But with the sound of small arms fire still heard in the distance, the most difficult and potentially volatile part still lay ahead.

As the surrender party approached the 3-inch gun, it became unbelievably quiet. Maybe it was because the Japanese had been told of the surrender. Whatever the reason, despite the severe strafing of the position an hour earlier and being surrounded by close to 100 Japanese, somehow they had held out.

Maybe it was because of the spirited defense put up by Elrod, Tharin, Hanna, Jim Hesson, and the rest, or maybe it was Paul Putnam's words, "This is as far as we go." However it happened, when Devereux identified himself and yelled twice that the island had been surrendered and to drop their weapons, judging the number of Japanese troops seen surrounding the position, he knew it was a miracle that they had held out.

Of the eleven Marines and 18 civilians who had taken part in the fight, only 15 were still alive. Of those, only one man, Frank Tharin, was not wounded. Of the 18 civilian construction workers who had stayed, fifteen were killed.

Sadly, George Gibbons, one of those killed, was the son of Fred Gibbons, one of the three who had survived.

Frank Tharin led Devereux over to Putnam, who along with John Hanna, was just crawling out from under the gun platform.

"[Putnam] looked like hell itself," said Devereux. "He had been shot in the jaw. His face was a red smear."

Putnam said, "Jimmy, I'm sorry. Poor Hank is dead."

Devereux walked over and looked at Elrod's body. "He lay there with his eyes open, defiant, [a] grenade ... tightly clenched in his hand."

Three years and 8 months later, his signature on a recommendation for the Medal of Honor for the courageous young Marine captain would help send it on its way to the Congress of the United States.

On the opposite side of the platform lay the bodies of Robert Bryan and Paul Gay, two civilians that had originally helped man the 3-inch gun with Lt. Hanna. The other two, Eric Lehtola and Corporal Ralph Holewinski, had survived.

Lying next to Gay and Bryan was bloodied but still-breathing Holewinski. Firing perhaps the last shots fired in defense of the gun, he had killed two Japanese who, evidently thinking he was dead, had mistakenly ignored him as they moved in close to the platform. "When Major Devereux came along with the white flag, I had three bullets left. I was glad it was over as I thought I was about to die."[53]

It was close to ten o'clock when Devereux led the surrender party through the brush and onto the runway toward where he expected to find the bodies of four of his Marines. The fact that the airfield hadn't been blown up led him to believe that Kliewer and the three men who had been sent to the generator must have been killed before they could set it off. He was wrong.

When the four Marines who had been fighting off the most recent enemy attacks from the east saw a group of men coming from that direction carrying a white flag, their first thoughts were that it was a trick.

Stopping some 20 yards from the position, Major Devereux cupped his hands around his mouth and yelled to them to lay down their arms, that the island had been surrendered.

One of the men grabbed Kliewer's arm. "Don't surrender, Lieutenant," he said. "It's a hoax. Marines never surrender."[54]

Studying the situation for a moment, Kliewer shook his head, stood up, and raised his hands. The other three men followed. It was over. Needless to say, his comment later that "it was a difficult thing to do" was silently repeated by every Marine on Wake Island that morning.

"We gathered in the crews of [the] two .50 caliber machine guns still holding out at the end of the runway and pushed on toward the sound of small arms fire in the direction of Camp One," said Devereux. While heading in that direction, he remembered thanking God that Kliewer had not blown up the airstrip while they were crossing it. Even if they had lived through it, he thought, "the Japs would have murdered us all for what they considered an act of treachery."

A few yards past the end of the runway, they came up behind 50 or so Japanese in a fire-fight with troops they could not see. "They were giving ground when they saw us," said the surprised Marine commander.

Despite the white flag and that there were only two Marines standing among the 20 Japanese in the surrender party, some turned and fired in their direction. "Then," said Devereux, "a bunch of them charged us with bayonets."

Fortunately, one of the Japanese officers stepped in front of the two startled Americans, shouting at them until they stopped.

Of course, the troops Devereux "could not see" were Arthur Poindexter's beefed-up Mobile Reserve Force, who, in less than three hours, had retaken nearly a mile of ground they had conceded to the Japanese when they'd pulled back to Camp One.

Although the closer they got to the end of the runway the more difficult the fighting had become, Poindexter was still confident they would soon link up with Marines he hoped were holding the airfield. His confidence was buoyed even more when one of his men yelled, "Hey, Lieutenant, a mob of Japs are coming down the road with a white flag!"

Thinking that the Japanese were surrendering, he ran over to take a look. "Indeed this was an astonishing turn of events," he said. "Perhaps our people around the airfield had gained the upper hand and reversed the tide of battle."

Preparing to accept the enemy surrender, he told his men to cover him "in case there [was] any funny business," then stood up and started walking toward them.

"Only when I was perhaps 60 or 70 yards from the white flag did I recognize the voice of Major Devereux, who desperately shouted at me to drop my rifle, take off my helmet, and put my hands behind my head."

He was shocked, not only because it was he who had been ordered to surrender, but because Major Devereux's diminutive stature, as he called it, hadn't stood out in the group of enemy soldiers until he heard his voice.

"Not until then did I realize that he was in fact a prisoner of war."[55]

The Japanese in the surrender party, at first sight of the tall, slender Marine, rifle in hand, grenades hanging on his shirt pockets, and face blackened like a commando by some sort of flash cream, didn't quite know what to make of him. When he reached up to remove the grenades from his shirt pocket, not sure what his intention was, they all quickly backed up.

"Have your men stand up and leave their weapons on the deck," Devereux yelled again. At that point, as they complied with the order that was relayed back to them by Poindexter, the same Japanese who a few minutes before had come at Devereux and Malleck yelled "Banzai!" and charged toward them.

For a second time one of the officers with the surrender party interceded, and the enemy troops lowered their rifles and backed off.

After watching the Japanese march his men down the road toward the runway, Poindexter joined the surrender party. Walking toward Camp One, he was surprised at the large number of Japanese troops that lined the road. A lot more had either come ashore since they had fought their way from Camp One, he thought, or maybe the dense brush on the north side of the road had neutralized any attempt to organize an attack against his rear, which, up to the surrender, had remained unchallenged.

As the party neared Camp One, Poindexter, with Malleck close behind holding the white flag high over his head, yelled in the direction of the men manning the perimeter he had established on the edge of the camp to surrender.

The water tower at Camp One was located a few feet off the road in the middle of the camp area. After the men, reacting to Poindexter's order, stood up and stepped out into the clearing, a Japanese in the surrender party spotted the American flag still flying from the abandoned tower.

"When the Japs saw the flag," said Devereux, "some broke into a run, cheering and yelling, and one began climbing the tower. I looked at the men. They were staring at the Japs with burning eyes. Fists were clenched. They were at the breaking point, the crazy point where a man will go against a gun with bare hands.

"I snapped, 'Hold it! Keep your heads, all of you!'"[56]

Unknown to him, on the far western side of the tower, Sergeant Dave Rush, a Marine machine gunner who apparently had not heard the surrender order or noticed what was going on in the center of the camp clearing, had taken dead aim at the enemy soldier climbing up to remove the flag. Fortunately, at the last second he spotted the group of Americans standing in the clearing with their arms raised above their heads. Realizing that it was over, he slid the bolt out of his gun and threw it as far as he could, then stood up, raised his hands and walked toward the clearing.

Had he fired, the consequences may have been a little more than "extremely embarrassing," as Devereux put it when he learned later just how close Rush had come to pulling the trigger.

On the Wake side of the Wilkes Channel, some 300 yards west and out of sight of the Camp One clearing, like Rush, Gunnery Sergeant John Cemeris, in charge of the last .30 caliber machine gun position on the island, had not been informed of the surrender, either. When he saw the low-flying Japanese float plane that had been circling over Peale bank head toward him, he aimed and opened fire. When it passed overhead, black smoke was pouring from its engine.

Back at Camp One, everyone, including the Japanese in the surrender party, saw what had happened. "I saw the Jap jettison his bombs," said Devereux. "It was beautiful shooting, but [could make] things a little ticklish for us because our Jap escort also saw it." Devereux and Poindexter looked at each other, then, accompanied by one of the officers and a few riflemen from the surrender party, hastened down the road toward where the shots had come from.

"Stand up and put your hands over your heads," Poindexter yelled as he neared the sandbagged position. Four men stood up and, with surprised looks on their faces, slowly raised their hands.

Devereux, up to that point having avoided a serious encounter with the Japanese over the surrender, said to himself, "I've got one last thing to do."

Like his decision to blow up the runway to deprive the Japanese from using it, he had also planned to block the Wilkes Channel, the only access to the lagoon, by blowing up a barge he had loaded with dynamite. Because of the loss of communications and the reluctance of the civilian in charge to set it off without orders, when he reached the channel he found the barge still tied up where it had been left.

"I [decided] to tell the [Japanese] lieutenant about it," he said. "Nothing could be gained by trying to hide it, and an accidental explosion might cause the Japs to massacre us."

Relieved that the surrender was at last over, Devereux was surprised when the officer directed him to the boat dock. As he, Malleck, and Poindexter, who were still with him, stepped onto the barge to take them across the narrow channel, he asked him why they were being taken to Wilkes.

"That was when I learned that Marines still held [the island]," said the surprised little major.

About the time the surrender party reached Camp One an hour or so earlier, Marine lookouts on Wilkes, who had been watching Japanese ships maneuvering off the island, reported to Captain Wesley Platt that landing boats were heading toward the channel. Platt quickly phoned Lt. John McAlister and told him to man his 5-inch guns and blast the enemy barges out of the water. A few minutes later, McAlister called back, telling him that bombs from the air attacks that had been going on since eight o'clock that morning, had damaged the guns to the point where they could not be repaired.

After a quick trip to see for himself, Platt drove over to Battery F to check on the condition of the 3-inch guns. Finding that they, too, had been damaged, he told McAlister, Gunner McKinstry, and Sergeant Raymond Coulson to grab two .30 caliber machine guns and as many men as they could find and head for the channel to meet the Japanese.

As the group of perhaps 50 men trudged their way along the beach, they were attacked by a Japanese plane from the carrier *Hiryu*, which dropped a bomb that killed 21-year-old PFC Robert Stevens. His death marked the last Marine to die in combat on Wake Island.

It was close to one o'clock when the surrender party disembarked onto Wilkes and started up the beach toward the far end of the island. Although Platt's headquarters were over a mile away, not knowing exactly where contact with his troops might occur, Devereux right away yelled, "This is Major Devereux! The island has been surrendered! Put down your arms!" There was no answer. A hundred yards or so up the beach, he yelled again, "The island has been surrendered! Don't try any monkey business!"

"There was still no answer," he said. "We heard nothing [and] saw nothing."

What he did see, however, were several destroyers and the landing barges that Platt's men were on their way to hopefully stop from getting ashore.

A few seconds later there was a flash from a gun on one of the destroyers. "[A] shell burst at the water's edge," said Devereux. "A moment later a second [one] exploded. It was nearer ... then a third ... within 50 yards of us. I wanted to crawl into a hole, but we kept walking. We were scared but ... could not show it before the Japs."[57]

At that point, one of the Japanese officers "did what he should have done at the first shot," said the angry Marine commander. "He ordered a signalman to give the destroyer the word to cease fire." He later said that he had never been more relieved than when the Jap officer took cover so that the surrender party could, too.

After the firing stopped, the party started up the beach again, with Devereux calling out from time to time that the island had been surrendered. About 1:30, one of the men from the front of Platt's column ran back and told him that he'd seen a group of enemy soldiers boldly walking up the beach toward them. He did not mention seeing a white flag. Platt told his men to take cover while he went forward to reconnoiter the situation.

Staying to the brush just off the beach, about 50 yards from the surrender party he spotted three men in Marine uniforms, and one had a white flag. Hearing one yell, "We have surrendered!" he recognized the voice as that of Major Devereux.

As Platt stepped out into the open and began walking toward them, Devereux walked forward to meet him. "It's over Wes," he said. "It's over. We've surrendered."

Behind with his men, tough Gunner Clarence McKinstry, unable to believe it until he saw the two men talking to each other, angrily stripped his .45 and tossed the parts into the surf.

And so, the final battle of Wake Island, the opening shots of which had come from Wilkes early that morning, officially ended with the surrender of the island where it had started. Although the fighting was over, what followed would be more difficult and frightful for many of the captives than were the life-and-death situations they had faced before the surrender.

On Wilkes, after separating the enlisted men, who were marched off toward the channel, the four officers, Devereux, Platt, Poindexter, and McAlister, were led to the 3-inch gun position. As they neared the battery, they heard the Japanese talking excitedly and motioning at the vast number of dead comrades that littered the ground around the position. A moment later everything went silent. The Americans wondered what was up.

Two Japanese had been examining the bodies of three men who were clustered close together when one of the corpses suddenly stood up. It startled everyone. Although slightly wounded, he had been playing dead until, as Devereux put it, "He heard the Japs jabbering as they stared at the litter of dead."

The Americans led the Japanese to Captain Platt's command post, where the only two Japanese prisoners taken in the battle for Wilkes had been tied up with communication wire. After they were released, a Japanese officer and Lt. Poindexter began searching the area for wounded survivors. They would find none. As they went from body to body, one of the prisoners who had just been released followed them. Poindexter didn't understand why until they came across a body, who, when the young man saw it, dropped to his knees next to it and sobbed. The officer told him that it was the boy's brother.

Further on, the two men found the body of a dead officer who had been shot in the face. The Japanese officer pulled out a small white flag with a big red "meat ball" in the center and laid it over the dead man's chest. Poindexter remembered that the flag had Japanese writing all over it. At the request of the officer, the two men picked up the body and started down a path toward a truck that was being loaded with the corpses of other dead Japanese.

Along the way Poindexter spotted a can of pears. Having not eaten since the night before, he reached down and picked it up. After loading the body on the back of the truck, the two men jumped up on the tailgate, where they shared the pears. The Japanese then opened a tin of cigarettes, encouraging Poindexter to take several. They would be the last the young lieutenant would have for a long time.

Private Wiley Sloman, who had been shot in the head during the battle to retake the 3-inch gun that morning, had been put on a stretcher to wait for transportation to the hospital. When the Japanese came across his semi-conscious body, they rolled him off the litter into the bushes so they could use it to carry their own dead down to the channel.

Lt. John McAlister actually saved Sloman's life twice. The first came when he convinced two Japanese who were ready to shoot him that he couldn't stand up and walk out of the bushes with his hands up because he was badly wounded. The second came when he sent two civilians back to find him and bring him out. Although it would be two days before they were allowed to get him, he survived.[58]

Meanwhile, Major Devereux, Captain Platt, and John McAlister had been led down the beach, where they met up with the Japanese whom Platt was on his way to engage when told to surrender. Devereux, who recognized the Japanese officer as a full lieutenant, could see that he was not amused when the officer escorting them made his report.

"The lieutenant kept scowling at us," he said. "I imagine he had learned how many men that day's work had cost them."

And what of those losses? In addition to the estimated 95 killed on Wilkes, 62 enemy bodies were found around Putnam's position. Devereux was told by the Japanese that their losses amounted to close to 350. American losses were only 29, 15 Marines, and 14 civilians.

The search and transportation of bodies on Wilkes went on throughout most of the afternoon. Gunner McKinstry, who had been marched to the channel with the enlisted men, worried that one of the two enemy survivors might recognize him because of his long red beard. Finding a knife, he painfully dry-shaved his face as inconspicuously as possible.

It was close to two o'clock when the three officers got back to Camp One.

"We saw the Jap landing force commander ... with the wounded hand, talking to Commander Cunningham and Commander Keene," said Devereux. "When they got in a truck, [we] climbed in after them. Nobody tried to stop us. We drove to the [temporary] Jap headquarters near Hanna's gun, where the Jap commander continued to question [the two men]. One of the things he wanted to know was where the women were."

Taking a pencil and paper, Keene wrote, "No women on island." The Japanese officer looked dumbfounded.

"It was now about 2:00 P.M., and I had not eaten since six o'clock the night before," said Devereux. "The Jap officer offered us some canned food." Even after he ate the raw fish, which he remembered tasted pretty good, he said he felt dead inside. "I had just walked six miles under guard, most of the time with my hands in the air, and my body ached from weariness," he said. "But I do not think that was the reason ... it was at last the full realization of what had happened — our best had not been good enough." It was what Devereux called "the death of pride." More accurately, it was the feeling of humiliation.[59]

While they were finishing up the last of their raw fish meal, Devereux spotted a group of Marines being marched toward them.

"Most were stripped to their skivvies," he said. "Some had [no] shoes and were limping barefoot on the coral." Captured on Wilkes, they had walked over two and a half miles under those conditions and were, as he said, "exhausted, hungry, dirty, and there was no hope."

Walking in front of them was mustachioed Sergeant Edwin Hassig, a tough, barrel-chested, 20-year Marine. When he spotted the group of American officers, he turned and said to his men, "Snap outta this.... Goddamn it, you're Marines."

"Hassig was at right guide [when they passed]," said Devereux, "shoulders back, mustache defiant, and the men — weary scarecrows — were marching in perfect cadence, heads up and eyes front ... like a regiment on parade. I felt pride at the sight of them marching by" [and] at the bewilderment on the faces of the Japanese."[60]

As groups of Marines were rounded up from Wake and Wilkes, they were marched up the road fronting the two hospitals and Devereux's command post. Regardless of their physical condition, they were stripped to their shorts and, with hands tied behind their backs with wire that was looped around their necks, they were herded into the two hospitals.

As more and more were brought in and forced into the small concrete dugouts, the situation became critical. Packed like sardines with no room to sit down, some men passed out. Others, in the near suffocating environs, became sick and vomited. The weaker they became, the more difficult it was to keep from relaxing their arms and strangling themselves. For the wounded men, whom the Japanese made no effort to help or separate, the situation was even worse.

In the Marine hospital on the far southern end of the group, Gunner John Hammas, an old Shanghai Marine with some fluency in Japanese, asked an elderly enemy officer to free Dr. Kahn so he could look after the wounded.

"You doctor, too?" he asked.

Hammas told him that he wasn't.

"Are you an officer?"

"Yes sir," he replied.[61]

At that he ordered the guards to untie both Hammas and Dr. Kahn. A while later Hammas approached the officer again, this time convincing him to loosen the wires around the prisoners' hands and remove the nooses altogether. He agreed.

Although the conditions in the Marine hospital had improved, it was far from that in the civilian hospital on the opposite end. Fortunately, the situation for both was ended when the Japanese, realizing that they had overestimated the capacity of the two dugouts, let the Marines out and marched them onto the airstrip. By the time the civilians were rounded up from Peale and herded onto the field, over 1,500 men were crowded onto the coral runway.

As the afternoon wore on, the question of what was going to happen to them was speculated by everyone. When the Japanese set up machine guns facing the lines of trussed-up, half-naked prisoners who were captured earlier, everyone was convinced it was to massacre them. That their fears were correct was acknowledged when Japanese admiral Sadamichi Kajioka, who had come ashore earlier to take formal possession of the island, got in a heated 15-minute argument with the officer who had ordered the machine guns. In the end, the admiral prevailed, forcing the officer to order his men on the guns to stand down.

Just before dark, the last of the Marines to surrender were led onto the airfield. They were the men from Battery A on Peacock Point, whose position the Japanese had apparently overlooked until they walked out under a white flag.

All afternoon, battery commander Clarence Barninger had watched the Japanese round up everyone, strip them, and march them away. Not wanting to have the Japanese come upon them in the dark, he decided to voluntarily surrender. It paid off, as his men were the only ones among a handful of other prisoners allowed to keep their clothes.

It is not known how many officers were among those half-naked prisoners being held on the airstrip. Possibly only one, Lt. John Kinney, who, it will be remembered, as one of the walking wounded from the hospital, was stripped, tied up, and forced to march barefoot to the airfield. Without his uniform to identify him, he most likely was the only officer on the field.

Just before the sun went down, remembered Kinney, the Japanese "decided that there was nowhere for any of us to run, so they untied us and allowed us to pick up a few pieces of discarded clothing from where other prisoners had stripped." Outside of that, they were given a little bread and water, and forced to sleep, if they could, on the runway, where off and on during the night they were pelted by rain and cold winds from the lingering storm of the night before.

As for Commander Cunningham, Major Devereux, and most of the other officers on Wake, they were taken to the Camp Two area, where they were housed in what Cunningham referred to as two slightly damaged guest cottages that were located next to his old bombed-out quarters.

The last detail completed that afternoon occurred near Hanna's 3-inch gun. Lt. Frank Tharin, John Hammas, and a group of 30 Marine volunteers were allowed to bury the Americans who had been killed in the fighting around the gun. Of the 16 bodies that were placed in the 4-foot-deep mass grave, four, including Hank Elrod, were Marines. Of the 12 civilians who were buried alongside them, eight would be honored posthumously with the Bronze Star for their contributions that night.

Chapter 2

Bataan's Final Hours

On December 23, 1941, a decision was made that would set the stage for the 3-month siege of Bataan Peninsula. The decision, made by General Douglas MacArthur, commander of the American and Philippine army in the Islands, had been planned long before the war broke out.

Years before, in anticipation of war with Japan and the circumstances that presented themselves on the twenty-third, a plan called War Plan Orange-Three (WPO-3) was drawn up. Based on the probability that the island of Luzon could not be held, WPO-3 directed a withdrawal into the Bataan peninsula, where, together with Corregidor and the Manila Bay forts, a 6-month delaying action would take place until, hopefully, reinforcements would arrive.

Unfortunately, WPO-3 — which provided that Bataan would be stockpiled with food and medicine and that roads, air fields, and well-laid-out lines of defense would be built well in advance — was discarded by MacArthur two months earlier. Anticipating that his American and Philippine army would be prepared to successfully defend Luzon if and when the Japanese attacked and that WPO-3 was too defensive in nature, MacArthur got Washington to void its directives in October 1941.

He was caught, therefore, in a state of partial preparedness; of his army of 75,000 men, approximately 65,000 were Philippine army troops, barely half of whom had completed basic training before the war. Not only were they ill prepared, but ill equipped as well. The only men who could be called real soldiers in the islands were from the Philippine Division. Some 10,500 in number, it was made up of three infantry regiments, two of which were the highly trained and respected Philippine Scouts. The third regiment, the U.S. 31st, was the only all–American unit in the Islands. A third Philippine Scout regiment, the 26th Cavalry, originally commanded by Jonathan Wainwright, was the last true horse cavalry unit ever to see duty in U.S. history.

Along with a handful of P-40 fighters and a half dozen PT boats as sole representatives of the air forces and navy, there were also two National Guard battalions of light tanks and 75mm-toting half-tracks and two Guard anti-aircraft regiments. Both had arrived just days before the war started. Although there were several 155mm artillery units attached to the Scouts and Philippine army, the ever-present Japanese air force pretty well kept them silenced throughout the campaign.

Many of the weapons used on Bataan were of World War I vintage, as was the ammunition. Outside of the U.S. 31st and Scout regiments, who were issued Garand M-1s, Philippine army troops used well-worn 1903 Springfield and 1917 Enfield rifles. Both hand grenades and ammunition for their World War I Stokes mortars were of similar vintage, causing misfire rates in both as high as 75 percent.

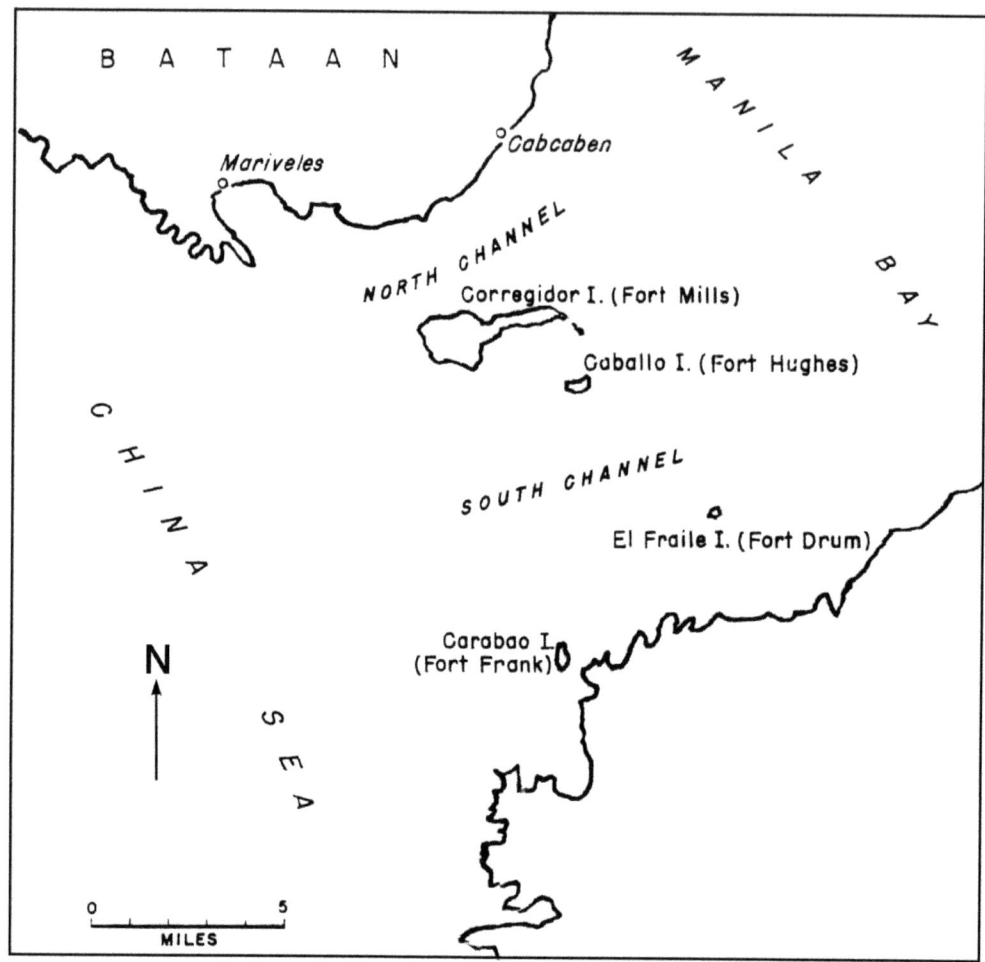

The failure to implement the pre-war preparations outlined in WPO-3 was the greatest contributor to Bataan's plight. In the end, it can be said that the army on Bataan lost the battle to starvation and disease as well as to the Japanese. Had the peninsula been stockpiled with enough food and medicine to support its army, the story of its fate may have been different. Just two days before the first Japanese attack on Bataan on January 11, and in the face of running out of food in 30 days, the entire army was put on half rations. But by the middle of March, the 35-ounce-per-day ration had dwindled to 17 ounces—barely one-fourth of what was considered a full 4,000-calorie, 71-ounce issue.

Two weeks before the surrender, a medical officer attached to the Provisional Tank Group said that "the average man in his unit had lost 30 to 40 pounds." Of the 100 Philippine Scouts in one 155mm battery, only four were strong enough to lift the 98-pound shells up to the breeches of the guns. On March 15, I and II Corps commanders both estimated the combat efficiency within the two corps to be down to just 25 percent. "Men are actually weak to the point of staggering when they walk after any burst of energy," wrote one officer of the Filipinos in his unit.

Not only was the Bataan ration to blame. Magnifying the starvation diet was the widespread epidemics of both malaria and dysentery. Wrote an American officer about their effects on U.S. 31st Infantry troops: "Approximately 50 percent of the regiment is down with malaria or dysentery at all times. Those who were up and around were either just recovering or coming down with one or the other of the two diseases." Of the two, it was malaria in the end that took the highest toll. The malaria-infested jungles of Bataan, coupled with the depletion of the supply of quinine for use as a prophylactic in mid–March, led to an average of 1,000 men per day reporting to sick call with the disease.

On the evening of March 11, 1942, General Douglas MacArthur, his wife, young son, and staff of seven generals left Corregidor and Bataan for Mindanao in the four remaining PT boats. MacArthur had been ordered to Australia by President Roosevelt to lead the fight to retake the southwest Pacific and eventually the Philippines from the Japanese.

Although many on Bataan feared the ordering of the general out of the islands meant that the Philippines had been written off, most still believed that help could arrive. Young private James Wall with an air corps ordnance unit probably reflected fairly accurately how most men felt. "Even after MacArthur left," he said, "we couldn't believe that the United States, with all its power and resources, couldn't come to our rescue." Air corps officer Lt. Edgar Whitcomb commented that "despite the fact that rumor after rumor was proving false day after day, we had faith and hope so strong that we embraced each new rumor as if it were the first we had ever heard." Colonel Ernest Miller of the 194th Tank Battalion added that he "never gave up hoping." "Faith in Uncle Sam," he said, "kept the spark alive." Lieutenant Tom Garrity, an air corps officer with General Wainwright, wrote in his diary on February 3 that he had missed his guess about help arriving by February 1 but that he was "willing to compromise and make it March 1. "I don't know how long we can hold out here because the front line troops need rest. At any rate, I continue to hope for the best — that old photo finish." Colonel Richard Mallonee with the 21st Field Artillery, wrote in his diary that "we continued to hope and have faith in our leaders, in our ability to hold out, and in our government's efforts to send a relief expedition that would arrive in storybook fashion." In his estimate of the situation, he wrote, "there was one favorable fact: Sooner or later the relief expedition would have to arrive."

The battlefield situation on Bataan between the time of the opening battle on January 11 and the end of March had gone through several phases. The Americans and Filipinos were forced to withdraw from the hastily prepared first line of defense on January 25, falling back to what would be the final line near the center of the mountainous peninsula. At that point, between late January and the last week of March, the Japanese, after a botched invasion of the west coast and failing to gain against the new line, withdrew to lick their wounds and send for reinforcements.

On the U.S. side, the 30-day lull that accompanied the Japanese withdrawal saw, among other things, a confused situation at the command level. When General MacArthur left the Philippines on March 11, without notifying Washington he planned to retain command from his new headquarters in Australia. Senior among the general officers left in the command was Major General Jonathan Wainwright, at the time commander of Bataan's I Corps. On the night of March 9, General Richard Sutherland, MacArthur's chief of staff, called the exhausted Wainwright on Bataan, telling him that the general wanted to see him. "Too tired to ask why," the sleepy-eyed I Corps commander scribbled on his pad, "boat ... Mariveles ... noon," hung up, and went back to sleep.

It was early the next afternoon when Wainwright entered the Malinta Tunnel on Corregidor and headed for the headquarters lateral. There he was met by Sutherland. General

MacArthur was "up at the house" some 400 yards east of the tunnel, so Sutherland filled him in while they walked. "General MacArthur is going to leave here and go to Australia," he said. "He's going to divide his Philippine forces into four subcommands, himself retaining overall command while in Australia. You will be placed in command of all troops on Luzon." "All troops on Luzon" for all practical purposes meant those on Bataan only, as "General George Moore [would] remain in command of the harbor defenses and fortified islands in the bay." MacArthur met Wainwright on the porch of the cottage, where the two men talked for a half hour or so before saying goodbye. Shaking hands, MacArthur said, "When I get back, if you're still on Bataan, I'll make you a lieutenant general."

"I'll be on Bataan if I'm still alive," Wainwright retorted, then turned and walked away.

The man MacArthur picked to take Wainwright's place as I Corps commander was Brigadier General Albert Jones, who, along with all general officers on Bataan, was informed of the changes on March 12. Wainwright, as Bataan's first commander, told them that MacArthur "had been forced, by order of the commander in chief, to leave." "I watched their faces as I spoke," he said, "but ... soon saw that they understood. They realized as well as I what the score was."

One of the top priorities on Wainwright's list as Bataan commander was to increase the rations for his men. On March 15, he went to Corregidor to see Brigadier General Lewis Beebe, who had been MacArthur's supply officer. Finding that he "had no control over their issue, which irked [him] a bit," the old cavalryman returned to Bataan "with heart made heavier" by the knowledge that he would have to trim his already meager ration issue "by another third in order to exist until April 10." Unknown to the disappointed Wainwright, things within the next six days were to happen that would give him not only the authority to increase Bataan's rations himself, but much more.

When General MacArthur left for Australia on March 11, he planned to remain in tactical command of the Islands. Washington, however, was never notified of this and therefore assumed that General Wainwright, as senior officer still remaining in the Philippines, had taken over.

On March 17, with the unknowing Wainwright back on Bataan, General Beebe, who had been assigned the position of MacArthur's deputy chief of staff, received a message dispatched to the "Commanding General USAFFE [U.S. Armed Forces Far East]." It read, in part: General MacArthur has arrived in Australia and has been assigned to supreme command. The President and the War Department felt justified in agreeing to his new assignment because of confidence in your leadership and the demonstrated fighting morale of your army.

It concluded by stating that the Philippines were still under General MacArthur's supervisory control, but "because of the isolation of your command, you are instructed to maintain direct communication with the War Department and submit daily reports." Although obviously meant for Wainwright, Beebe forwarded it on to MacArthur, accompanied with a plea to please notify Washington of the new command alignment. MacArthur did not respond, however.

Two days later on March 19, confusion mounted. It was started by a message from President Roosevelt, the contents of which told of Wainwright's appointment to lieutenant general. Before the day was over, two more messages came in, both from Chief of Staff General George C. Marshall, both recognizing him as the new commanding general. Beebe was left no choice other than to recognize Wainwright, which he did the next night.

Meanwhile, Wainwright, busy on Bataan, had remained completely oblivious to what was transpiring until receiving a call from the distraught Beebe on the night of March 20. Over a very bad phone connection, causing Beebe to literally yell the news to Wainwright, the surprised Bataan commander was barely able to hear about the two most important promotions of his life: one to lieutenant general and the other to commanding general of all United States Forces in the Philippines, known officially from then on as USFIP.

At 10:00 sharp the next morning, brand new Lt. General Jonathan Wainwright, who "did not sleep much that night," was standing on Quarantine Dock opposite the old Philippine port of entry Quarantine Station in Mariveles waiting for transportation to his new assignment—a job, that according to Washington, he had already been working at for ten days.

To take his place on Bataan, Wainwright picked an old artilleryman, Major General Edward P. King, senior American officer remaining on the peninsula. Before he left, Wainwright presented him with his old command trailer. "It was not much of a gift," he said, "nor was his role an enviable one."

On the enemy side, the position of commanding general had, since the latter part of January, not been an enviable one either. The Japanese timetable of conquest of the Philippines was, of course, long overdue. General Homma was the only theater commander who had thus far been stopped. Following the general withdrawal of Japanese troops from their assault positions on what was called the Bagac-Orion line in early February, Japanese Imperial Army Headquarters in Tokyo rushed a team of high-ranking generals to the Philippines to find out what had gone wrong. After a thorough inspection tour, the headquarters observers had to agree with General Homma's conclusion—"Bataan could be subdued only if additional troops were [sent]."[1]

After an inspection tour of Bataan by Lt. General Takeji Wachi, a newly appointed chief of staff to General Homma, he concluded that "the morale of the troops [was] completely broken down and they confined themselves to the bottom of ravines. In the face of too many defeats, their morale could not be sustained.... The Japanese army," he concluded, "[had been] severely beaten." The decision made, beginning in mid–February Japanese troops were beckoned from all over occupied Southeast Asia, a beckoning that revealed just how damaging the Filipino-American stand on Bataan had been to Japanese overall war strategy. Of the 50,000 troops to be involved in the final assault, 80 percent had to be withdrawn from newly occupied or still-active theaters. The roundup of troops included 11,000 from China, diverted while actually en route to assignment in Indo-China, 4,000 from Hong Kong, and five battalions of infantry from Japan. Additionally, both existing units on Bataan were bolstered by 3,500 replacements each from the home islands.[2]

For the air phase, two heavy bomber units of 30 planes each were transferred from Malaya. The Japanese navy also contributed 27 of its planes, bringing the overall number of aircraft available for the Bataan operation to close to 100.

As the month of March drew to a close, the Japanese military buildup continued in proportion to their attempts to break Filipino morale. Considered the possible weak link in the U.S. position on Bataan, the Filipinos were hit hard during this time with everything from anti–American propaganda leaflets to "Ticket to Happiness" surrender handbills instructing them how to walk away from their predicament and go home. Battlefield loudspeakers also tried to convince them to give up, all to no avail.

On the American side, although most remained convinced that help would arrive, more damage was done by well-meaning, friendly radio broadcasts from the States than anything. The program *Freedom for the Philippines* broadcast nightly from station KGEI in San Francisco left many dispirited and homesick. Lieutenant Edgar Whitcomb with air corps communications at Cabcaben Field noted that after a few weeks of KGEI, "only a handful of hollow-eyed, ragged soldiers hung on, trying to glean a word of hope.... It was heart rending to see them turn away evening after evening and walk back to their area without a word." Captain Allison Ind, also with the air corps, wrote that he heard the "Jack Benny hour tonight — KGEI. The first since before this crazy, upside-down world became a real one. Finally shut it off. Does funny things."

Lieutenant Henry G. Lee with Philippine Division headquarters on Bataan wrote a poem reflecting the feelings of the men around him. Different from Hewlett's, Lee wrote:

> I see no gleam of victory alluring
> No chance of splendid booty or of gain
> If I endure — I must go on enduring
> And my reward for bearing pain is pain
> Yet, though the thrill, the zest, the hopes are gone
> Something within me keeps me fighting on.

With the marked increase in enemy patrol and air activity in the latter days of March, General Wainwright scheduled a meeting of his two corps and nine division commanders on Bataan to discuss the likely point of attack of the coming Japanese offensive. That it would come against the II Corps was obvious. The rugged terrain and dense jungle that dominated General Jones' I Corps all but eliminated it from attack. The II Corps, occupying the eastern half of the peninsula outside of Mt. Samat, the most dominating high-ground position on the line, was open and sparsely jungled.

The Japanese, deciding, as the Americans had guessed, to launch their attack against the II Corps, had to first decide what to do about Mt. Samat. From U.S. positions on the 2,000-foot-high mountain, they had both visual and artillery command of the entire line. Of the three choices Homma had — to bypass the mountain, flank it, or hit it head on — the Japanese commander chose the latter. First, it would be something the Fil-Americans (Filipino-Americans) wouldn't expect, and second, if successful, the anticipated toughest part of the fight would be over. The date and time scheduled for the opening of the final offensive was 3 P.M., Friday — Good Friday — April 3.

On the U.S. side, by the third week in March, it had become obvious that the Japanese had initiated their pre-offensive softening up and probing operations. Official USFIP communiqués, originally concealing or watering down the true situation on Bataan, for the first time began delivering more candid pictures of what was happening. On March 24, for example, Communiqué No. 158 noted that "our positions in Bataan were heavily bombed this morning by 54 Japanese heavy bombers of a new type." It went on to mention that "several sharp encounters occurred between hostile ground forces." Again on March 27, a communiqué noted "a number of sharp clashes between patrols," also that there were "troop and truck movements behind enemy lines which indicated that increased activity may be expected.... Japanese dive-bombers [also] attacked our rear areas."

Relative to the air attacks on the rear area, on the night of March 27, several men from a small quartermaster detachment near the barrio of Cabcaben on the southeastern tip of the peninsula were called out on a burial detail. Burying the dead was one of the jobs of the quartermaster, but this call was a little different. Judging from the size of the detail, the men thought that they must be going to bury a whole army.

On the morning of the twenty-sixth, Japanese bombers in one of the six air raids made on Corregidor that day knocked out one of the freezer units in the Rock's cold-storage plant. With no freezer units on Bataan, Corregidor was forced to store and issue the daily ration of carabao meat to the troops on the peninsula. Twenty-four thousand pounds of carabao—nearly two days' meat allotment for Bataan—was threatened by spoilage with the shutdown of the freezer unless it could be transported across the North Channel and issued. But the beefed-up Japanese air force, which by then had begun its around-the-clock bombing of Bataan, Corregidor, and anything afloat in the channel, delayed the loading until dark. By dawn the next day, the lighter carrying the meat was tied up at the dock at Cabcaben. But again, because of the ever-present Japanese planes, it couldn't be unloaded.

That night, as quartermaster supply trucks pulled down to the dock to unload the meat, some 32 hours after it had been removed from the refrigeration unit on Corregidor, there was no need to tell anyone that it was too late. The gentle onshore breeze, carrying the undeniable odor of spoiled meat, met the nostrils of the detail when they reached the dock. The meat was loaded onto trucks and driven into the jungle and buried. The quartermaster detail wasn't burying an army after all, but if things like this continued to happen to the starving Bataan soldier, it wouldn't be long.[3]

Among the prime targets for Japanese air attacks were suspected U.S. artillery positions. Colonel Richard Mallonee, senior instructor with the Philippine army's 21st Field Artillery, wrote of the devastating bombings everyone on the peninsula was exposed to, that "every few minutes one plane would drop down, lift up the tree branches, and lay one or two eggs. Every vehicle that tried to move, every wire-laying detail, infantry patrol, every individual moving in the open was subject to these spot bombings." Also noted was a marked increase in the volume and accuracy of enemy artillery fire. Indications came that the Japanese were not just pre-registering their guns for the offensive, but had brought up heavier caliber pieces as well after the installation of an observation balloon on the eastern slopes of Mt. Natib.[4]

Its effects can be best understood, perhaps, by reading two entries made in the Bataan Diary of Major Achille Tisdelle, an aide to General King. Back on Monday, March 16, after writing of the "routine bombing and shelling" that day, he noted that "the Japs now have an observation balloon just out of range of our 155s." Little did he speculate that 15 days later, after noting that the "Nip artillery [had been] raising hell," he would discouragingly write, "If we could only get that damned balloon."[5]

With the arrival of 60 twin-engine Japanese bombers from Malaya in mid–March, the preliminary air assault on Bataan was in full swing by the end of the month. In fact, from about March 22 on, as reflected in Major Tisdelle's diary, there were "heavy bombings in front and in rear areas." Also, "night bombing raids were initiated on our front." His entry for Monday, March 30, began the same way as his previous entries: "Enemy bombers exceptionally active." But there the similarity ended, as the next line astonishingly read: "Bombed Hospital No. 1 today, reported killing 7 and wounding 11."

There were two field or general hospitals on Bataan, both located in an area known as Little Baguio. Located just off the road leading to the barrio of Mariveles on the southern end of the peninsula, they both had been established after the late January withdrawal from the first main line on Bataan. Hospital No. 1 was established in the abandoned buildings and sheds of an old motor pool. Number 2, without a single permanent structure, was set up among the tall trees and jungle a mile or so east of Number 1. The only advantage No.

2 had over No. 1 was that it was completely hidden from the air by the dense foliage under which it was located. The buildings that housed No. 1, on the other hand, were out in the open, and therefore liberally marked with giant red crosses painted on roofs and on a huge layout of galvanized sheets in the center of the compound.

The attack, which came at 7:30 that morning, killed 15 — one American medical corpsman and 14 Filipino mess attendants who had taken shelter in a slit-trench that took a direct hit. That night, over Manila radio station KZRH, men listening to their radios on Bataan and Corregidor heard the Japanese make a formal apology for "the unfortunate bombing of the hospital. It was a mistake." Seven days later a second, more vicious attack would prove that the bombing on March 30 was not a mistake.[6]

As anticipated, what was to be the final Japanese assault on Bataan opened on April 3. Also, as planned, the enemy attack was launched against U.S. positions on Mt. Samat. What was not planned or anticipated, however, was the ease with which the Japanese pushed the starved and exhausted Filipino troops back. In fact, the American line had fallen back so fast that the Japanese had to halt their offensive a full day and a half to allow their supply trains to catch up.

On the U.S. side, the surprising collapse of the Philippine army troops manning the Samat front brought General Richard Parker, II Corps commander, to order the entire Philippine division into the fight. The three regiments, the U.S. 31st and Scout 45th and 57th Infantries, had been held in reserve for just such an emergency. However, judging by the physical condition of the Americans of the 31st alone left little doubt of the success of the operation.

Major Eugene Conrad of the 31st's 2nd Battalion wrote that "before we could move, we had to first eliminate all men who were unable to march. About 20 men per company [30 percent] were so sick with malaria and dysentery, they were unable to even start." Major Everett Mead of the same regiment added that "some men who could hardly walk moved out with their battalions; they had left sick beds to join their outfits, not wanting to be left behind." Colonel Ernest Miller of the 194th Tank Battalion noted that members of the 31st were in such poor physical condition that they "could march for only about ten minutes and then had to rest." There was little doubt, as the division moved forward into the darkness of the night of April 4, 1942, that the handwriting for the entire command was, as General Wainwright said, "already vivid on the wall."

On the afternoon of April 5, Easter Sunday, General Wainright, after a visit with General King for an "overall picture of what was happening on Bataan," headed north to get the details of General Parker's counterattack plans. Captain Tom Dooley, the general's aide, driving "like a wild man, [as] time was indeed precious," skidded the jeep to a stop under a clump of trees near Parker's II Corps headquarters. As the dust-covered Wainwright, wearing goggles to keep the dirt out of his eyes, entered the tent, he was met by Colonel Harrison Browne, chief of staff of the Philippine division. Browne, on loan to II Corps headquarters to help General Parker who had been down for several days with malaria, was just leaving.

Wainwright proceeded to meet with the gaunt, fevered II Corps commander, whose look of despair reflected the hopelessness of the situation. Lines on Parker's maps indicating the extent of Japanese gains looked like a red-colored lasso dropped over the shoulders of Mt. Samat. With "misgivings as to the outcome," Wainwright approved Parker's plan, which he hoped would restore the ground lost in the first two days.

On the way back, Dooley, according to Wainwright, "drove so hard that he broke an axle." The few minutes' delay in securing new transportation gave them pause to watch a small convoy of troops as they passed on the way to the front. It was a sad sight. The men were all terribly thin, mere shadows of what they once were. Their heads were down, bouncing and rolling with the bumps in the road. The sight was still with Wainwright later that evening on Corregidor when he phoned the chief quartermaster, Brigadier General Charles Drake. Wainwright asked him if there was anything at all that could be done to increase the rations on Bataan. Drake told him there was plenty of rice and a little flour and that there were 45,000 C-rations being held for emergency. Double the rice and flour and hand out all the C-rations except enough for 5,000, he told Drake. Send anything that can be spared.

During the next 24 hours on the peninsula, unit mess sergeants were made to feel like Santa Claus. Portions were doubled. Bakeries were back at work baking bread. There was salmon again, and tomatoes, and even cigarettes. The 2nd Battalion of the U.S. 31st Infantry got their food drop on the evening of April 6. "We received about 12 cans of C-rations per man, also cigarettes," remembered Major Conrad of that unit. "We were told they came from Corregidor." Captain John Gulick noted that his Scout coast artillery unit even got "a few cans of abalone, and wonders of wonders, some cigarettes." At a Philippine army artillery unit, an additional reaction to the surprise issue of rice and salmon was recorded. "We thought," remembered Lt. Ambrosio Peña, "it meant that the mile-long relief convoy had finally arrived." Unknown to the Filipinos and to probably most of the Americans, when these rations were gone, there would be no more. The troops on Bataan were having their last supper.[7]

Of course, the counterattack by the Philippine division and a handful of tanks from the 194th Tank Battalion failed. By the morning of April 7, for all practical purposes, three Philippine army divisions on line across the II Corps front when the battle opened five days earlier had ceased to exist.

As the Japanese prepared to direct their offensive down the Bataan east coast, what was left of the U.S. defenders prepared to dig in along the south bank of the San Vicente River that formed a natural defense line diagonally from the coast to Mt. Orion, then west behind Mt. Samat. The key, unfortunately, to holding the hastily organized line depended on being able to link the eastern end with the I Corps. Outside of having to pull back in coordination with the II Corps' withdrawal, as anticipated, the I Corps had seen little activity other than enemy patrol action.

Because of the dense jungle, the battle for the area behind Mt. Samat came down to who controlled the network of roads, called trails, that had been built by army engineers before the battle. Of the nine different trails in the contested area behind and around Mt. Samat, by midday of April 7, five had been irretrievably lost to the Japanese.

For the U.S. stand along what was called the San Vicente River line, the key road junction of Trails 6–8 immediately behind Samat would have to be held. Unfortunately, it couldn't be. Its loss not only jeopardized any hope for success in stopping the Japanese, but, for all practical purposes, ended any chance of saving Bataan.

As successful as the Japanese army was during the first five days of the offensive, much of the credit for its success went to its air force. So intense were enemy efforts to keep the reeling army on Bataan on the run that even attacks on Corregidor were suspended. After launching its 120th air raid against the island on April 5, all attacks for the next few days were ordered against Bataan only. Averaging 150 sorties and 90 tons of bombs each day, Japanese planes saturated roads, bivouacs, command posts, troops moving forward, troops withdrawing — everything. The bombing caught the 201st Engineers, who had been ordered into the fight as infantry, moving up into position on the sixth. According to its commander, Major Harry Fischer, "flying 300 or 400 feet off the ground where they couldn't be seen through the thick jungle, they had a field day." Major Clarence Bess recorded the two-hour long bombing of the 31st Infantry Service Company that same day as the "worst it had experienced on Bataan." After one flight of dive-bombers "had released their bombs, one plane would remain and strafe the area until another flight appeared." Colonel Ernest Miller wrote that "Japanese bombers and strafers pounded [him] unmercifully" on April 7. "They came in veritable clouds — wave after wave. At times the sky was almost black with them."

The officer in charge of U.S. efforts to make a stand on the San Vicente was Brigadier General Clifford Bluemel. Despite the failure to hold the 6–8 trail junction, and with it, the imminent collapse of the entire line, Bluemel refused to concede it.

Two days earlier on April 5, the fiery general was given command and the responsibility of organizing a line of defense along the river. Few unit histories whose men took position on the San Vicente fail to mention the personal efforts of Bluemel during that period. As men straggled across the river throughout the afternoon of the fifth and into the morning of the sixth, many were met by Bluemel, who "personally attempted to organize the resistance." With rifle in hand, he and several other officers had prodded, talked, threatened, but in most cases forced a semblance of a line along the south bank.

Around ten o'clock on the morning of the seventh, a two-and-a-half ton truck loaded with artillery ammunition from a nearby ordnance depot was passing the entrance to Hospital No. 1 when it was pounced on by a Japanese dive-bomber. The well-aimed single bomb made a direct hit on the truck, blowing it up and its two occupants. The men standing guard at the hospital gate dove into a nearby slit-trench at the sight of the diving enemy plane, only to be buried alive by dirt and debris from the ensuing blast.

The "screech of Nip dive-bombers" sent Dr. Alfred Weinstein and hospital Chaplain William Cummings, at that moment crossing the middle of the hospital compound, diving for cover. The concussion from the exploding truck momentarily knocked both men unconscious. Not knowing how long they were out, "bleeding from nose and ears, drums shattered [and] concussed," the two men got up and "stumbled on towards the wards." The tremendous explosion knocked almost everyone in the hospital compound down. Patients were bounced off their beds onto the floor. In the orthopedic ward, where arms and legs were suspended in traction, men who had been tossed to the floor only to be left dangling by their tied-up extremities screamed to be cut down. Other men in the ward, knowing they couldn't be moved to a safe place, began to sob.

Father Cummings and Captain Weinstein, in the meantime, half stumbling and half running, made it safely across the center of the compound. Cummings, attracted by the screams of the orthopedic patients, entered the ward. Weinstein, from the surgery ward nearby, witnessed Cummings' first few moments with the men. "OK, boys, OK," he said. "It's all over. Calm down. The planes have gone." Climbing to the top of a small metal table in the middle of the ward, he said, "OK, men. Let's say a prayer together." Arms outstretched, he began, "Our Father who art in heaven." The screaming stopped. Men quieted. Some joined in. The work of the nurses and corpsmen became easier.[8]

But the raid wasn't over. In fact, it really hadn't begun. Lieutenant Juanita Redmond, on duty in one of the open-sided, tin-roofed, converted motor pool sheds known as a general medical ward, heard someone outside yell, "They're coming back!" Bearing down on the mess hall and the doctors' and nurses' quarters, the Japanese scored direct hits on both. Again patients bounced like rubber balls off their beds onto the hard cement floors.

With sights centered on a giant red cross atop one of the buildings, the Japanese dove again, laying their last stick of bombs among the row of wards. According to Lt. Redmond, who was in one of the wards that was hit, the "bomb pulverized the sheds, smashed tin roofs into flying pieces, and broke [wooden beds] jaggedly like paper matches."[9]

The blast left only one end of her ward standing. A big hunk of its galvanized roofing was "blown into the jungle." Mangled bodies, many impossible to identify, lay partially buried by debris. Arms and legs had been "ripped off and flung among the rubbish." Elsewhere in the compound, amid the screams of those newly wounded and those dying, a hospital corpsman was climbing up a tree to cut down the mangled body of one of the patients who had been blow there by the bomb blast.

"Shaking and sick at their stomachs," nurses and attendants feverishly pulled at wreckage under which men might still be alive. The upper limbs of the tall pine tree in front of the surgical ward would remain draped with blankets, pajamas, linen, sheets, shattered arms, legs, and tin roofing metal for days afterwards.

With the suffering and pain came also sympathy and concern. An American soldier named Freeman, "our boy with no legs," remembered Lt. Redmond, was knocked out of his bed and buried under debris. When found, the first thing he wanted to know was if "Miss Redmond [was] alive." Not far away in the next ward, nurse Willa Hook was knocked down by a falling bunk bed. "You all right, you all right, Miss Hook?" she heard. Dazed but okay, she raised her head and looked into the concerned face of a young Filipino soldier who, ironically, was another "boy with no legs." A survey of the casualties showed 73 had been killed outright in the raid, and 117 more injured or wounded. Of those, 16 would die later, some from shock. The cost in hospital personnel was light: no one killed. Along with Father Cummings, who was wounded in the shoulder, three nurses and two medical corpsmen had also been hit. Remarkable was one aspect of the damage done to the beds in the hospital—of the 1,600 or so estimated to be available for use before the raid, only 65 were left standing.

Physical damage to the hospital was extensive. One of the general medical wards was a total loss. The pharmacy had also been hit, leading to the loss of most of what was left of the drugs. A crater 40 feet across and 16 feet deep was left in the middle of the compound.

While clean-up crews worked to salvage as much as possible, patients were being transferred to Hospital No. 2. Doctors, like Weinstein, were standing over the operating table working on a steady flow of new wounded that would keep them there for 24 hours. Nurses and corpsmen too, worked long into the night, as did the burial details. And sleep, if it came at all, would come in a foxhole.

That same morning back on the San Vicente, despite General Bluemel's heroic efforts to make a stand, it would not be realized. Men who were sick, starving shadows of what they once were could give no more. The morning opened with a three-hour long artillery bombardment of U.S. positions, punctuated regularly by the usual air attacks. At the same time, 4,000 men of the Japanese 67th Infantry Regiment struck the easternmost edge of the line. Fil-American units in position along the San Vicente when the attacks started that morning were made up of the remnants of five regiments. By mid-morning, three had been routed from their positions, leaving U.S. 31st and Scout 57th Infantries to go it alone.

Obviously, it couldn't be done. Finding its right completely open, the 31st followed by the 57th were ordered to pull back and establish a line along Trail 46, a little over a mile to the southeast. Finding Trail 2, the only access to 46, in enemy hands, both units were forced to make their way cross-country. All semblance of organization was soon lost. The men, many sick, some wounded, and all dog tired and hungry, were no match for the difficult terrain. It became, according to Major Eugene Conrad of the 31st who went through it, "every man for himself. Units became separated, the men straggled, and it was extremely hard to keep any contact at all." Troops of the two regiments, beginning their trek as organized units, ended it as stragglers. Because of this unfortunate breakup, they would never again fight as anything more than a remnant force.

Meanwhile, General Bluemel's almost personal fight to keep his reeling command intact had continued throughout the morning. As the day before, many a soldier's path was blocked by the rifle-carrying general as they fled the broken San Vicente line. But, unlike the day before, many, including Americans, were now ignoring him.

Major Clarence Bess of the U.S. 31st, witnessed Bluemel that afternoon, "rifle in hand, trying to collect units streaming to the rear and form them along a delaying position." "This," said Bess, "he was unable to do." Around one o'clock, however, the exhausted, disheartened general got an unexpected lift. Rifle still in hand, "moving slowly and reluctantly southward," he was somewhat surprised at the sight of a lone American officer actually moving forward. He was again surprised and even "cheered up a bit" to find that the officer, Major William Chandler, had been sent north to find him. Help in the form of the 26th Cavalry, he was told, had arrived.[10]

Bluemel had not known that the 26th, long since on foot as infantrymen since their horses had been slaughtered for food, had been assigned to him from I Corps reserve the night before. Chandler told him General Parker had conceded all chances of holding on the San Vicente and ordered him to try again from the south bank of the Mamala River, the next most defensible position.

To gain time for Bluemel to reestablish on the Mamala, the relatively fresh 26th was dispersed across Trail 2 and told to "execute a delaying action, with which," according to Chandler, "they had become so familiar." Around three o'clock that afternoon, close on the heels of the last of the retreating 31st Infantry, Japanese 8th Infantry troops ran into the 2nd Squadron line. The 26th, veterans at the delaying action, stopped the 8th cold. The ensuing lively battle was a short one, however, as they were soon outflanked on both sides and forced to withdraw back through the 1st Squadron's position a mile behind.

There, for the first time, the cavalrymen were hit by the combination of air and artillery bombardments that had been ravaging the II Corps since April 3. Major Chandler, taking note upon the 26th's arrival of how "open and sparsely covered" and therefore subject to "hostile artillery fire and bombing" the II Corps appeared, was to more than realize his fears. The attacks, "more severe than anything the regiment had ever been through before," broke the Scouts' hold on the trail. The 1st Squadron, catching the "brunt of the fire, was forced to pass the junction on either side by short rushes in small groups." Casualties were "high, and a much reduced Troop A and only a portion of Troop B reached the Mamala River." With word of the withdrawal to the Mamala, General King sent his chief of staff, General Arnold Funk, to see General Wainwright on Corregidor.[11]

"His face was a map of hopelessness of the Bataan situation," reflected Wainwright upon seeing Funk. And Wainwright knew why. Earlier that day, he had ordered King to launch a counterattack east out of the I Corps against the western edge of the enemy's II Corps salient. General Beebe, calling for Wainwright, told King that the 11th Division was to attack east in a general line with Trail 8 and link up with the II Corps on the Mamala River.

King told Beebe that he couldn't attack. "The troops are so exhausted that they could not move a hundred yards out of their foxholes before collapsing."

"Nevertheless, those are your orders," said Beebe.

"Very well," answered King and then hung up.

General Funk, however, had come not only to explain to Wainwright that it couldn't be done, but to tell him that things were deteriorating so rapidly on the peninsula that General King "might [even] have to surrender." Unknown to him, the Philippine commander was hamstrung. "Under no conditions" could he allow Bataan to be surrendered.

On April 4, he had received orders from General MacArthur, endorsed by General Marshall in Washington, stating emphatically that "under no conditions should [Bataan] be surrendered.... Any action," he continued, "was preferable to capitulation." Bataan was ordered, in so many words, to fight to the death; the troops, as MacArthur more tactfully put it, were to "give a good account of themselves."

Interestingly enough, the details of MacArthur's ill-founded plan, which included a "feint" by the I Corps followed by "a sudden surprise attack by the II Corps," astoundingly directed that it should not be launched until all "food or ammunition failed." In other words, although the Japanese had steamrolled over more than 30 square miles of Bataan real estate in less than five days, and although 70 percent of the command had malaria and dysentery and over 90 percent were suffering from near acute malnutrition, things weren't quite bad enough to initiate MacArthur's plan.

Wainwright paused, looked up at Funk, "a picture of weariness," and said, "Go back and tell General King that he will not surrender. Tell him he will attack. Those are my orders."

Disbelievingly, tears filling his eyes, Funk reminded Wainwright of just how bad "the situation [was] over there. You know what the outcome will be."

"I do," replied the heartsick Wainwright, unable to speak more.[12]

Crestfallen, Funk left the headquarters lateral and headed back to Bataan with the news. By the time he reached General King's headquarters, however, something had happened that brought a little relief to the situation. It started with King receiving a call from his I Corps commander, General Albert Jones. The fiery Jones, who had been informed of the counterattack in person by King's operations officer, Colonel James Collier, was dumbfounded. He told Collier that the attack, scheduled for four o'clock that afternoon, couldn't possibly be mounted before 4:00 A.M. the next day. Furthermore, 11th Division troops were too weak to even make the precipitous Pantingan River gorge, let alone drag their artillery with them.

With Jones' report, King got both Jones and General Wainwright on a 3-way telephone hookup. After several minutes of deliberation, Wainwright gave in. The decision to attack was left to King.

The Bataan commander wasted no time in ordering General Jones to stand down. "I'm taking the responsibility myself and order you not to attack," he said. In fact, it was agreed by both men to pull the still intact but highly exposed I Corps right flank back about four miles parallel with the Mamala River. By the afternoon of the 8th, if all went well, the Bataan front would again appear as a straight line across the peninsula. But it wouldn't.

After the II Corps withdrawal from the San Vicente to the Mamala River had been acknowledged on the afternoon of the seventh, General King pulled out all stops in making an attempt to hold the Japanese there. In addition to the Scout 14th and American 803rd engineers, whom he had given to Bluemel earlier as infantry, King ordered men of the 4th Philippine Constabulary Regiment out of their beach defense positions along the bay and into the line.

Despite this, however, a stand on the Mamala wouldn't be realized. General Bluemel hadn't liked the chances the south bank of the river had presented him the moment he saw it. The higher, much steeper north bank would give the Japanese complete command of the line, making it virtually untenable even before the fight began. Additionally, the resulting breakup of the 57th and 31st Infantries during their strenuous cross-country trek from the San Vicente that afternoon had rendered them impotent as organized fighting units. It was much the same for the stragglers from the other three regiments who had been routed from the line.

Another unit, the 201st Engineer Battalion, had been overrun and captured even before it reached the Mamala. Wrote its commander, Major Harry Fischer, whose men were "practically dead ... from fatigue, hunger and dysentery [anyway], we were so tired that the idea that the Japs finally had us didn't bother us a bit."[13]

Around nine o'clock that night, Bluemel ordered the Mamala abandoned in order to gain a few hours' rest and to reorganize what was left of his army—one more time. Two and a half miles to the south lay another river—the Alangan—whose prominent southern bank would, if nothing else, make it much more defensible at the outset than the Mamala.

And so, slowly, painfully, men who had seemingly expended the last bit of energy they possessed digging in on the Mamala, arose to move south once more. Leaving the 26th Cavalry to cover the withdrawal, men moved out across pitch-dark roads and trails, many hanging on to one another to keep from becoming separated or lost, men who were sick with fever or with wounds dropping out along the way.

An American with the 31st, suffering from dysentery, had to stop five different times to relieve himself, each time finding it more and more difficult to catch up. Finally, after the fifth time, he gave up, sat down and waited for the Japanese. Fortunately, he was picked up by the 26th Cavalry, who, covering the withdrawal, were the last ones out.

Later that night, General Wainwright, upon hearing of the withdrawal from the Mamala, penciled a message on his yellow-lined note pad for Washington, which read, in part, "Continued heavy enemy pressure, constant bombing, strafing, and shelling of front line units forced all elements of the right half of our line in Bataan to fall back. A new defensive position is forming on the high ground south of the Alangan River."[14]

But the "new defensive position" referred to by Wainwright on the morning of April 8 offered a pathetic sight. The II Corps, listing 26,000 effectives on April 3—not including the U.S. 31st and Scout 57th—could muster only 1,600 men on the Alangan—including the 31st and 57th—for what would be its last stand. The Americans alone, entering the fight just three nights earlier with 800 men, were down to just 120 riflemen.

Depleted as it was, the handful of Americans and Filipinos who were still standing on the new U.S. line (and standing they had to remain, according to one American, "to stay awake"), by dawn of April 8 had been hurriedly dispersed up and down the Alangan.

The bulk of the II Corps withdrawal had been accomplished over two routes: the East Road and Trail 20, some two miles inland along the base of the Mariveles mountains. For the sake of control, General Parker had decided to split his command at this point, giving the eastern half to Colonel John Irwin. Having no more than 1,200 men to work with, Irwin's main charge was, of course, to hold the important East Road. General Bluemel, in command of the rest of the II Corps, spread his men across the remaining mile and a half of the river bank from Trail 20 east. Although on paper his strength was shown at eleven battalions, in reality it was close to just two—1,360 men.

As it arrived, Bluemel assigned his exhausted army to its position on the new line. For the third time within the past 48 hours, the battered remnants of the II Corps found themselves hurried into a strange, unprepared, and unreconnoitered position.

It was little wonder that men who had not eaten or slept in nearly four days got confused or were unable to respond, for only two of the five units actually ended up in their assigned positions. They were the 14th Engineers and the 26th Cavalry—both Philippine Scouts—who were assigned to the left and right sides of Trail 20, respectively. From the right of the 26th all the way to Colonel Erwin's sector, the U.S. line appeared a sieve as, unknowingly or perhaps unavoidably, the American 31st had left a 1,000-yard gap between themselves and the 26th on their left, and 500 yards between them and the 57th on their right. Worse, the American 803rd Aviation Engineer Battalion, assigned as the connecting link between the 57th and Irwin's flank, unable to make contact with troops on either side when it reached its position, had continued south.

When informed that a gap of a half mile existed between the two forces, Bluemel phoned General Parker for reinforcements. He was told that troops couldn't possibly be there before dark. That was over 12 hours away. "That'll be too late," said Bluemel. Unless the gap was filled immediately, they could be "damned sure the enemy would have it by then." You'll have to hold with what you've got until then, he was told. Bluemel slammed the phone down and angrily went out to assess his chances.

Japanese foot soldiers, in the meantime, having crossed the Mamala River, were some two hours away. But their air force wasn't. Around ten o'clock, enemy reconnaissance planes discovered the Americans and Filipinos digging in along the south bank of the Alangan. An hour later, the Japanese fighters and bombers struck. The focal point of their attack on the eastern end of the line were remnants of the Philippine Army's 31st Division, the Constabulary's 4th Infantry and 2nd Engineers and the Provisional Air Corps Regiment.

The junction of the East Road and the mouth of the Alangan River converged at the upper end of a horseshoe-shaped curve that forced the road to run parallel on both sides some 300 yards before it again turned south. It was from where it passed directly in front of the defender's side that the battle to halt the Japanese would take place.

Arriving in their assigned positions in the middle of the night, they'd not been able to reconnoiter their positions until that morning. "We didn't have any shovels, so we began to look for a good defensive position," said Captain Mark Wohlfield of the American's 2nd Battalion. "As we moved up ... to the main ridgeline, the Japanese planes found us.... I gave the order to go beyond the ridge, which had practically no cover, and to get to the wooded area beyond. Some of our men were blown into fragments. Some of the trees were blown down; the grass was on fire; the smoke was everywhere."[15]

Not only did the 2nd Battalion get hit hard by the Japanese planes, so did its 1st Battalion and the Philippine army's 31st Infantry on its right. In fact, so unrelenting were the air attacks that Lt. Colonel Frank Loyd, an American instructor with the Constabulary, found nothing but empty foxholes, abandoned equipment, and dead bodies on his inspection of the positions originally occupied by the two units.

Credit for organizing the defense by the Constabulary went to three men: Colonel Rafael Jalandoni, 4th Division commander, Lt. Col. Loyd, and Lt. Col. Vicente Torres of the 2nd Engineer Battalion. With a clear, unobstructed view from their high-ground positions above the road, it was decided that the best chance for success was to ambush the Japanese from where they had dug in on the south side of the river.

Around noon, signs that the enemy was close came when the up-to-then steady stream of refugees and vehicles heading south had disappeared from the road. When lead elements of the Japanese 67th Division reached the opposite bank of the river, it appeared by their lack of caution that their movement would continue to remain unchallenged. That was about to change.

Waiting until they crossed the river and reached a spot abreast the Constabulary's line of foxholes on the ridge, the Filipinos opened fire on the unsuspecting Japanese. Surprised and staggered by the volume of fire coming from the ridge, for the first time since their opening attack on April 3, the Japanese were stopped dead in their tracks. Some pulled back toward the river. Most took cover in the cagon grass on the opposite side of the road. In fact, it was from the concealment offered by the chest-high grass that allowed them to organize and counterattack the Constabulary positions.

For an hour the battle raged back and forth. At one point, when it appeared the Japanese were poised to overrun the command post, Col. Jalandoni, with a handful of hurriedly rounded-up service personnel, led a bayonet charge against the startled enemy, chasing them back across the road. The sight of their commander leading the assault galvanized the rest of the Constabulary men, who, under the leadership of Frank Loyd and already twice-wounded Vicente Torres, routed the Japanese, vehicles and all, back across the river.

Low on ammunition and in desperate need of reinforcements, an officer was sent back to II Corps headquarters to ask for help. He arrived back with nothing but bad news: there would be no reinforcements or ammunition; they were on their own.

Although faced with an impossible situation, Jalandoni refused to give up the roadblock that he felt was the only thing stopping the Japanese from rolling up all of Bataan. Despite his honorable intentions, for all practical purposes, it would cost him what was left of his entire regiment, which started when the entire 2nd Battalion slipped away unnoticed when its exhausted commander fell asleep. Unknown to the remaining 1st Battalion and 2nd Engineer troops as they awaited an anticipated second frontal attack, the Japanese, with tanks and infantry, burst out of the jungle behind the startled Filipinos.

It was over in minutes, as those not killed or wounded fled in all directions. Fortunately, all three officers escaped. Wounded Vicente Torres was picked up and transported back to Hospital No. 2, where he would receive three Purple Hearts and the Legion of Merit from the U.S. Army and the Distinguished Conduct Star from his own army.[16]

In Bluemel's sector, it was a fight of a different kind. There, Japanese incendiaries had set fire to the tall, dry grass and clumps of bamboo throughout which the U.S. 31st and 57th were digging their foxholes. Exhausted men were forced to beat out fires and clear areas around their foxholes just to avoid being burned out of their positions. Bluemel himself, by then "nearing a complete state of exhaustion, but," according to Major William Chandler of the 26th Cavalry, "still refusing to spare himself," was supervising preparations of the roadblock of Trail 20 in anticipation of the inevitable stand to be made by the 26th and 14th Scout Engineers sometime that afternoon. While awaiting the arrival of the Japanese, an example of the futility of the situation within the crumbling II Corps occurred.[17]

Around 2:00 P.M., four 75mm-carrying half-tracks, under the command of Lieutenant Colonel Joseph Ganahl, arrived to help support the Trail 20 roadblock. The SPMs (Self-Propelled Mounts) were promptly placed in position to cover the high ground north of the river. "With artillery support for the first time in the war," commented Major Chandler, "we began to feel that the forthcoming struggle might not be so one sided after all."

But that feeling was short lived, however, as moments later "enemy tanks were reported on the East Road, and Ganahl's guns were ordered [there] ... just 30 minutes before the Japs hit our roadblock. It's doubtful," lamented Chandler, "if [Ganahl] ever reached the East Road, and besides, the enemy tanks turned out to be ours anyway."

But the tanks that appeared about 4:00 P.M. at the Trail 20 roadblock "were decidedly not friendly," said Chandler. But again, futility, for although the Japanese tanks were unable to either penetrate the roadblock or back up along the narrow trail, neither did the Scouts have the necessary weapons to knock them out. Despite not being able to use the tanks, Japanese infantrymen arrived "by the truckload, and were soon swarming [all] over the terrain to [our] front."

Earlier that afternoon another Colonel Irwin, Colonel Constant Irwin of General Wainwright's staff, had come over from Corregidor to General King's headquarters with some special orders.

One had originated some two months earlier on February 3, when General MacArthur told General George Moore that if Bataan's fall ever appeared imminent, he wanted the entire Philippine division brought to Corregidor. To Wainwright, the imminent time had arrived. But two of the three regiments, the 31st and Scout 57th, were too heavily engaged on the Alangan to be pulled out. That left the 45th, which, from its reserve position in the still-quiet I Corps, alone was selected. After securing transportation for his regiment, 45th commander John Doyle and his staff headed for Mariveles by car.

The second order was for the evacuation of all the nurses and a few of the doctors from Hospitals 1 and 2. Transportation to the docks was arranged for that evening along with boats to take them to Corregidor. Arrangements were also made for two more groups—the last Corregidor would officially take. They were the few remaining navy men at the Mariveles Section Base and three coast artillery units on loan to Bataan from Corregidor since January.

In the meantime, back on the Alangan, despite the gallant and stubborn fight made throughout the afternoon by the Scouts and Constabulary men, the inevitable had occurred: the Japanese had discovered the gaps in the line. It wasn't until 7:00 P.M., some three hours since the first Japanese assault against the roadblock, that Bluemel got word that the 31st and 57th had abandoned their positions on the Alangan. With no other choice, he ordered the 14th Engineers and 26th Cavalry " to disengage and head south down Trail 20."

Although it was never known, it is very probable that the breakup of the Alangan River line that evening was the turning point in General King's decision to surrender some nine hours later. In retrospect, from that time on, events were recorded that leave little doubt of it. They began at 7:00 P.M.

With news that the Alangan had been abandoned an hour earlier, the Bataan commander, completely exhausted of reserves, ordered members of the 200th and 515th antiaircraft units to report, as infantrymen, to the ridge immediately to the south of Cabcaben airfield.

About four miles up the road, the last pathetic remains of the II Corps were trying to form along a ridge, too. This one overlooked the Lamao River. But, as had happened after each successive withdrawal, there were fewer men to work with. Of the 1,000 or so who were there, it is safe to surmise that less than 20 percent were capable of carrying on the fight.

Even General Bluemel, their seemingly indefatigable leader, also appeared as if he could give no more. While soaking his feet in the middle of the river he didn't even know was the Lamao, he was told that General Parker wanted him on the phone at his recently abandoned C.P., a half mile down river. Bluemel said that if Parker wanted to talk, "... tell him to get the phone to me."

Captain Franklin Anders, 57th intelligence officer, who helped string the wire from the old C.P. to Bluemel, along with several other officers listened to the blistering, one-sided conversation that followed. Speaking with Lt. Col. Howard Johnson, Parker's chief of staff, he said:

> You sit there on your dead tails in your comfortable, well-lighted C.P. and draw a line on a map with your grease pencil and tell me to hold it. I am here in pitch dark, with no map and only a vague idea where I am. I have been fighting and falling back on foot for the past 72 hours. I have no staff, no transportation, no communications except the phone I hold in my hand. My force consists of remnants of the only units that have fought the enemy and not run from them. The men are barely able to stagger from fatigue and lack of food, which we have not had for over 24 hours. Yet you cannot send me one of your many fat, underworked staff officers to show me where I am to deploy the handful of men I have. Where is the food we need to revive our starving bodies? Where is the ammunition we need to fire at the enemy? Where are the vehicles and medics to treat and evacuate our wounded? I'll form a line, but don't expect it to hold much past daylight.[18]

Meanwhile, to help slow the enemy down, King had his chief of staff, General Arnold Funk, call Corregidor's Seaward Defense Commander Colonel Paul Bunker to see if he could bring any of his big guns to bear on the East Road above the Lamao River. Bunker told him that he could reach as far north as Limay. Fifteen minutes later, batteries Smith and Hearn opened up. Off and on for the rest of the night, the big 12-inch shells would be heard whistling northward into the teeth of the advancing Japanese army.

Back in January, General MacArthur had selected at the time Captain, later Colonel, Carlos Romulo to be the voice of a daily radio program from Corregidor to the people of the Philippines. Called *The Voice of Freedom*, Romulo made over 300 broadcasts to those who were able to secretly listen over radios that they were forbidden by the Japanese to have. Because of the broadcasts, the Japanese put a "Wanted — Dead or Alive" price tag on Romulo's head for the "propaganda of lies being conducted" as the voice of freedom. Realizing this, and the possibility that there may not be another chance to get the little Filipino off of Corregidor, General Wainwright sent for him that afternoon.

When Romulo entered the headquarters lateral, Wainwright, sitting behind his desk at the far end of the tunnel, stood up. "I'm ordering you off Corregidor," he said.

"What do you mean, Sir?"

"Bataan is hopeless," he said, handing Romulo his orders. "At seven tonight, take the little launch to Bataan. Go to the Bataan airfield. From there you will take off for Mindanao."

Formalities over, Wainwright stepped around the desk and grabbed Romulo's hand.

"God bless you, my boy," he said, shaking it warmly. "Tell President Quezon and General MacArthur I will do my best to the end."[19]

Three hours later, "pockets ... bursting" with letters from friends to be mailed home, Romulo climbed into a waiting jeep outside Malinta Tunnel for the short ride to the dock. As they drove down the hill looking at Bataan, he wondered "what was taking place across that three-mile stretch of water. At that very moment on the other side of that "three-mile stretch of water," a few select people had been having the same thoughts about Corregidor. They were the nurses and three doctors from Hospitals 1 and 2 who had just been notified that boats were waiting to take them there.

At Hospital No. 1, someone yelled, "Be ready to leave in 15 minutes, and take only what you can carry."

"What's happening?" wondered Lt. Juanita Redmond. "Why are we being ordered out?"

All the doctors and corpsmen had come to see them off. It hurt to say goodbye. "Farewells were hasty and tearful," remembered Captain Alfred Weinstein, "kisses sweet and salty."

As the two buses carrying them turned right out of the compound for Mariveles Harbor, Captain Nelson, in the lead bus, turned and said, "Girls, there's going to be a lot of trucks, soldiers, and civilians on the road. There'll be a great deal of confusion." In a voice turned somber, he said, "Bataan has fallen!"

"It shocked us into silence," Lt. Redmond recalled. Slowly, however, all began to realize "how [they] had been hiding from the thought [of it], refusing to believe it would happen," but now that it had come, few were surprised. What about the girls at Hospital No. 2, someone asked?

"They've been ordered out, also," Nelson answered. Yes, they had. But since No. 2 was closer to the dock at Cabcaben, they had been directed there.[20]

On the ridge behind Cabcaben airfield, one 37mm gun and some 1,500 men from the 200th and 515th AA artillery, who, it will be recalled, were ordered there by General King earlier, formed what was to be the last line of defense on Bataan.

"It was dark by the time the trucks parked behind the line we were to form," said Corporal Hubert Gator of the 200th. "We then ... marched single file down the ridge overlooking the runway. I didn't believe the line we formed was much more than a mile long. Each man dug his own foxhole. There was a shortage of shovels, so most of us spent the night digging with our bayonets. To a man we expected the next day to be our last on earth."[21]

Down at Cabcaben Field, Lt. Edgar Whitcomb, as the day wore on had witnessed "more and more men ... straggling through [his] camp." All had the same story. "Each had been separated from his unit during the attack in which most of his outfit had been wiped out."

"Oh, God, it was terrible," said one man. "They bombed and strafed us all day along the road."[22]

Colonel Richard Mallonee, on his way to contact Colonel John Erwin on the Alangan that afternoon, commented when he reached the East Road that "bombers were working the road again and it was a shambles, choked with refugees, military and civilian. Hardly a hundred yards was without its ditches lined with dead. One bomb hit near a running soldier; and when the smoke settled, only the torso was in the center of the road."[23]

Around 8:30, the launch carrying Colonel Carlos Romulo to Bataan after a harrowing trip across the North Channel, pulled up and unloaded its passengers at what was left of the Cabcaben dock. A few minutes later, standing on the edge of the East Road waiting for his transportation to Bataan Field, Romulo remembered thinking it funny that all the traffic was coming his way. "I didn't dream it was retreat." he said. Moments later, his mind was jolted into reality, however, when the driver of the car commandeered for his ride north told him that it would be impossible to get through to the airfield. Nevertheless, orders from Wainwright directed them to try.

Less than a hundred yards up the semblance of what once was a paved, two-lane highway, Romulo realized what his driver was talking about. "Such a mélange of vehicles swarming together was surely never seen before in the world," he wrote later. "Truckloads of soldiers jammed together so that they could not slump with the weariness that was written on their haggard faces ... ambulances crammed with men and command cars filled with haggard-faced officers ... all headed for the bay, for the shoreline that was the end of the world."[24]

For a few lucky ones, the shoreline wasn't quite the end of the world, however. For the nurses and doctors from Hospital No. 1 who had arrived at the Quarantine Dock in Mariveles around 9:30, it would be a two-and-a-half-hour wait for the boat to Corregidor — a wait that few would forget, but all would live through. "Bombers came over while we waited," remembered Lt. Redmond, "but as we didn't know where [the foxholes] were, we stayed on the dock."

Despite his own orders for the navy to destroy its facilities on Bataan to avoid capture, evacuating the nurses for the same reason, ordering the 45th Infantry to Corregidor, and telling Carlos Romulo that Bataan was hopeless, General Wainwright had still not issued the order for Bataan's surrender.

On his desk, staring him in the face, were the April 4 orders from General MacArthur not to surrender, but to attack. The timing of MacArthur's counterattack plan, which, as mentioned earlier, was not to be launched until either food or ammunition ran out, was perfect. Bataan's food supply, with the issuance of the last 45,000 C-rations earlier, was now exhausted.

At 11:30 P.M., Wainwright had the Corregidor switchboard connect him with General King on Bataan. Despite knowing that his exercise in futility couldn't be carried out, he told King that the pressure had to be taken off the II Corps before it was too late.

King told him that it was already too late.

Nevertheless, Wainwright ordered him to reinforce the "suppressed II Corps" with units of General Jones' I Corps, and then attack "northward toward Olongapo and Subic Bay" with the rest.

Stunned, yet still answerable should he fail to notify I Corps of the plan, King called Jones. Jones, as outspoken as General Bluemel, particularly concerning what he considered "asinine" command decisions, told King that MacArthur's plan was "ridiculous." His men had just completed a tortuous four-mile withdrawal to the banks of the Binuangan River in compliance with his order of the night before. They had nothing left.

King did not press it. He would not order an attack that was doomed to failure even before it started. There would be no counterattack by the I Corps. King looked at his watch. Both hands were at 12. It was Thursday, April 9, 1942 — the beginning of what would be recorded as Bataan's last day.

The weary Bataan commander called General Funk and his operations officer, Colonel James Collier, in for a conference. Together they reflected on the meeting they had had two days before with frontline commanders. When questioned about what percent of their units were still considered effectives—defined by King as a soldier who could walk 100 yards without staggering and still have the strength to shoot—they unanimously agreed it was no more than 15 percent. Together they retraced the old lines on the map of Bataan, looking like the rungs of a ladder leading to the firepits of hell itself: San Vicente, the Mamala, the Alangan, the Lamao, and, before long, the Cabcaben. Was there a chance? Could the Japanese be stopped before reaching the high ground above Mariveles?

They looked at the words "Provisional Coast Artillery Brigade" (200th and 515th Antiaircraft Battalions) penciled in as the defense of the Cabcaben line. The Japanese would be in Mariveles no matter what happened by tomorrow night.

"II Corps as a tactical unit no longer existed," reflected Collier. Just behind Cabcaben were the refugee camps and the hospitals with over 13,000 defenseless patients already "within range of enemy light artillery," no place to fight a battle.

"I've decided to surrender," General King said. But, knowing the position Wainwright was in with MacArthur's "no surrender" orders, he decided to put his own two stars on the line and not notify the commanding general until he had already contacted the Japanese. "I don't want [Wainwright] to be compelled to assume any part of the responsibility," he said.

Like the notification of the death of someone who had been terminally ill for some time, to everyone in the room, it was no surprise. Yet, remembered Colonel Collier, it hit us "with an awful bang and a terrible wallop." By the time General King left for his trailer to begin outlining his surrender terms for the Japanese, "there wasn't a dry eye present."[25]

Slowly the agonizing wheels of capitulation began to turn. Word went out at 2:00 A.M. to the large engineer and ordnance depots above Little Baguio to destroy everything. Motor pools were told to destroy all vehicles. Artillery and antiaircraft guns were ordered spiked. Of the remaining 50,000 gallons of precious gasoline, 40,000 were ordered dumped. The quartermaster was ordered to hold back 10,000 gallons to hopefully be used to transport the defeated garrison to POW camps. Unit commanders were told to bury their records and then have their troops report to the Mariveles airfield at dawn to surrender.

Before word of the surrender reached what was left of what could be called the air corps on Bataan—two P-40s, two P-35s, and a Navy Grumman Duck, the commanding officer of Bataan Field, Captain Edward Dyess, already knew of the imminent collapse.

Around six that evening, Dyess had received a phone call alerting him that the Japanese had broken through at the Alangan and were now less than two miles away. With what was left of his air force in jeopardy should that be true, he grabbed pilot Jack Donaldson and told him to take off in Dyess' old P-40 and to bomb and strafe the approaching Japanese. More importantly, he told him if this was a false alarm, "come in and land. [But] if the Japs are as close as they tell us, rock your wings and keep going for Cebu."

Fifteen minutes later Donaldson was back, "bomb racks empty. ... He rocked the plane like hell and kept going."

Dyess relayed the information over the phone to air force headquarters at Little Baguio, where he was told to begin evacuating the remaining pilots in the planes that were left. In the event the Japanese broke through, he pulled the two P-35s out onto the field "with their motors running." First out was Captain "Ozzie" Lund. Lieutenant Randy Keator, who had happily stuffed himself into the baggage compartment, went with him. Next he called Captains Ben Brown and Hank Thorne at the headquarters shack above Bataan Field and told them that a P-35 was waiting for them. "They both refused to go," wrote Dyess, "but as field commanding officer, I sent them off."

With Brown and another pilot, Lt. Larry McDaniel, crammed in the baggage compartment along with a half-dozen 30-pound fragmentary bombs to "drop on the advancing Japs," Thorne somehow cleared the field.

Word then came down that Captain Joe Moore had taken off from Cabcaben Field in the last P-40. That left only one plane, the old Grumman Duck. But things didn't look too good for it to even leave the ground.

Ironically, it was Moore who had last flown the Duck on April 6. Returning from Cebu with a load of medical supplies, it blew a cylinder about 80 miles south of Bataan. Moore, a skilled veteran pilot, was able to nurse it back to Cabcaben for what he thought would be the last time. But it wasn't the last time.

In a small cave at the head of Cabcaben Field, head mechanic Leo Boelens and Lieutenant Roland Barnick were busy working on the engine of the old Duck when Dyess drove up see how things were coming. Three pilots who were assigned to go if they could get it running, Lieutenants Stewart Robb, "Shorty" Crosland, and Bill Coleman, came out of the cave to meet him. Dyess told them to keep their eyes open for another passenger, a Colonel Romulo "sent over by General Wainwright from Corregidor." Boelens and Barnick, who was to be the pilot, working on the engine, overheard Dyess. They looked at each other. That'll make six, four more than she had seats for, they thought.

"What about you, captain?" one of the pilots asked Dyess. "When are you going to leave?"

"I still have some men to take care of," he said, avoiding the question. Unknown to the three men as they watched him drive off into the horrible night, one of them was there because Dyess, although ordered out, had refused to leave.

"Not too far away, the sixth man, Colonel Carlos Romulo, was sure he had missed his plane. Around ten o'clock he had seen Hank Thorne's P-35 head out from Bataan Field and turn toward Corregidor. "There goes my plane," he thought. For over two hours, he and his driver had been literally fighting their way against a "swarming outgoing tide of vehicles and men fleeing south." At least half a dozen times he had jumped out and pleaded for help. None came. He remembered seeing boys "of seventeen or eighteen ... dragging their guns and stumbling in the dust. Some walked with spraddled knees, like old men, falling and rising and staggering on."[26]

They reached Bataan Field only to find it abandoned, but fortunately they ran into an officer with new orders for Romulo from Corregidor. "Word had been left ... that I was to go to Cabcaben and ask for Lieutenant Barnick. There was a plane there."

Meanwhile, work on the old Grumman Duck at Cabcaben had been progressing. They were just ready to test the motor, when someone yelled, "Lieutenant Barnick?"

"Is that Colonel Romulo?"

"Yes!" exclaimed the relieved little Filipino in a voice that he said "could have been heard in Tokyo." But after seeing the old Duck, which he thought "looked like something reclaimed from a city dump," the "sickly" feeling that he had had earlier when he thought he had missed his flight returned.

"Let's test the motor," said Barnick.

Romulo "crossed [his] fingers and prayed while the boys spun the propeller." Miracle of miracles, it started. At last, they were off. At exactly "eighteen minutes past one," remem-

2. Bataan's Final Hours

bered Romulo, the six men crawled into the plane. With four men literally stuffed into the oversized pontoon well, Barnick started the engine.

It kicked right over and began to vibrate. "Quit shaking the plane," shouted Barnick to the four men. They weren't. But something sure was—at that very moment Bataan was being rocked by a heavy earthquake.

"If this thing flies, I'm a genius," Romulo remembered Barnick saying earlier. Little did he or the other passengers know that part of what he meant was due to the fact that he had never flown a Duck before.

Barnick related later in a letter to Romulo his version of the next few seconds. He wrote:

> There was no light in the cockpit, so I was forced to use a flashlight. On takeoff, I discovered that the propeller would not change pitch—the equivalent of starting an automobile in high gear. I succeeded in taking off from Cabcaben Field by bouncing the plane and then retracting the landing gear. As we cleared the end of the field we settled within a few inches of the water. Our load was too great, but I managed to maintain altitude by running the motor wide open.[27]

Unable to gain any more altitude, Barnick handed a hastily scribbled note down to the passengers: Throw out all extra weight! Hurry! It said. Everything went, baggage, tin helmets, parachutes, radio equipment, sidearms, even a chunk of floorboard.

"That seemed to give the old Duck a new lease on life,' said Romulo. "She soared upward—50 feet." The plane, with Barnick "swearing so loudly that we could hear down below," continued to climb. Its destination: Panay Island, some 225 miles to the south.

The earthquake that had rocked the old Duck before it took off, and which was severe enough to make the skipper of an approaching American submarine think he had run aground, was widely felt on Bataan. Amid exploding 12-inch shells from Corregidor batteries Hearn and Smith on the Japanese advancing along the East Road, and amid the explosions of 500-pound bombs being set off by army air corps ordnance at various bomb dumps, for some it was difficult to differentiate between the vibrations. At 2:00 A.M., however, two back-to-back explosions occurred that everyone felt—Bataan's death knell.

Behind Little Baguio on a hill known as Cemetery Ridge, men had been preparing for over an hour to blow up Bataan's main engineer supply depot. The oil had already been drained "from what cars and trucks remaining in our motor pool," wrote Corporal Robert Levering of the engineers. "Then we set the engines racing wide open."

At 2:00 A.M. "our cache of 500,000 pounds of explosives was touched off," Levering continued. "Seemed as if the old volcano on Mt. Bataan had come back to life." Seconds later, with dirt and debris "still falling around us ... magazines of the nearby 75th Ordnance Depot let go. The sky boomed with explosions of heavy shells and all kinds of small arms ammunition."

Army sergeant Jerome Leek was driving a truck on the East Road near the turnoff to Mariveles when the two explosions, so close together as to be interpreted as one, occurred. "Must have been the largest ammunition dump in the Philippine Islands," he thought.

He continued on another quarter mile and then pulled off at a familiar supply dump. In a nearby tent he aroused a sleepy second lieutenant and said, "Sir, our big ammunition dump just went up. It looks like the end if we don't try to save it."

"Save it, hell," answered the young officer. "Our own engineers blew it up. Bataan has fallen, you know."

"Bataan has fallen?"

"Yeah, Bataan has fallen. You are on your own."

Not too far away, several others had the feeling that they were on their own, too. They were the nurses from Hospital No. 2, who earlier had headed toward the dock at Cabcaben where the boat scheduled to take them to Corregidor was waiting. But the trip to the dock against the endless stream of vehicles and men had made them late. The boat, if there ever had been one, was gone. Carlos Romulo saw them on the Cabcaben cutoff road "fleeing toward the waterline, where there might or might not be a boat to carry them to Corregidor." It was a sight he would never forget.

But there was still a chance ... if they could reach Mariveles. By the time they got back onto the road, however, it didn't seem to make any difference which way they were going. Traffic would crawl along, then stop, move a few feet, and then stop again. They had driven over and through wreckage, bypassed shell holes, and even had to wait for a body to be removed from in front of them before continuing. From the back end of the foul-smelling garbage trucks they were riding in, they were living Bataan's death.

Around 1:30 A.M., they slowly drove past the road leading to their hospital from which they had started some five hours before. A half hour later, not far from the turnoff to Hospital No. 1, they were held up. "They're going to blow up the ammunition dumps," someone said.

A few hundred yards away in his foxhole inside the Hospital No. 1 compound, Dr. Alfred Weinstein was waiting for the same blast. "At the appointed hour," he wrote, "the skyline behind the hospital was illuminated with an eye-searing glare ... the earth trembled as if shaken by a giant fist, [and] the air was filled with the roar of released energy. Blast followed blast," he said, "until it seemed as if my already ruptured eardrums would be ripped from their moorings."[28]

Back on the road to Mariveles, traffic began to move again. Along with everyone else, two strangers who had hitched a ride on one of the nurses' trucks back at the Cabcaben turnoff were happy to be moving again. The two, air corps officers from Cabcaben, had received orders to report to Kilometer Post 184, north of Mariveles. Had they known that by the time they would reach their destination they would be directed to surrender to the Japanese, they wouldn't have been quite so pleased to be getting under way.

But maybe it wouldn't be such a surprise after all, considering what they had witnessed earlier near Cabcaben. It happened when one of the officers, Lieutenant Edgar Whitcomb, leading a group of 20 men over a jungle trail, reached the East Road. "There we were greeted by a sight that made our blood turn cold," he remembered. "The entire road was packed with vehicles of all kinds, each one overflowing with combat-weary soldiers. Both sides of the road were choked with soldiers unable to find a place on a vehicle. I was so surprised and stunned by the sight," he said, "that I was unable to speak for a few minutes."[29]

As the long column of vehicles resumed its slow crawl toward Mariveles, the wheels of a mission important to the lives of thousands on Bataan were also turning. Following his decision earlier that morning to surrender Bataan, General King's primary task was to somehow communicate with the Japanese beforehand as to those desires. Colonel Everett Williams and Major Marshall Hurt, two bachelors on the general's staff, were selected to make the initial contact at dawn.

King handed Williams an official two-page "memo of instructions" to be used as a guideline in arranging a formal surrender meeting with General Homma later that morning. To cover the possibility that the Japanese should decline his offer, the memo instructed

Williams to "ask him terms under which he [would] accept the surrender of the Luzon force on Bataan."

Listed were several points of consideration toward which King wanted Japanese attention drawn — such as the dangerous proximity of the two hospitals to the current battle zone, the fact that, because of the unusually poor physical condition of his command, it would take quite some time to organize and deliver them as prisoners of war, and that he had already "issued orders" to have them delivered "by motor transportation ... to places as might be directed." Lastly, hoping for their immediate release, he directed attention to "the vast number of civilians present in Bataan" who had remained "in no way connected with the American or Philippine forces."

It was decided that in order for Hurt and Williams to reach the Japanese lines by dawn, they should leave Little Baguio around 3:30 A.M. At 2:00 A.M., the two men were sitting in one of the headquarters shacks when the II Corps ammunition and dynamite stores went up less than 800 yards away.

Hurt had just finished addressing what he feared might be his last letter home and was talking on the telephone when "a terrific explosion occurred ... followed by a second." He started for the door. Just then another blast rocked the "whole earth," and the shack began to break up. This was followed by a forth explosion. "The window [fell] on my head," he dimly remembered, "and lumber [fell] all around," as did rocks, tree stumps, and chunks of concrete.

Williams helped his benumbed comrade up the hill to the safety of General King's dugout. Although wobbly, Hurt was still "determined to go."[30]

Major Achille Tisdelle, who lived through the experience with Hurt and Williams, recorded the two explosions in his diary as the most terrific he "had ever heard. ... In the morning, our overhead cover [tops of trees] was gone and there were many empty shell cases all over the camp. It is miraculous we came through this."[31]

A few minutes after the explosions, the light from General Wainwright's extension began flashing on the Corregidor switchboard. It was General Lewis Beebe, his chief of staff, asking to be patched through to General King's headquarters. Wainwright, who had not heard from King since ordering him to counterattack at 11:30, was wondering how it was progressing.

The explosions, however, had momentarily disarranged the telephone communication system on the peninsula, and instead of getting King, General Bluemel answered. He was still up on the Lamao River trying to organize the pitiful handful of men from his disintegrated II Corps into some kind of fighting force. It was impossible.

Bluemel told Beebe that very thing. Beebe, relaying instructions from Wainwright, told him that he was on his own, that the commanding general would approve "whatever action he deemed best." After hanging up, Beebe tried to ring through to General King's headquarters again. "That line is still out, sir," he was told by the operator. They had to wait.

Anxious as ever about news of his counterattack yet still unable to reach Bataan headquarters, Wainwright rung General Jones at I Corps. General Beebe was still talking for the commanding general, whose slight deafness made it almost impossible for him to hear anything because of the existing poor conditions. Beebe asked how Jones' plans for the attack were progressing.

Orders for the attack had not yet been given, Jones answered.

Beebe told him to stand by, that he would probably be receiving them any minute from General King, and then hung up.

The fact that Jones still hadn't received orders to attack drew no reaction from Wainwright, strongly indicating that the Philippine commander hadn't expected it anyway. Further evidence along those lines surfaced a few minutes later, at 3:00 A.M., when King, after hearing of Beebe's conversation with Jones, phoned across to Wainwright. Beebe picked up the receiver.

"I want a definite answer as to whether or not General Jones will be left in my command regardless of what action I may take," King said.

Beebe relayed the question to Wainwright, who nodded his head yes. "General Wainwright says you're still in command of all forces on Bataan," Beebe answered.

The subject of why King, after three and a half hours, still hadn't informed his commanders of the counterattack wasn't even broached by Wainwright. Nor did King mention that in less than 30 minutes he would be sending two men forward with white flags to implement the surrender he had ordered three hours earlier.

About that same time not too far away from General Wainwright's headquarters in Malinta, a small boat was being tied up to the island's North Dock. Minutes later, a group of weary army nurses and three doctors from Hospital No. 1 were seen trudging their way up the dock toward waiting trucks. They had left the Quarantine Dock in Mariveles at midnight for what was usually a 45-minute trip across. Three nightmarish hours later, they thankfully stepped ashore on Corregidor.

Over at Little Baguio on Bataan, explosions were still being felt and debris was still falling as engineers and ordnance crews continued to destroy their depots.

In a blacked-out dugout at nearby Bataan Headquarters, a man looked at the green, luminous dial of his watch. It was 3:15 A.M., time to get started for the front. Colonel Williams and Major Hurt, the officers selected to carry word to the Japanese of General King's desire to surrender, left the dugout and headed for the main road.

After a quick stop at Hurt's tent for a piece of bedsheet that could be used for a white flag, "we commandeered a reconnaissance car and a motorcycle escort and were off," said Hurt. Latest word put the front north of Lamao at somewhere around Kilometer Post 152, a little more than three miles away.

The two men started out but, of course, found the traffic impossible. Deciding to abandon the car, Hurt remembered that Williams looked at his watch, grabbed the white flag, "climbed on the rear of the motorcycle and took off."

Left to follow the best he could, Hurt began working his way through the "maze of traffic, worming through crouching, demoralized, beaten foot soldiers." It was 4:00 A.M. He remembered what was written on the copy of instructions in his pocket: "You will proceed ... in time to arrive at our front lines by daylight." Bataan was down to its last two hours.

Back at the navy section base along the east shore of Mariveles harbor, the last of the four tunnels that had been dug into the hillside to accommodate navy supply, communications, and hospital services on Bataan had just been dynamited closed. As soon as it was completed, a small fleet of motor boats filled with the last of the section base personnel shoved off for Corregidor. As the last three boats, loaded mostly with exhausted crewmen from the just-scuttled sub-tender USS *Canopus* cast off, a tremendous explosion erupted from the northernmost of the four tunnels. Commander Earl Sackett, skipper of the *Canopus*, witnessed what followed from one of the boats:

The whole hillside seemed to erupt in an orange burst of flame, hurling huge boulders half a mile out into the bay.... Evidently, gasoline drums stored in the tunnel had broken open when the entrance was dynamited, and fumes in the corked-up passage had built up a gigantic explosive charge. Our three boats were squarely in the path of that deluge of destruction. Two of them were struck with massive boulders, one of them sinking instantly under an impact which sheared off the whole stern, leaving the three occupants struggling in the water.[32]

The other damaged boat did not sink, but boulders crashing down through its canopy killed an officer and three men. Nine of the men were hurt, some seriously, by the "rain of heavy rocks," but two of the three boats were still able to make it across to Corregidor.

By 5:00 A.M., Major Hurt, after "saying a few prayers ... bumming a few rides, and doing a lot of walking," was within about three quarters of a mile of Lamao. He had been virtually all alone on the road for the last half hour. There, in the faint, early morning light, sitting in a jeep parked next to Kilometer Post 155, Hurt recognized Colonel Williams and a driver.

Hurt climbed into the back of the jeep and the three men started forward. It was still quiet "except for the far-away explosions of the dumps and the chattering teeth of our driver," he said.

After crossing the bridge over the Lamao River, they ran into Lt. Colonel Joe Ganahl, who, with a few tanks and half-tracks and a handful of troops, represented the entire covering shell. Colonel Williams told him that it was all over, that he and Major Hurt had come forward to meet the Japanese and surrender Bataan.

Leaving the three men alone to wait for the enemy, at 5:30 A.M. Ganahl turned his tiny armored column around and disappeared into the early morning light. An hour later they were still sitting. There were still no Japanese, and it was now broad daylight. Interestingly, Bataan had folded up so fast within the last six hours that the Japanese army had found it tough to keep up.

Since "nothing has happened, we start slowly forward to make contact," said Hurt. "After a mile, everything is still deserted and quiet. We see and hear nothing."

They crossed the bridge over the Alangan River and started up the hill on the other side. Unlike the Lamao River they had just passed, judging from the wreckage and debris, it appeared that somebody had put up a pretty good fight at the Alangan. Just then, a large group of Japanese soldiers came onto the road. "We stop the car, raise our hands, and wave the white flag," wrote Hurt later. Yelling, they "rush at us with their bayonets flashing. Is the end here?"[33]

Ironically, less than a hour earlier, a yell of a different kind was heard over the same question. At 6:00 A.M., when General King was confident Hurt and Williams either had or would soon be in contact with the Japanese, he phoned General Wainwright to tell him what he had done. Lt. Colonel Jesse Traywick, who took the call, rushed to the commanding general with the news.

Wainwright was shocked. "Go back and tell him not to do it!" he yelled.

The night duty officer hurried back to the phone. It was too late, he was told. Contact with the Japanese had already been made.

"I had my orders from MacArthur not to surrender Bataan," wrote Wainwright later, "and therefore ... could not authorize King to do it." But he was quick to show that he had "no criticism" of the Bataan commander for doing what he had done. "It was a decision which required great courage and mental fortitude."

Wainwright's next thought was how to tell General MacArthur. Sitting at his desk contemplating just how he would explain it, he began writing:

> At six o'clock this morning, General King, commanding Luzon force, without my knowledge or approval, sent a flag of truce to the Japanese commander. The minute I heard of it I disapproved of his action and directed that there would be no surrender. I was informed too late to make any change, that the action had already been taken. Enemy on east had enveloped both flanks of what was left of the II Corps and was firing into the hospital area, which undoubtedly prompted King's action. I had ordered the I Corps to attack north, but the attack did not get off. Physical exhaustion and sickness due to a long period of insufficient food is the real cause of the disaster. When I get word that terms have been arranged, I will advise."[34]

Over on Bataan, meanwhile, the men who would carry that word were, at that moment, not at all sure they would live. Colonel Williams and Major Hurt, it will be remembered, were being rushed by a platoon of bayonet-wielding Japanese soldiers. A minute or so later, a noncommissioned officer appeared and ordered the soldiers, who had already begun ransacking the jeep, to put everything back. "We heave a sigh of relief," said Hurt.

Williams pulled out General King's surrender instructions and showed them to the sergeant. Seeming to understand, he climbed into the jeep and motioned them to drive on. They soon passed more enemy soldiers who "stare at us and do a lot of talking. Before long, we were turned over to an officer who, in turn, relayed us further to the rear."

"We pass several exhausted 31st Infantry soldiers being herded along by the Japs," wrote Hurt. "A rope is tied around the wrist of each, but they tell us they are not being treated badly."[35]

At Kilometer Post 146 they stopped and got out of the jeep. Seated at a small rickety table was Major Kameichiro Nagano, whose detachment had been assigned to capture the East Road. Hurt and Colonel Williams, carrying their white flag, entered the clearing and were introduced to Nagano. No one saluted. Nagano did not stand up.

The interpreter read Williams' surrender instructions.

The two Americans answered several questions which, among other things, included challenges to their authority to surrender Corregidor. Nagano, at Williams suggestion, agreed to set up a meeting with General King at the Bataan Agricultural Experimental Farm Station back near the Lamao River bridge. Colonel Williams was left behind while Hurt, escorted by four Japanese tanks as far as the Lamao River, was sent on alone to bring back General King.

"How long?" his escort asks.

"Two to four hours depending on traffic," he told him.

"Speedo," the Japanese said as Hurt pulled away, "speedo!"

As the American began his difficult journey to pick up General King at Little Baguio, back at Mariveles dawn had offered no more than an extension of the dreadful night before.

The line of garbage trucks carrying the nurses from Hospital No. 2 had filed slowly through the smashed remains of what was once the pleasant barrio of Mariveles. The only thing left standing, remembered one of the nurses, was the statue of what looked like a saintly lady pointing off toward the rising sun.

The trucks passed the turnoff leading up the West Road, rumbling on toward the old Quarantine Station and the dock in front. On the last truck the two army air corps officers who had hitched a ride from Cabcaben earlier that morning jumped off. "Better come along to Corregidor with us!" one of the nurses shouted.

2. Bataan's Final Hours

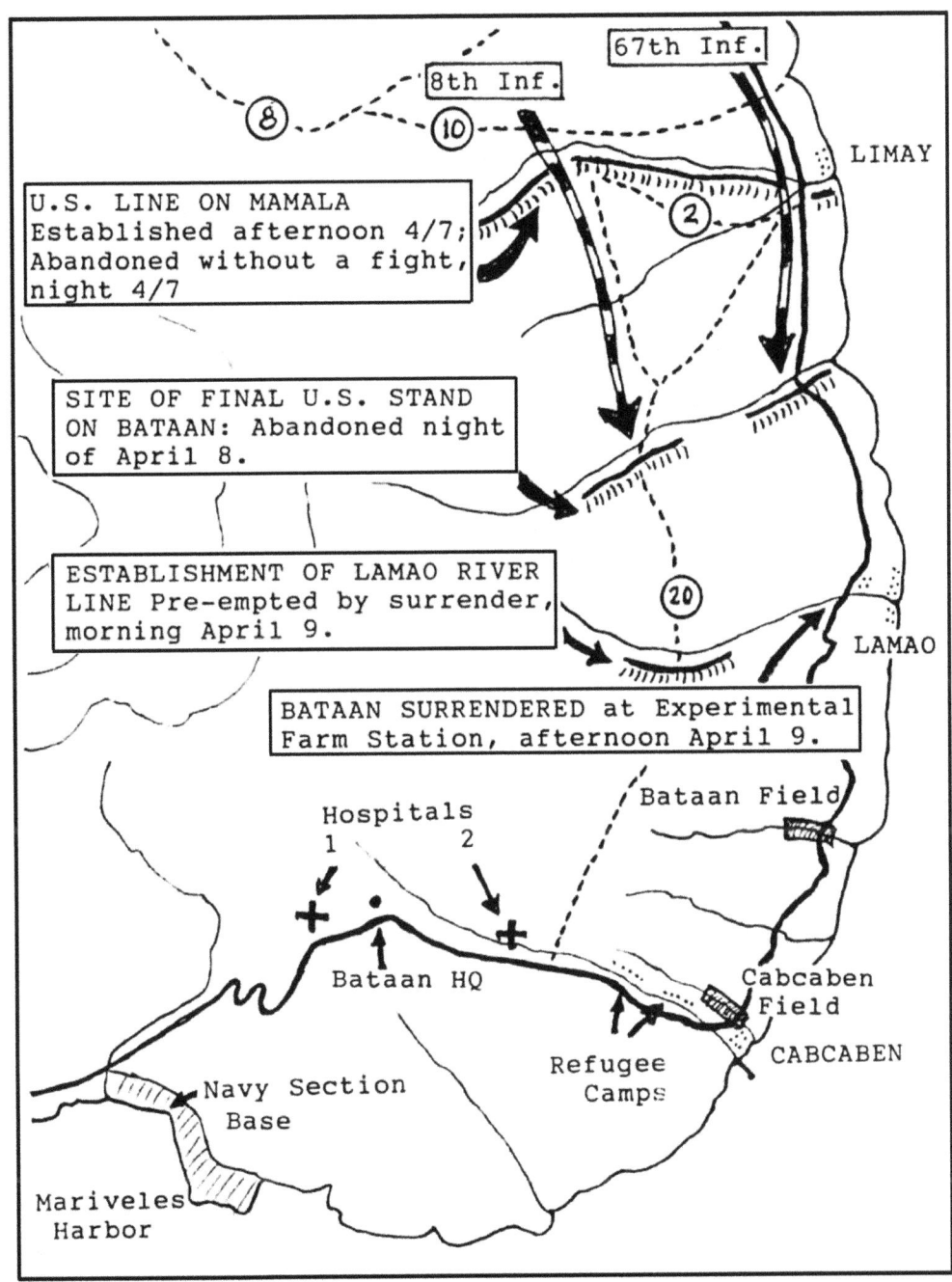

"Sure like to," answered one, "but we have to go up to meet the rest of our outfit north of Mariveles."

"Good luck to you, then."

As the trucks continued on through the maze of abandoned vehicles toward the waterfront, one of the nurses stood up to take a look. "There's no boat!" she cried. "No boat!"

They'd been bouncing about on the back end of stinking garbage trucks for close to ten hours, had missed one boat at Cabcaben, been held up for over an hour by the explosions of the engineer and ordnance depots, stalled, been pushed by a half-track, had one truck break down, forcing its occupants to make it on foot, and now, no boat.

Exhaustion, by then, had anesthetized the fears and anger of most. Seemingly no longer caring about the boat, within a few minutes, practically all were sound asleep in roadside ditches or shelters near the dock.

Like the nurses, many men had hopes of making it to Corregidor when they reached Mariveles that morning. Few did. "The most unforgettable sight of all," remembered Navy Lt. Commander John Morrill, watching through binoculars from Corregidor, "was the groups of men standing on the south Bataan shore in the early half-light of the morning, beckoning and signaling with flashlights for help.... How many were ferried across, we never knew."[36]

Over on Bataan, meanwhile, several hundred men, mostly Americans from units stationed on the southern end of the peninsula, had gathered just off the West Road in a huge open field adjacent to Kilometer Post 184. Those who had started out for there that night were told that they were going to organize for a last-ditch stand against the Japanese. By daylight, however, the picture had changed.

The two officers who had hitchhiked over from Cabcaben on the back of one of the nurses' trucks were headed for Kilometer Post 184. They had picked up a ride on a truck moving south just outside Mariveles. Many of the vehicles heading toward them, they noticed, were displaying white rags and sheets as they passed. But it wasn't until they reached their destination and were told that Bataan had surrendered that they realized that the sheets were really white flags.

Many others, by then, had heard the news of the surrender. Reactions varied. Some men cried. Most swore. A few tried for Corregidor. Some contemplated escaping into the hills.

Because of the anticipated reactions of the Americans to the surrender orders, a few officers were dispatched to the area around Mariveles to round up stragglers as they filtered in from the roads and jungle trails. Everyone by this time was looking for a way to get to Corregidor. Under the guise of leading them to an isolated spot on the beach where they would be met by a boat that would take them to the Rock, it was announced instead that they were to discard their weapons and wait for capture by the Japanese. It's a wonder, under such circumstances, that the bearer of such news was not shot by one of his own men.

Engineers at the main supply dump on Cemetery Ridge had just finished destroying their equipment when word of the surrender reached them. Their reactions, recorded by Corporal Robert Levering of that unit, reflect the feelings and response of most soldiers. "Some men," he remembered, "didn't want to surrender." Down at Mariveles they had heard "men were abandoning the peninsula like rats leaving a sinking ship.... Bancas and leaky boats were selling to the highest bidder."

"Several wanted me to join them in an escape party up the mountain," he said. But we "gave up the idea when we considered that we had no food or medicine to ward off starvation and disease in the jungle." Finally, with the attitude of "not caring very much about what might happen, we started for Mariveles airfield, where all troops were ordered to assemble."[37]

The rumor of men "abandoning the peninsula like rats." was true if they were lucky enough to find a banca. Probably because of the presence of the unmolested Japanese air force, there was no Dunkirk-like evacuation of the hundreds of men who had retreated to the southern tip of the peninsula during the night and early that morning. Despite this, it is estimated that close to 2,000 somehow made it across the three-and-a-half-mile North Channel to the Rock. Of those, it's safe to say that they all did it on their own.

Of those did, two men, Privates Andy Miller and Ernie Mallon of the Provisional Air Corps Regiment, following their withdrawal from Sector B on the seventh, that morning discovered a banca on a beach just south of Cabcaben. Remembered Miller, "We found an old banca that had an outrigger on one side and two good [outrigger] supports on the other side."

After finding a piece of bamboo to replace the missing outrigger, the four men (they had been joined by two men during the night) were about to shove off when six Filipinos wearing Philippine army blue denim outfits suddenly jumped in and sat down in the middle of the boat.

"It was obvious that we were not going to get to Corregidor without them," said Miller. "[Around 11:30 A.M.] we finally got under way, using boards for paddles. There were ten people in the banca ... [but] only four [Americans] paddled. The Filipinos never paddled.... We paddled like mad for about a half hour and probably got about one fourth of mile off the beach. It seemed like were being swept to sea three feet for every foot we made toward Corregidor."

By 1:00 P.M. they were far enough off the beach to get a good look at Bataan. "There were Jap planes all over the place, still strafing and dive bombing," he said. "A couple of times a ... plane came flying by to take a look at us ... but never fired. I remember thinking at the time, [that] there had to be a better place to be than sitting in a banca in Manila Bay, between Bataan and Corregidor."

Around four o'clock, four and a half hours since they shoved off, Miller guessed they were about halfway. "About this time we saw a navigation buoy ... and tied up to it. [It] was about six feet square with a pole sticking up in the center. I leaned up against [it] and fell asleep. About 6:00 P.M. a navy patrol boat came by and shouted at us to stay put, that they would be by later to pick us up. They did. As soon as we were picked up, the boat was dive bombed.... The bombs dropped short but showered us with water from the explosions.

"We were given food on the boat, the first we had had in the last two days. I was exhausted and slept on the boat all night." Early the next morning, some 18 hours since they'd left the beach below Cabcaben, the boat pulled into the South Dock at Corregidor. "As we walked into the entrance to Malinta Tunnel," said Miller, "we met some other men who had done the same as Ernie and I had. Very nearly all of us who made it were assigned to beach defense."[38]

When it was light enough, binoculars were broken out for a look at what was happening across the 3-mile-wide channel. Although it wasn't much, they could tell one thing for sure: "If King did surrender, some of the Japs don't know about it," said one man, alluding to the enemy planes seen still bombing and strafing.

He was right. Until General King could make his surrender official, the Japanese air force had been instructed to continue their attacks on Bataan. Of that order, King himself need not have been told, for no sooner had his surrender party left Little Baguio than they were strafed off the road by a Japanese fighter.

Major Achille Tisdelle, carrying a white flag in General King's jeep, wrote in his diary that they were bombed and strafed by "three fleets of dive bombers ... all the way, repeatedly." Colonel James Collier, carrying the flag in the lead jeep with Major Hurt, was a little more specific, stating that they were attacked no less than once every 200 yards, forcing everyone to dive into ditches or behind trees each time.

"Colonel Collier and I ran out of the ditch and waved the white flags hoping the Japs would see them," continued Tisdelle. "If they did," he said, "they paid no attention."[39]

It was now ten o'clock. The surrender party had been on the road for an hour and had only progressed a mile and a half. If the next mile was as tough, chances were they wouldn't make the Japanese lines alive, and there would be no formal surrender of Bataan.

About that time in the Press Relations Office back on Corregidor, Philippine army major Salvador Lopez wasn't sure he could do what he had to, either. Word had come from General Beebe, Wainwright's chief of staff, that although nothing official had been heard from General King's headquarters, they should begin preparing the announcement of the fall of Bataan.

Lopez, one of the principal writers of *The Voice of Freedom* scripts since the beginning, was given the job. He looked up at his companion, Lieutenant Francisco Isidoro, who would translate what he wrote into Tagalog, the native language, and Lieutenant Norman Reyes, who would read it in both languages over *The Voice of Freedom*. "I don't think I can do it," he said. "Mechanically," he remembered, "I placed a sheet of paper in the typewriter and began writing.

> Bataan has fallen. The Philippine-American troops on this war-ravaged and blood-stained peninsula have laid down their arms. With heads bloody but unbowed, they have yielded to the superior force and numbers of the enemy....

In all, Lopez would write 282 words of "the epic struggle that the Filipino and American soldier put up" on Bataan—a 282-word epitaph filled with praise befitting the "intrepid fighters [who had] done all that human endurance could bear." "The flesh must yield at last," he wrote in moving conclusion, "endurance melts away, and the end of the battle must come. Bataan has fallen, but the spirit that made it stand—a beacon to all liberty-loving peoples of the world—cannot fail."[40]

Yes, Bataan had fallen, but still not officially. The American half of the surrender party, about the time Lopez had finished writing his announcement, had been received by Major Nagano at the Agricultural Experimental Farm Station near Lamao. They had been two hours traveling the three miles from Little Baguio. They had been harassed and strafed continuously by the Japanese air force for the first half of their journey, until an enemy reconnaissance plane acknowledged their white flags just outside Cabcaben.

Through an interpreter, Nagano told the frazzled, disheveled Americans as they sat down that he was not authorized to make the arrangements himself, but that a member of General Homma's 14th Army staff was on his way.

A few minutes later, a 1940 Cadillac, still shining through its coat of red Bataan dust, arrived and out stepped Colonel Motoo Nakayama, Homma's senior operations officer. As

Major Tisdelle remembered: "General King and all the rest of us [including Colonel Williams who they found waiting for them at the Farm Station], stand up when he strides in. No one salute[d] on either side and no one [shook] hands."

"We arrange ourselves around the table," Tisdelle continued. "I cross my legs but a Jap officer knocks my feet down. I light a cigarette, but he knocks it down too." He glanced over at King, braced stiffly in his chair in front of Nakayama. "I never saw him look more a soldier than in this hour of defeat," he remembered.[41]

General King, reflecting on his history at that moment, remembered that almost to the minute, 77 years before, April 9, 1865, General Robert E. Lee was meeting with General U.S. Grant at Appomattox. Like Lee, King lamented that he, too, "would rather die a thousand deaths" than to do what he was about to do.

Nakayama's interpreter opened the conversation. "You are General Wainwright?" he asked.

King identified himself as the commander of the army on Bataan.

"Where is General Wainwright? We want to see General Wainwright."

King told them that he had "no means of getting in touch with Wainwright" and that he was only representing his command in the negotiations.

"Japanese cannot accept surrender without Wainwright," emphasized the interpreter.

Again King patiently explained that he had no authority to speak for Wainwright or to surrender Corregidor either, as he had also been asked. "Finally the Japs appear to be convinced," Tisdelle observed, "so the aide blurts: 'You will surrender unconditionally!'"

King explained that his forces "were no longer fighting units" and that he wished an armistice period so he could prepare his "army for deliverance as prisoners of war." He also requested that the air bombardment be lifted.

The Japanese air force was ordered to bomb until noon, he was told. "You will surrender unconditionally!"

"I desire to surrender with these four conditions," King went on, listing the points he wished the Japanese to honor. Would his men be treated as prisoners of war under the provisions of the Geneva Convention?

"You will surrender unconditionally!" was again the response. It was absolutely impossible, continued the interpreter, for Colonel Nakayama to negotiate for the surrender of Bataan only. If the forces on the peninsula wished to give up, it would have to be done "voluntarily and unconditionally ... [by] each individual or each unit."

"How will the prisoners be treated?" King asked again. Would they be protected by the rules of the Geneva Convention?

"Of course," came the reply, "we are not barbarians. Will you surrender unconditionally?"

At that moment, a flight of Japanese planes roared over the trees heading south. Realizing that each minute of debate meant death to more and more of his shattered command, the Bataan commander nodded in agreement. Nakayama then asked him for his sword.

"I have none," King replied, rather shocked.

The Japanese appeared even more surprised. "They jabber some more," wrote Tisdelle, "but finally decide that the crazy Americans can surrender without sabers."

At 12:30, Major Hurt and Colonel Collier, who were standing some distance from the surrender scene, saw the four Americans stand up, take out their pistols, and lay them on the table in front of the Japanese. With terms apparently agreed upon, General King called

Collier and Hurt over and instructed them to take a jeep south. "Move all American and Filipino troops south of Cabcaben. They are to be assembled by unit for surrender," he told them.

Back at Bataan headquarters in Little Baguio, meanwhile, Brigadier General Arnold Funk, King's chief of staff, who had been nervously waiting for official word of the surrender, got a phone call. It was from Corregidor. It was news he had been waiting for, but it was not about the surrender.

Around eight o'clock that morning, calling as to the whereabouts of his nurses who had supposedly left Bataan for Corregidor sometime during the night, he was astonished to hear that the girls from Hospital No. 2 were missing. They'd missed their boat at Cabcaben, he was told, and were not at Mariveles either. Funk told them to send a boat back to find them. They weren't sure they had one to send, came back the reply.

Only through a lot of "vim, vigor, and swearing," to put it mildly, did he finally get them to promise to send a boat back to look for them.

At dawn, when the nurses from Hospital No. 2 arrived at the empty Quarantine Dock, nurse Dorthea Daley Engle (she had married a soldier on Bataan on February 14), like everyone else, succumbed to the demands of physical exhaustion and fell asleep. The next thing she remembered was being aroused by the noise of people cheering. Raising up out of the drainage ditch where she had been sleeping, she soon saw why. It was a boat, the *Mitchell* from Corregidor.

To avoid becoming a sitting duck for the ever-present Japanese air force, the skipper pulled in, hurriedly took on a dozen nurses, and then pulled out into the bay. At that moment, a Japanese plane dove down and dropped its bombs some distance behind the dock. Despite the big explosion, none of the nurses were hurt. Once more the rescue craft came in, took on a few passengers, and then pulled out. After the third time the dock was empty.

An hour later, as the little engineer launch edged up to Corregidor's North Dock, a runner was dispatched to the communications lateral in Malinta Tunnel. "Notify General Funk that his nurses from Hospital No. 2 have arrived," he was told.

After giving the switchboard the message, the courier paused for a moment to listen to the noon broadcast of *The Voice of Freedom* coming in over one of the many civilian radio sets in the tunnel. The voice was an unfamiliar one. The man, identifying himself as Lt. Norman Reyes, began, "Bataan has fallen. The Philippine-American troops on this war-ravaged and blood-stained peninsula have laid down their arms."

Three hundred miles away, on the edge of a dusty little auxiliary fighter strip on the east coast of the island of Panay, a half dozen men gathered around a radio carrying the same message. They were Lieutenants Barnick, Robb, Boelens, Crosland, and Coleman. The sixth man was Colonel Carlos Romulo, the "last man off Bataan," as Barnick had called him, and except for the old Grumman Duck, the man who would be back on Corregidor reading the very same message they were listening to.

Romulo didn't think he could stand hearing Reyes' message read through. "I turned," he said, "with some crazy idea of running somewhere. Barnick's big arm reached out to steady me. He was crying too—the husky soldier from North Dakota, the wisecracking flier, the tough guy. We stood there on that airfield at Iloilo, an American flier and a Filipino soldier ... tears running unashamedly down our cheeks. And we didn't give a damn who saw us."[42]

2. Bataan's Final Hours

Bataan had fallen. But the many unusual circumstances, increased because of the chaotic state of affairs within the shattered command, promised that the actual surrender would be a touchy one. The lack of communication, of course, was the greatest contributor to the confusion on both sides. By and large, troops in the II Corps, who had borne the brunt of the fighting since April 3, didn't have to be told it was over. By the morning of the ninth, they were through. Officially or unofficially, it made no difference. Yet there were a few diehards who still had to be convinced.

One of the first confrontations with the Japanese over the surrender occurred just north of Cabcaben on the East Road. Only the fortunate arrival on the scene of Major Hurt and Colonel Collier saved it from becoming serious. The two Americans, heading south from Lamao with two Japanese officers, arrived just in time for Collier to jump from his jeep and step in between a Japanese tank commander and a feisty Philippine Constabulary major, seconds away from blowing the Japanese "in two" with his drawn and cocked .45.

"Colonel, this SOB demands my surrender," said the major, voice shaking, "and I am not going to ... and if he makes a move to give a command, I'm going to shoot him in two."

Collier calmly explained that Bataan had been surrendered to the Japanese less than an hour before. The major, shaking his head, disgustedly turned his pistol over to Collier and walked back to tell his troops who were dug in some 150 yards away.

At 11:00 A.M. over on Trail 20, remnants from General Bluemel's Lamao River force, withdrawing south toward Cabcaben, ran into a regimental-size enemy force that had worked its way in behind it and was blocking the trail. A firefight had erupted between the Japanese and the 26th Cavalry's 1st Squadron, Bluemel's advance guard. Having hoped to avoid contact with the Japanese front line troops in case they may not have received news of the surrender, Bluemel, despite the protests of several American officers, was not about to stop the fight. Before going much further, however, word was sent back that white flags had already been uncased across the U.S. front. The fiery general, according to Major William Chandler of the 26th, "reluctantly decided to send forward a white flag in hopes that the hostile unit had heard of General King's surrender. Whether or not they had was never determined, but they did accept it."

Meanwhile, in the jungle a mile or so to the west, G Troop of the 26th Cavalry, which had split off from Bluemel's force, had run into two American military policemen who informed them of the surrender. The officer in charge, Major Don Blanning, decided to make for Signal Hill on the southwestern slope of Mt. Bataan, where it was rumored a last stand was being organized. After an hour or so of unsuccessfully trying to locate the trail leading across the foot of the mountain, however, Blanning gave up. Calling his gallant little band of Scouts together for the last time, he gave them the opportunity to either surrender or escape. Wisely, wrote Major Chandler, they "elected to trust the jungles rather than the Japs."[43]

As will be remembered, General King, the night before, had ordered what was left of the 200th and 515th New Mexico National Guard antiaircraft units to move into defensive positions along Cabcaben ridge — the last line of defense on Bataan. Although like with Bluemel, word of the surrender had reached the commander of the 200th before daylight, again it would probably be the Americans who had to convince the Japanese of it.

It wasn't long before the Japanese appeared in front of the 200th position on the edge of the East Road. Despite offering no resistance and a number of well-placed white flags, the lead elements of enemy tanks and trailing infantry moved cautiously down the road.

At that point, suspecting they hadn't been informed of the surrender, Major Paul Schurtz, regimental supply officer with the 200th, with a white T-shirt tied on the end of a bamboo stick, went forward with hands up to meet with the Japanese.

Ignoring the white flag, he was immediately knocked down and clubbed by Japanese soldiers until stopped by an officer from one of the tanks. Although it wasn't, as Corporal Hubert Gator said, their "last day on earth," for a few moments it appeared he might be right.

The one regimental-size unit still unaccounted for that morning was the all–American Provisional Air Corps regiment. Following its 1st Battalion's route from the Alangan River on the eighth, as an organized fighting force it no longer existed. In fact, when Captain Mark Wohlfield took muster on the morning of the ninth, only 75 of the original 770 men of the battalion could be found.

What happened to the balance of the 1,500 or so airmen who made up the regiment before the Japanese April 3 offensive, was what happened to most of the surviving 28,000 II Corps troops.

What occurred was perhaps best described by Sgt. Sam Moody of the same regiment. At dawn of April 6, from their still-unchallenged position on the II Corps front, he said that a few ragged, filthy, bloodied men "straggled into the area. 'The Japs are coming!' one soldier screamed. 'They're just a couple of miles away. We're done. Everybody is running like hell.'" And running they were.

"In a matter of minutes, humanity was pouring down the roadside from our area, heading almost nowhere. Just running, fleeing from the enemy in any way they could. Trucks labored along the road. Soldiers, many without weapons, plodded along, barely able to keep their bodies aloft, tripping as a drunken man does when he's thrown out of a bar. Officers and enlisted men of every rank. Some carried rifles. Some carried nothing. Many were bare headed and some wore nothing but trousers.

"The word came to evacuate. We didn't know where. We couldn't even tell if the order had come from an appointed source. Everybody just started to move out. We got up, were ordered by someone to march to Mariveles, then left to ourselves."[44]

Meanwhile, the order eventually leading to the fate of the 75 men who alone represented the entire Provisional Air Corps regiment came early in the morning of the ninth.

"Along about 2:00 A.M. ... I got a message to make contact with the unit on my left flank," said Captain Wohlfield. "After marching in the dark for an hour or so, we came upon some troops from the 31st Infantry. An officer asked who was in command. I told him I was. The officer was General Bluemel. 'How many men have you?' he asked. He said he had about 600. Now he had 675."

After taking cover in a thicket, they were shelled out of their position by Japanese artillery. "I moved the men onto the road near Lamao," remembered Wohlfield, "then down into a valley leading to Trail 20. As the sun came up, we started taking small arms fire from the jungle. We shot back ... until I heard a whistle. The word that we were surrendering passed down the line. It was about eleven in the morning.... I had a real feeling of relief. It was like a heavy load had been lifted off my back. It was over! It was over!"[45]

About that same time in a remote area near Little Baguio, a scene quite contradictory to what was happening throughout most of southern Bataan was unfolding. It was, of all things and of all times, a poker game involving the men of the 194th Tank Battalion who had been ordered to pull back to that area the night before. They were informed of the surrender early that morning.

At 7:00 A.M. the battalion commander, Colonel Ernest Miller, was handed a message with one word: "Blast." Miller wrote, "Black Thursday had arrived," as it was the signal to "destroy all vehicles, guns, and ammunition." Miller ordered his tanks and half-tracks spread out over the area. Fuel valves inside the tanks were broken off so as to flood them with gasoline and then set fire.

"The armor plate on the tanks was subjected to such intense heat that it was made useless except for scrap iron," noted Miller. "We also fired 37mm armor-piercing shells into the tank and truck motors. Gasoline was dumped into the cabs and bodies of the trucks. Weapons were stripped and parts thrown into the blazing vehicles, stocks were smashed, gun barrels heated and bent around trees."

Miller then ordered a detail of men to go to a nearby Quartermaster Ration Distribution Point in hopes of getting some food. Despite the acknowledged fact that Bataan had already surrendered, the officer in charge refused to issue either food or rations without proper authority. Captain Clinton Quinlen, in charge of the tankers, according to Miller, "used his initiative," and took what he wanted, "even while being threatened with court martial.

"We had more to eat that day than we [had] ... since the start of the war," remembered the battalion commander. With stomachs full for the first time in weeks, men relaxed to wait for the Japanese. Some slept, some actually played poker or shot craps. "I never participated in a game of chance," remembered Miller, "which meant so little as that one."[46]

The Japanese, although close by, did not move in to take the 194th until the next day, April 10.

Not too far away from the 194th's bivouac, close to 2,000 men within the Hospital No. 1 compound would not be so lucky as to realize the same 24-hour grace period. Surrender or not, it was business as usual for the doctors and hospital staff until the Japanese arrived. Surrender or not, 1,800 patients would still need tending.

Earlier that morning, Colonel James Duckworth, commanding officer of the hospital, after notifying his staff that the fight was over, ordered Red Cross flags taken down and white bedsheets raised in their place. Not long afterward, a column of Japanese tanks was seen coming down the road. Colonel Duckworth and two fellow officers went to meet them at the hospital gate. With guns from the lead tank trained on the three Americans, a Japanese general and an interpreter climbed out and jumped to the ground. Duckworth saluted and said that he was surrendering the hospital.

"You have Japanese wounded in your custody?" the interpreter asked.

"Yes, forty-two," Duckworth replied.

"Send them here immediately."

A few minutes later, 30 or so Japanese walking-wounded filed out of the prison ward and lined up in front of the general. "There was much bowing, scraping, saluting, and questioning," observed Captain Alfred Wainstein. Before long the general turned to Colonel Duckworth. "These soldiers say you have treated them well.... How many have you killed?"

"None," answered Duckworth, "although there are many who are still seriously ill.... Some of these may die."

"Show them to me," he ordered.

"Of all the wards," continued Weinstein, "fate had destined that the Nip ward was to suffer least from the recent bombings.... Showers were functioning, latrines were working, the roof was intact. The slopeheads, wearing clean pajamas, were lying on surgical beds covered with clean linen. Candy and cigarettes were on their side tables."

The general was pleased with what he saw and asked to be taken on a tour of the rest of the grounds. Near the center of the compound, he paused and pointed to the huge unfilled bomb crater in the middle of the grounds. "A Japanese bomb," explained Duckworth. "One hundred patients had been killed and a ward completely destroyed."

"Too bad," the general said with apparent concern. "That is unfortunate."

Then, turning to Duckworth, he repeated again that his wounded had been treated very well and that he had decided to use the hospital for the next few days as headquarters and bivouac for his tanks. "I shall instruct my men to refrain from interfering with you or your duties," he said. "Carry on with your work."[47]

Duckworth and his staff would be allowed to carry on for a month and a half at Hospital No. 1 before leaving for their prison camp.

Under the tall trees of the same Little Baguio forest some two miles to the east, the staff of Hospital No. 2, unfortunately, would find carrying on much more difficult.

Both staff and patients of the hospital, with its quarter-square mile of open wards, had spent most of the night and morning in slit trenches, many dug conveniently underneath their beds, dodging Japanese bombs and stray bullets.

Around 3:00 pm., with word that the surrender had taken place, Colonel James Gillespie, hospital C.O., ordered white bedsheets displayed next to his Red Cross flags. For the next five hours, and for the first time in days, doctors and medical corpsmen went about tending their over 7,500 patients without the roar of heavy guns or rattle of small arms fire. The quiet seemed strange, almost out of place. It wasn't until eight o'clock that evening that the first Japanese officers and a handful of soldiers arrived.

Calling the staff together, the officer in charge, an arrogant major named Hisashi Sekiguichi, announced that he was taking over the operations of the hospital, firmly stating that everyone was a prisoner of war and could be shot for disobedience.

After listening to the major's speech, Colonel Gillespie asked him if there was a chance of increasing the size of the rations of the patients.

If your own army didn't feed you enough, he retorted, then he didn't see why he should "feed them any more than they'd been receiving."

"That night," according to Colonel W.H. Waterous, a member of the staff at No. 2, "Japanese soldiers roamed at will through the hospital area, relieving everyone of watches and any other item they wanted." Few of those who were allowed to sleep after that went to bed without the ominous feeling that the presence of Major Sekiguchi portended trouble.

Their instincts proved correct, as at dawn they were told that sometime during the night, the American woman refugee (married to a Filipino naval officer) convalescing in the officer's ward with her new baby of two months had been gang-raped by the Japanese in the presence of everyone there. Later, while most of the staff was sitting down at their meager breakfast of steamed red rice, an American medical corpsman ran up with the news that the Filipino patients were all leaving. The chief surgeon, Colonel Jack Schwartz, led the line of doctors out of the mess hall toward the open wards.

Schwartz stopped one of the patients. "Where are you going?" he asked.

The Japanese had freed all the Filipinos. They were going home, he was told.

Word of this started when some Japanese soldiers, without authorization, even from Major Sekiguchi, ordered the staff of a small Philippine Scout medical detachment camped on the edge of the hospital area to join the line of men marching north out of Bataan. At the sight of the Scouts moving out, rumor spread that the Filipinos were being freed to return home.

Schwartz and his fellow doctors went from ward to ward and soldier to soldier trying vainly to convince them that they were in no condition to leave, that the whole thing was a trick. Struck with mass hysteria, few listened and almost none remained. Amputees, using tree limbs for crutches, joined the pathetic procession. A row of blind patients formed a human chain behind one of the walking wounded and headed for the road. Men holding their hands over fresh stomach wounds to keep them from breaking open staggered out — most to become just another one of the hundreds of corpses that, within a few days, would line the roads leading out of Bataan.

Colonel Waterous, whose clinic was near the lower end of the hospital, "could see the never-ending column of men from the upper wards moving down the road towards Cabcaben ... all moving like cattle on their last mile.... This went on," he remembered, "for 48 hours." There had been over 5,000 Filipino soldiers in beds under the trees of Hospital No. 2 before the incident. Fewer than 600 remained.[48]

Later that same day, several batteries of Japanese field artillery positioned themselves in a circle around the hospital. Anticipating return fire from Corregidor as soon as the Japanese opened up, Colonel Gillespie asked Major Sekiguchi if the hospital could be evacuated or at least relocated.

Nobody, said the major, would leave until Corregidor had fallen.

He was right. It wasn't until six days after Corregidor surrendered that the Hospital No. 2 site was abandoned and the staff and patients attached to Hospital No. 1.

The situation surrounding the surrender of the I Corps on the jungled western half of the peninsula, of course, was much different from that of the II Corps. I Corps units had gone virtually unchallenged except during the opening hours of the enemy's April 3 offensive. And the only withdrawal had been as a strategic necessity brought about by the rapid collapse of the II Corps.

Word that Bataan was going to be surrendered came to I Corps commander General Albert Jones around 2:00 A.M. on the ninth. Jones had been prompted to call General King at Little Baguio about that time following the detonation of the engineer and ordnance depots above Mariveles. "What's going on?" he asked King.

Explaining that the II Corps ammunition dumps had just been blown, King told him that he was surrendering at 6:00 A.M. "Put white flags all along your front ... destroy your artillery and machine guns and stand by for further orders."

Jones agreed to spike his artillery, but said he'd hold off destroying his small arms until the last minute. "Use your own judgment," said the despondent Bataan commander, and then hung up.

As opposed to the situation on the II Corps, the absence of fighting or, in some cases, even contact with the Japanese on the west coast, offered I Corps no hint of how bad things really were throughout the command. Where II Corps units didn't have to be told that Bataan was through on the night of April 8, men scattered throughout the quiet I Corps, even when told, still didn't believe it. If there was a chance for an incident, it would be here, and here it happened.

On April 8, General Wainwright, it will be remembered, had issued orders to withdraw the Philippine Division (31st, 45th, and 57th Infantries) to Corregidor. The only regiment able to free itself was the 45th, which started south that night from its positions in the I

Corps. Despite this, the 45th was unable to make it to Mariveles in time to be picked up and met its fate on Bataan with the rest of the division.

With surrender still unanticipated in the I Corps, the 1st Battalion of the 1st Infantry Regiment of the Philippine army's 1st Division was ordered to relieve the Scout 45th Infantry from their positions near the junction of Trail 8 and the Pantingan River.

The next morning, April 9, the battalion fired on a column of Japanese 65th Brigade troops as they attempted to cross the Pantingan. A good-sized firefight ensued. But before long, the outnumbered Filipinos began withdrawing westward over Trail 8 in hopes of receiving help from the 11th Division, into whose area they were being pushed.

The frustrated 1st Battalion commander did not know, however, that the 11th, which had received its orders to surrender, had already abandoned its frontline positions and had begun to stack arms about a mile to the southwest.

Late that afternoon word was received by 1st Division commander Colonel Kearie Berry that a battalion from his 1st Infantry Regiment was in the middle of a big fight with a large Japanese force near the junction of trails 8 and 9. He was stunned. Why hadn't they surrendered? he wondered.

By the time Berry could react, the game-but-outnumbered 1st Battalion had been pushed back over Trail 9 into the 1st Division area. The only thing standing between it and total annihilation was the impenetrable jungle that had continuously held the Japanese to the confines of the trail.

Grabbing what units he could to help, the worried division commander moved forward with the hope that the Japanese would still accept his surrender after what had happened. Upon reaching Trail 9, Berry placed the two battalions he brought with him astride the trail behind the battered 1st and then went forward to find out why it hadn't surrendered. The startled battalion commander's answer was simple — he hadn't been informed that he was supposed to.

It was twilight on the morning of April 10 when Berry and two Filipino officers, vigorously waving a large white flag, cautiously moved across Trail 9 toward Japanese lines. After 50 or so agonizing yards, several Japanese soldiers appeared. One of them was the regimental commander, who, with no apparent disdain over what had happened, accepted the surrender. Although over, it wouldn't be forgotten, however, nor go without repercussion.

The first repercussion came that night. Eleventh Division troops, upon receiving the order to surrender that afternoon, according to their commander, General William Brougher, were waiting for their captors "with large bonfires built in all directions and white flags displayed." Unaware of the altercation between the 1st Division and elements of the Japanese 65th Brigade, which was still unresolved at the time, "the Japanese came in with machine guns blazing and shot into our soldiers disarmed and huddled in their bivouacs. The men were terrified and took off down Trail 7 toward Mariveles" leaving guns and even food behind. "In my C.P.," Brougher continued, "we debated ... the merits of sticking it out or following the men to the rear. With machine gun bullets whistling all around, we decided to follow them, and took off."

By ten o'clock the next morning, Brougher, with help from his staff, had rounded up most of his division and was ready to try again. Once more, white flags were displayed. This time, however, the Japanese honored them and peacefully accepted the surrender.

The disappointment that registered among the proud, confident Filipinos of Brougher's

11th Division when the surrender was announced was noted by its commanding officer. "Strong men wept like children," he said. "Those that had been willing and heroic in the desperate conflict were the ones who were most completely overcome with emotional collapse on having to surrender."

No one had been more confident or was more let down than Brougher himself, who wrote afterwards, "We had worked unstintingly for two months building an impregnable defense in our subsector front and felt that we could hold the Japs indefinitely."[49]

The surrender of various I Corps units continued throughout the entire day and into the night of April 10. The corps commander, General Albert Jones, interestingly enough, might have been the last man on the peninsula to surrender. Although I Corps headquarters was captured on the evening of the tenth, the Japanese officer in charge waited until the next morning before officially accepting Jones' capitulation.

Up on Signal Hill, a prominent observation point about three-fourths of the way up the western slope of Mt. Bataan, several hundred Americans and Philippine Scouts had been gathering since the night of April 8. Exactly why men were ordered to Signal Hill is not clear. Many heard it was to organize for a counterattack.

General Max Lough, commander of the Philippine division, relayed an order from General Parker to his division command post that it had been established there "to set up a defensive position and fire on the Japanese only if they attacked."

Nevertheless, it wasn't until late in the afternoon of the tenth that the American troops were ordered down off the hill by the Japanese. At dusk, wrote Lt. Henry G. Lee of the U.S. 31st, "our column moved out down the Signal Hill road, which was crowded with our Scout comrades whom we were now forced to leave behind. Many had already gone into the brush, refusing to surrender. At the foot of the road," Lee continued, "columns were stopped and thoroughly looted by a body of Japanese infantry. Finally we were allowed to proceed to Kilometer Post 181, where we were again searched and herded into a prisoner-of-war enclosure. We were never again together as a unit."[50]

The access road the Americans took from Signal Hill to K.P. 181 on the West Road was actually part of Trail 7. It was the only north-south trail, other than the West Road, on the western half of the peninsula. About six miles north of the Signal Hill turnoff up Trail 7, it junctioned with Trails 8 and 9. About five winding miles east over Trail 8 was the junction of Trail 29. On the morning of April 11, Lieutenant Reynaldo Perez of the Philippine army's 41st Division, along with a handful of other men from miscellaneous units, arrived on foot at the junction to find "hundreds of Filipino soldiers seated on the ground on the south side of the trail" guarded by Japanese soldiers. Upon sight of Perez and the men with him, the Japanese ordered them to sit down with the rest of the prisoners.

About noon, a high-ranking Japanese officer, identified as Lt. General Akira Nara, commander of the 65th Brigade, drove up. Upon seeing the large number of Filipino prisoners sitting beside the road, he stopped and beckoned the Japanese officer in charge over to his car. After a brief conversation with him, Nara drove away. Although no one at the time knew what was said, many would soon find out.

Japanese guards immediately began separating the officers and ranking non-commissioned officers from the enlisted men. Once this was done, the Filipino enlisted men were herded out onto Trail 8 and marched off toward Limay.

"A few minutes later," remembered Perez, "a Jap officer called our attention. In fluent English, he asked for the ranking officers. Among this group were two majors, whom he ordered to form the group into a company, three platoons, and a column of fours." As the company formed out on the road, Perez, for the first time, got a look at how many men there were. "I estimated that we numbered 300 officers and NCO's," he said.

Soon, several Japanese soldiers appeared carrying reels of telephone wire. Guards with fixed bayonets were increased. Perez was the second man in line. "The Japs commenced tying my file leader. His hands were tied behind him, and with the same telephone wire, my hands were likewise tied. All the men in each file were tied in tandem."

The Japanese, as soon as everyone, except the leaders of each platoon and ranking officers, were tied, started the columns down Trail 8 toward the Pilar-Bagac Road. "Our gait was very slow," recalled Perez, "for we kept pulling and dragging each other."

A few hundred yards down the trail, Perez spotted several army trucks. He was relieved. "I thought they would take us to a concentration camp," he remembered thinking, "but when I saw that the leading units were not getting in, my fears were confirmed. It was going to be a massacre."

Before long the columns were led off the south side of the trail into the jungle, file after file disappearing into the dense growth. They were halted on the edge of a steep, 100-foot-high bluff overlooking one of the tributaries to the Pantingan River and told to sit down. Because of the jungle, none of the other groups, although only a few yards away, could be seen. "There was a foreboding silence around us," said Perez. "I never prayed so much in my life."

Then it came. The explanation of what was about to take place. Over 300 Filipino officers and noncoms had been selected to pay for the mistake the battalion of 1st Infantry Regiment troops of the 1st Division had made. Uninformed of the surrender, it will be remembered, they had engaged a regiment of General Nara's 65th Brigade on the morning of April 9 in a fight that lasted over 20 hours. "Had you surrendered earlier," said the Japanese interpreter in Tagalog, "you would not have met this tragedy. Many of our soldiers died fighting against you."

Cries and pleas for mercy arose from the now-doomed Filipinos, but fell on deaf ears. Even requests to be killed by machine gun or rifle fire were denied. And then cries of another kind. They were "of my comrades," remembered Perez, "coupled with the beastly shouts of the butchering Japanese. My hair stood on end. I wondered what the Japs were doing to them."

Before long, he and the men in his column were to find out. Soon a Japanese officer, "brandishing a saber dripping with blood," led a dozen or so soldiers in behind the file of terror-stricken Filipinos. "Their bayonets red with blood," they readied for their grisly task. And then it began ... bayoneting and beheading. Now and then a shot. And with each thrust of sword or knife, an inhuman cry of pain.

When his turn came, Perez, with his back to his assassins, felt like he was hit in the back with a big club. "I felt an excruciating pain on my back." He had taken a single thrust from the 16-inch Japanese bayonet that went all the way through his body, making an exit wound in his stomach. But he was not dead or even unconscious. "My God," he thought to himself, "this is it. I did not dare move. I played dead."

His ordeal was far from over, however, as the officer next to him, the next man to be bayoneted, was pushed over the top of him. "He was lying on my right arm," he said, "then I felt the pain of the bayonet that had gone through him slowly pierce my arm. Again I dared not move for fear the Jap might give me the works again."

The "cold-blooded murders moved on," he continued, and "after a while there was quiet, except for the groans of the dying." Before long the Japanese came back to double check the bodies to make sure everyone was dead. "A Jap soldier grabbed me in the face and turned me upwards," said Perez. "I held my breath and kept my eyes closed. I was expecting another bayonet thrust. Thank God it never came."

About ten feet away another Filipino officer, Major Pedro Felix, of the 71st Division, had also been able to fool his executioners. Felix had miraculously survived not one but four bayonet thrusts from the Japanese and, like Perez, remained conscious through the entire ordeal.

Fortunately for the husky Philippine army major, unmoving, lying face down in the bloodstained dirt, the officer next to him had tossed his legs over his head and shoulders at the first thrust of the enemy's bayonet into his body, and then died. Concealed from the eyes of his killers, Felix was able to breathe freely and, after the Japanese moved on, actually opened his eyes and looked around.

It was dark before both men felt it was safe enough to try to free themselves. Both were weak from the loss of blood. Both were in terrible pain. Felix had actually tried to end it all by smothering himself, but failed.

"I had a big problem before me," Perez said. "Freeing myself was impossible. Then the unexpected happened. My file leader [Felix] was not dead after all. I whispered to him to get nearer to me. After some difficulty we managed to get near each other. I gnawed at his bonds and set him free. After resting awhile, he untied me also."[51]

It is, of course, impossible to know exactly how many men lived through this experience, or escaped to tell the tale. Three of the survivors came out with Major Felix, while Perez, after spending two days and three nights along a tributary of the Pantingan River, also made his way safely out of Bataan. (After the war, an American Bataan survivor, Sergeant Abie Abraham, working for U.S. Graves Registration, was led to the scene of the massacre by a local Filipino.)

Although certainly the worst, this was not the first nor the only incident of Japanese treachery. The brutality continued as the Japanese prepared their vanquished adversaries for movement out of Bataan. It was at dusty Mariveles air field, which, for the most part, had become the main assembly point of the Bataan troops, where another incident occurred to portend what lay ahead.

The foremost concern among Japanese soldiers over prisoners on Bataan became looting. It can be said with relative certainty that most of the more than 25,000 American prisoners would be searched no less than half a dozen times before reaching the prison camps.

The first thing air corps Captain Edward Dyess heard as he and his men reached Mariveles Field to turn themselves in on the morning of April 10 was, "Get rid of your Jap stuff." "Jap stuff," of course, meant souvenirs — a hobby most Americans had acquired during the three-month-long battle. "We did so, and just in time," he recalled, as Japanese soldiers soon ordered packs and duffel bags opened and their contents spread out.

As the Japanese guards began searching, things started getting rough. "I saw men shoved, cuffed, and boxed," Dyess said. "We were mystified. It was uncalled for. We were not resisting." Before long, the puzzling attitude of their captors was explained when a few ranks away, a Japanese guard held up a small shaving mirror. "Nippon?" he asked the American from whom he had taken it. The soldier nodded. Yes, it was "made in Japan."

"The Jap stepped back," witnessed Dyess, "then lunged, driving his rifle butt into the

American's face, and then lunged again. The Yank went down. The raging Jap stood over him, driving crushing blows to the face until he lay insensible." A few minutes later, it happened again. "A Jap was smashing his fist into the face of another American soldier, who went to his knees," only to receive a kick in the groin. "He too, it seemed, had been caught with some Japanese trifle."

On another part of the now hot, dusty, and crowded fighter strip, a scene of horror was unfolding that would bring even the strongest of prisoners to retch with abhorrence for their captors. As had been occurring with the men in Captain Dyess' group, an American air force captain was being frisked by a Japanese private. A routine search of one of his shirt pockets turned up some Japanese yen notes. An eyewitness later told Dyess that a big Japanese officer was shown the money. "Without a word he grabbed the captain by the shoulder and shoved him to his knees. He quickly pulled his sword out of its scabbard and raised it high over his head, holding it with both hands."

"There was a swishing and kind of a chopping thud," he told Dyess. "The captain's head seemed to jump off his shoulders ... hitting the ground in front of him ... rolling crazily between lines of horror-struck prisoners." Little did the men dream that this and similar scenes of murder and brutality lay before them.[52]

To complete the humiliation of defeat, one of the first groups of prisoners, as they left the airstrip at Mariveles on their march out of Bataan, were halted beside a small building. In front was a flagpole still flying an American flag. "Face the flag," they were told. The men turned around and looked up to see the Stars and Stripes being lowered to the ground and the Rising Sun hoisted in its place.

And so, as the men of Bataan began their march to prison camp, the last chapter in the "epic struggle," as General MacArthur described it, came to a close. What lay before them was 65 miles of hell. Sixty-five miles of brutal sun and heat — but of little or no food or water. Sixty-five miles of barbarity and inhumanity as no army in the history of the civilized world had ever known. So the Battling Bastards of Bataan, who had fought the good fight and earned the right to be treated with respect and civility due both victor and vanquished alike, before it was through would provide history with yet another story and title like no other ever written. It would be called the Bataan Death March.

CHAPTER 3

Corregidor's Final Hours

As mentioned in the last chapter, the key to holding Manila Bay against the Japanese was Bataan. If Bataan was to fall, Corregidor and the three island forts would follow.

Bataan surrendered on April 9, 1942.

Located just three miles off the southern tip of Bataan, Corregidor Island (Fort Mills), along with nearby Caballo (Fort Hughes), El Fraile (Fort Drum), a manmade, concrete, battleship-shaped island 4 miles south of Caballo, and Carabao (Fort Frank), 500 yards off Manila Bay's southern shore, in combination provided 92 coastal defense guns whose primary purpose was to defend the entrance to the bay against intrusion by an enemy fleet. Before the Japanese could claim victory in the Philippines, the four islands blocking the entrance to Manila Bay would have to be taken.

For its size (three and a half miles long and a mile and a half wide at its widest point), Corregidor was the most heavily fortified island in the world. Although protected by 23 fixed-position batteries, including 46 coastal defense guns ranging from 12-inch to 155mm, its primary weakness was that they were constructed in 1914 when the threat of being attacked from the air was never imagined. Although most fixed-position batteries provided adequate bomb- and shell-proof shelters for battery personnel, not a single weapon was protected from the air or from high-angle artillery fire. In fact, those batteries, with their guns located in the center of every gun pit, were jokingly referred to as the bulls-eyes by Japanese pilots.

Since the Japanese would be assaulting the island from Bataan, only half a dozen of the 23 batteries could be used effectively against them. This allowed them to concentrate exclusively on those guns from both the air and by artillery fire from the southern tip of the peninsula.

Relative to the latter, one of the major turning points in the siege involved the use of 240mm guns against the island. Both generals Jonathan Wainwright, Philippine Defense commander, and George F. Moore, Harbor Defense commander, made reference to the Japanese moving those guns into southern Bataan, which, around April 20, opened fire with devastating results. Wrote Wainwright: "Every installation on Corregidor visible from Bataan continuously objected to heavy enemy artillery fire. Our counter-battery fire brought overwhelming enemy 240-mm retaliatory fire down on the firing battery."[1]

Moore wrote that because of their high-angle fire, they were "able to blast our 12-inch mortar pits which flat trajectory weapons had been unable to reach." By neutralizing the counter-battery fire from mortars Way and Geary, Corregidor's most effective weapons were all but neutralized.[2]

One thing the 240mms did, however, was to force four of the 155mm batteries, whose guns were on wheels but located in fixed positions, to become roving batteries. To keep the

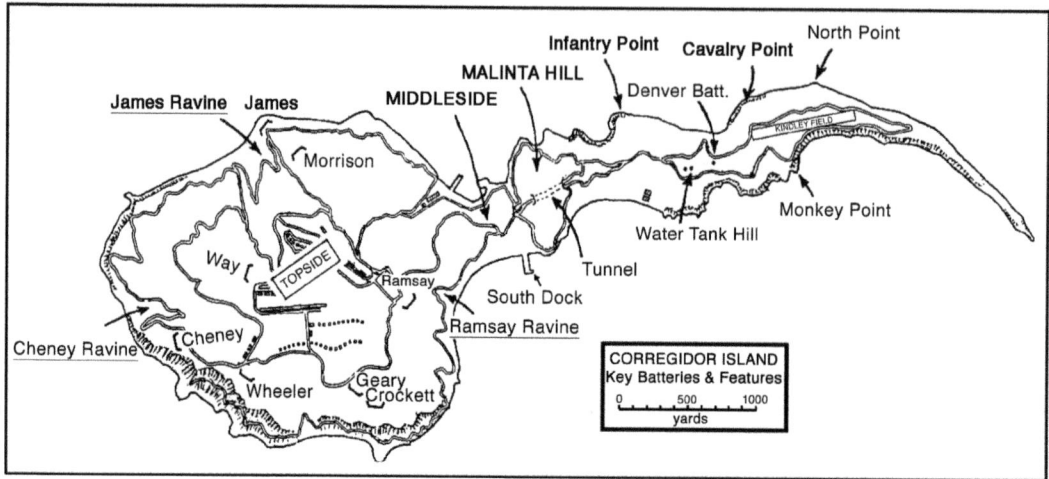

Japanese from blasting the known fixed sites, each night the guns were moved to a new unregistered position from which effective counter-battery fire could come.

"The plan worked splendidly," wrote Moore. "These batteries were our main dependence for counter-battery fire against the enemy batteries on Bataan until the surrender."

For the men whose position happened to be near a newly selected 155mm location, it wasn't always welcomed. "Fortunately," remembered Marine private Robert Farner, "when they moved one near our position, they gave us a half an hour to clear the area, for as soon as they opened up, it wouldn't be long before the Japs would pinpoint their location and blast the hell out of it and everything around it. As I recall, they only had time to fire a dozen or so rounds before moving the gun out of harm's way."[3]

Although the Japanese concentrated most of their efforts against Bataan throughout the latter days of March, on the twenty-fourth, the island got a taste of what was in store for it if and when the peninsula fell. Entries in the diary of Major General Moore for that day recorded the following:

> 0924 — Air Raid alarm No. 77 sounded.
> 0925 — 9 heavy bombers, a new type in the area, bombed Middleside, closely followed by 17 heavies bombing Topside.
> 0950 — 25 planes followed by 9 more made another attack. Meanwhile, artillery shells from enemy batteries at Cavite were bursting on Corregidor ... an ammunition dump of 75-mm shells on Morrison Hill was set off; exploded for hours.
> 1110 — All clear sounded 1435 — Air Raid alarm No. 78. 9 heavy bombers approached Corregidor from SE. Bombs dropped on Kindley Field.
> 1438 — 7 more planes from SE with more bombs. Shelling from mainland, also.
> 1529 — All clear 1552 — Air Raid alarm No. 79. 9 heavy bombers hit Kindley Field again.
> 1620 — All clear 2053 — Air Raid alarm No. 80
> 2115 — First night air raid. 2 medium bombers dropped incendiary bombs in Cheney Ravine. Bombed Bottomside.
> 2234 — All clear.[4]

Relative to the 0925 bombing of Middleside that General Moore recorded, one structure on the island that remained secure from both air and artillery attacks was perhaps its most famous feature — Malinta Tunnel. Located under Malinta Hill but referred to as Middleside, it was the heart and brains of the operation.

Consisting of 3 miles of reinforced concrete tunneling, along with its main, 1,400-

foot-long tunnel, there were 25 laterals branching off in both directions, each about 400 feet in length. Extending from one of the laterals north of the main passage was the hospital, located in a separate system of 12 laterals. On the south side of the main tunnel were two more branches, both extending from the same lateral. The first, consisting of 11 laterals, was used by the quartermaster. Past that section was what was called Navy Tunnel, which had its own system of laterals and entrance on the south side of Malinta Hill.

As obvious as it was for those involved in defending the island that the end was near, so was it for the hundreds working, living, dying, and hiding in Malinta Tunnel.

Civilian hospital assistant Maude Williams wrote in her diary about life in the tunnel: "Under the deepening shadows of death, life in the tunnel took on a faster, more intense tempo. The smallest and most simple pleasures became sought after and treasured as they became increasingly rare — an uninterrupted cigarette, a cold shower, a stolen biscuit, a good night's sleep. As the end drew near, there was a heightened feeling that life was to be lived from day to day. Many sought forgetfulness in gambling. Jam sessions attracted great crowds which gathered in the dark and hummed softly to the nostalgic swing of a haunting guitar, or low moaning trombone. Sometimes a nurse and her boy friend of the evening would melt into a dance ... while other couples would steal out into the perilous night. Others sought the consolation of religion."[5]

For most, however, life in the confines of the tunnel was anything but playing cards and listening to music.

Despite having the "security of solid rock overhead," as one of the nurses remembered, "we were constantly jarred by the force of [bombs and shells]. Bottles, dishes, any loose objects were flung from tables and shelves.... Smoke and dust filled the laterals, filling our eyes with tears and making breathing difficult."

Although temporarily safe from sudden death, the incessant bombing and shelling brought on a condition known as shelter shock, a term taken from the World War I condition known as shell shock. The tunnel rats, as some were nicknamed by a few of their sarcastic comrades, after a while refused to step outside the tunnel whose laterals were soon crammed to overflowing. Not all were military personnel. Over 1,000 of those lining the walls were Filipino laborers from the tiny barrio of San Jose who were caught on the island when the war started.

With the overcrowding and lack of water came sanitation problems. Soon the smell of urine and the body odor of the hundreds of unwashed men and clothes filled the air. Wrote Wainwright: "Many relieved themselves where they stood. For food they were issued canned rations, and the empty containers were added to the human filth on the pavement."

In the hours before the invasion, the hospital was forced to displace the men who had crowded into the laterals. Wrote Coast Artillery major Steven Mellnik, who was in charge of the Malinta Tunnel guard, "In the previous week (April 29–May 3), we had opened up six additional laterals to take care of the wounded. The tunnel system was now mostly hospital. As fast as we used up the supplies of food and ammunition, this storage space was turned into a hospital area."

"Every day it seemed that the lines of stretchers grew longer," wrote one of the nurses. "Convalescents were hurried to make room for fresh casualties.... And every day when the red light went out [announcing] that an air raid was over, the grimy, unwashed bodies would come in on their stained stretchers, many with eyes wide open with pain and fear."[6]

Surprisingly, according to Corregidor's chief surgeon, the number of extreme mental cases was small. He felt that since there was no escaping the situation, everyone grew to accept it. Another and perhaps more accurate assessment was that if those who cowered the days away in the safety of the tunnel caused trouble, they could find themselves issued a 1917 Enfield rifle and assigned to beach defense.

Diaries kept by both Moore and General Wainwright, clear up to the end, provide a brief outline of important events as they led up to the final hours. In the days leading up to the end, the ever-increasing shelling and bombing of the island led to several tragic incidents.

One occurred on April 15, six days after the fall of Bataan. Two of the most exposed gun batteries on the island were batteries James and Morrison on the northern Bataan-facing side of the island. Both batteries were destroyed even before the 240mms were employed.

To escape the heavy bombardment they were beginning to receive, Philippine army troops manning James and Morrison dug a tunnel against orders in the side of the hill whose entrance faced Bataan. On the morning of the fifteenth, most of the batteries' complements had taken refuge in the tunnel after it was determined that the Japanese had selected the two gun positions as their main objective. Wrote General Moore of the incident that followed: "During a heavy bombardment, part of the Philippine army personnel manning Battery James took shelter in excavation into Morrison Hill behind the battery. The intensity of the enemy fire collapsed the hillside above the entrance, suffocating 70 Philippine army occupants." Most of the bodies were never recovered.

On April 25, relative to another tragic incident, Moore wrote: "2158 [9:58 P.M.]— At this time a heavy shell exploded in the midst of a large group of men outside the west entrance of Malinta Tunnel causing about 50 casualties. Several were killed instantly."[7]

That night, after a day of air raids and incessant shelling, as occurred routinely every night, a large group of men had gathered outside the western entrance to Malinta to get a breath of fresh air and have a cigarette.

Up to that time, Japanese artillery had not fired on the island after dark. Sadly, the routine would change that night. From then on until the end, the Rock would receive enemy fire intermittently clear into the early morning hours.

About 15 minutes into their smokes, a 240mm shell exploded about a hundred yards from the group, making everyone dash for the tunnel entrance. To protect the main lateral from shrapnel, both portals had been fitted with makeshift, 10-foot-high, wood-reinforced, galvanized steel gates.

Concussion from the blast had slammed the gate tight shut. Unable to open it from the outside, men yelled and banged on the gate with their fists. Moments later a second shell hit, only this time about 50 yards away. Fifteen men were killed instantly. Of the many wounded, several would die later.

Lieutenant Juanita Redmond, one of the nurses who took care of the wounded, wrote the following about her experiences: "Some died before we could get to them. Legs and arms had been wrenched off; there were jagged flesh wounds; pieces of shrapnel stuck in ugly wounds; deaths from shock mounted no matter how frantically we worked.

"Once, as I stooped to give an injection to one they had just put down on the floor, I saw it was a headless body. I yelled at the corpsman, 'Must you do this?' 'It's so dark out there,' one of them said. 'We can't use flashlights. We feel for the bodies and just roll them onto stretchers.'"[8]

Ordered to remove the big toe of a patient whose foot was badly cut by shrapnel, she said, "When I dropped the toe from my instrument into the container in which we disposed of amputated parts, it fell into the open hand of an arm that had just been removed."

Needless to say, the incident that night brought an end to the nightly gathering outside Malinta as the frequency of shelling of the roads leading to both portals increased daily.

The only other recorded incident of some note regarding shells landing outside of the tunnel entrance happened on April 28. It involved General Wainwright.

That morning, intent on getting some air and making a walking tour of a nearby battery, about 40 feet inside the gate protecting the entrance, he had stopped to light a cigar when, as he said, "a 240mm shell hit the barrier with a splintering roar. The concussion was terrific. My head suddenly felt as if someone had rammed a red-hot pipe through one ear and out the other." The concussion was so severe that not only did it burst his left eardrum but damaged his right ear as well. "Since then," he said, "it has never [returned] to its old standard."[9]

Irrespective of the daily air raids, as an example of things to come relative to the growing intensity of enemy artillery fire from Bataan, on April 29, six days before the invasion, General Moore's diary showed that at 7:30 A.M., "enemy shells from Bataan hit Bottomside." Thirty minutes later, there was "extremely heavy shelling of both portals of Malinta Tunnel and North Dock." Twenty-one minutes later, he noted, "Enemy shelling Topside while observation plane overhead adjusts fire." At two minutes before ten, "enemy shelling near North Point" was noted. Thirty-three minutes later, "Battery Cheney under fire," followed six minutes later by "enemy shelling Malinta Hill." "James Ravine under fire" at 1047. The final entry at 1120 said, "Heavy shelling of Malinta Hill continued."[10]

Of the results to Corregidor's important North Shore beach defenses on that date, Marine lieutenant Robert Jenkins wrote that it was "practically impossible to get any rest or repair damage to our positions and barbed wire. Our field telephone system was knocked out; our water supply was ruined [drinking water had to be hauled from the other end of the island in large powder cans]. The island was enveloped in a cloud of smoke, dust, and the continuous roar of bursting shells and bombs. There were many more casualties than we had suffered in the previous five months."

What it was like to be caught in the open during an enemy barrage was recorded in the diary of Captain John Gulick, commander of Battery C, of the 91st Philippine Scout Coast Artillery Regiment. Caught with his Filipino driver, in part he wrote:

> To my terror it began to move towards us.... We began to run hoping to get around the side of the hill. The barrage walked after us at about a pace equal to our own.... Suddenly it shifted and came down about 400 yards in front of us and slightly to our left. We ran to the right.
> The curtain of fire shifted again and came down on our right moving towards us. It seemed as if the Jap artillery was playing cat and mouse with us.
> We ran down the old trolley tracks with barrages behind and on both sides of us. Suddenly again up ahead shells began to land. We reached a drainage ditch and threw ourselves into it ... we were so exhausted by then that we could only lie there panting and perspiring.[11]

Almost hidden in General Moore's diary for that day was that among the handful of Corregidor guns involved in counter-battery fire against Japanese was Battery Way.

The story of what led to it goes back to April 15, when Major Bill Massello was granted permission from General Moore to reactivate the then out-of-action battery. Despite its importance, its four 12-inch, 1890-model mortars had not been fired for several years.

Up to the fall of Bataan, Massello had commanded searchlight Battery Erie that had been sent across to help defend the peninsula back in January. Since their arrival back on Corregidor on the night of April 8, Massello and his crew of 100 men had been without an assignment. With some experience with fixed mortars, Massello volunteered to take over the battery, which included, among other things, successfully modifying their abundance of 640-pound armor-piercing shells into more effective anti-personnel rounds.

Since there had been no counter-battery fire from the up-to-then silent Way, the Japanese had removed it from their list of targets—that is until the afternoon of April 29, when Massello's gunners lobbed 80 rounds onto known enemy positions near Cabcaben, Bataan.

Once the Japanese discovered the source of the 640-pound shells that were blasting them, it seemed, as one of the Way crewmen remembered, like "we had become the only target on the island."

Wrote General Moore about that night: "Whole island raked by artillery fire until 2235; heaviest concentration being on Battery Way where, in spite of approximately 100 hits, two mortars still ready for action."

Like Bill Massello's 100-man searchlight battery taking over Battery Way, so was it the same for Battery Craighill on nearby Fort Hughes. A few days before the war broke out, three U.S. Navy river gunboats, *Luzon*, *Oahu*, and *Mindanao*, arrived from Shanghai and Hong Kong. After the fall of Bataan, the crews of the three ships were assigned to various gun batteries. The 60-man crew of the *Mindanao* was put in charge of Battery Craighill's four 12-inch mortars.

After successfully firing 26 rounds at Japanese positions on Bataan, they were judged qualified to take over the battery. Both Way and Craighill would be in it at the end.

"Two navy PBYs from Australia, via Mindanao, loaded with medicine and 740 mechanical fuses for 3-inch AA ammunition, landed in South Bay. Loaded with fifty passengers [including about 38 American nurses], the PBYs took off for Mindanao." So almost matter-of-factly wrote General Wainwright in his diary for that same night.

With the successful evacuation of all the nurses from Bataan on the night of April 8–9, there was a total of 88 American and 26 Filipino nurses on Corregidor.

At six o'clock that night, 20, not 38, nurses got word to report to the mess lateral at 0800. There they were handed orders by chief army nurse Maude Davison that told them they were being evacuated that night by PBY to Australia. They were told not to discuss their departure with anyone, and to take one musette bag that could weigh no more than ten pounds.

Of course, word of their leaving soon spread. Although the main criteria for being chosen was old age, illness, or being wounded, at least half a dozen on the list were considered the most attractive nurses by some who were not chosen. Two on the list refused to go. Forty-seven-year-old Josie Nesbit was one of those.

Lt. Juanita Redmond, one of those on the more attractive list but a veteran of 3 tough months on Bataan, commented that she felt like a deserter.

To conceal the engine noise of the two planes from the Japanese as they came in, General Wainwright had the navy order the crews of all the small boats around the island to race their motors. At eleven o'clock as planned, the roar of small boat engines was heard all over the bay. However, the two pilots, Lieutenants Leroy Deede and Tom Pollock, themselves worrying about engine noise, both cut their motors and glided in for a landing.

Along with several officers and the wife of one of the generals, the nurses, all dressed in khaki coveralls with white socks and white shoes, silently climbed aboard the two motor launches that would take them to their arranged PBY. General Wainwright was on the dock to bid them goodbye and Godspeed. Juanita Redmond, before she stepped into the launch, put her arms around the general and kissed him on the cheek.

"Oh, thank you, General," she said, tears streaming down her face.[12]

Unknown to those on the dock, two of the men manning the launch unloading passengers into Lt. Deede's plane were recognized as former crewmen. Both were taken on board.

A former crewman on Lt. Pollock's plane, Chief Radioman Burt Fuller, however, was not so lucky. Pollock, who was not told that he was on the launch, failed to see his old friend and sadly left him behind.[13]

Although both made it safely to Lake Lanao on Mindanao, Pollock's plane, with eleven of the nurses, was damaged and forced to leave its passengers. They were subsequently captured and returned to the civilian POW camp at Santo Tomas University in Manila.

From April 29 on, there was little letup in bombing and shelling of the island, each day seeing an increase over the day before. On April 30, as an example, Wainwright wrote: "Heavy air and artillery offensive launched ... with undiminished intensity. The whole island raked with artillery fire until 1035." On May 1, he wrote: "A total of 149 bombing attacks have been made against Corregidor during the 23 days since the fall of Bataan." In addition, he noted that there had been "thirteen distinct and separate bombing attacks" that day.

The next day, Wainwright messaged the U.S. chief of staff, General George Marshall, in Washington: "Corregidor and the other Fortified Islands subjected to continuous shell fire, the heaviest concentration yet experienced. During a 5-hour period, 12 240-mm shells have fallen per minute for a total of 3,600 hits." At 4:27 that afternoon, one of the 3,600 hits Wainwright referred to was made on the powder magazine of Battery Geary.

Of the half a dozen or so batteries on Corregidor that continued to threaten the Japanese, the two mortar batteries, Way and Geary, were the ones that were feared the most. Results of the ensuing magazine explosion blew up over 1,600 62-pound powder bags, resulting in the destruction of the entire 8-gun battery.

Everyone on Corregidor knew an explosion of epic proportion had occurred. It had rocked the island like an earthquake. Where the reinforced concrete-covered powder magazine had been, there was nothing but a smoking crater.

One of the battery's 10-ton mortars was actually ripped out of its traverse ring and hurled onto the golf course, an unbelievable 120 yards away. A second gun was torn from its mount and sent flying across the battery into and through a 3-foot thick concrete wall. The barrels of the remaining six guns of the battery were also knocked over or left inoperable by the blast. A slab of concrete from the roof of the powder magazine was hurled like a discus, landing 1,000 yards from the battery. A total of 56 men were killed outright in the blast. After 12 hours, four men entombed inside one of the battery plotting rooms were found alive by a group of engineers who broke through a 3-foot wall of concrete to get to them.[14]

On Sunday, May 3, under continued enemy pounding from the air and by artillery fire, a message from General MacArthur's headquarters in Australia was sent to Brigadier General Lewis Beebe, General Moore's chief of staff. It was from General Richard Sutherland, MacArthur's chief of staff.

Two days earlier on May 1, Beebe, Moore, and General Wainwright's aide, Johnny

Pugh, had tried to convince Wainwright, as commander of all U.S. forces in the Philippines, to establish a new headquarters out of harm's way on Mindanao, 500 miles to the south. All knew Corregidor's days were numbered. Wainwright refused. "This was General MacArthur's headquarters," he said, "and this is where I'll stay."[15]

At that point, initially without Wainwright's knowledge, Beebe took matters into his own hands. He contacted General Sutherland to see if MacArthur would order Wainwright out. Two days later, with Wainwright's knowledge of Beebe's request, the answer came.

"General Wainwright was assigned to his command by the War Department," messaged Sutherland to Beebe, "and General MacArthur has no, repeat, no authority to relieve him therefrom."

Had the decision been the opposite, Wainwright and his staff might have been passengers on what was to be the last ship to leave the besieged island. It was the sub USS *Spearfish* that Wainwright had requested stop to take as many passengers off the Rock as possible. With room for only 25, Wainwright selected 12 army and navy officers, a female dependent, and 12 nurses. One of the nurses was Gladys Mealor.

"No one had worked harder or was more valuable to her country than Captain Mealor, chief nurse in the tunnel," said Wainwright. Mealor, however, refused to leave "as long as there was a patient in the hospital."

"I considered ... this a truly great act of heroism," remembered Wainwright. "She knew as well as I that she was signing her captivity warrant."

As far as the rest, as before, the decision was left to Captain Maude Davison. The selection made, 54 army and 26 Filipino nurses and 21 civilian nurse-volunteers were left on the Rock in wait of the end.

At 9:30 P.M., the *Spearfish* surfaced off Corregidor and took on its 25 passengers. The sub, under the command of Lieutenant James Dempsey, was already on its fourth war patrol when he received the following message from sub headquarters in Fremantle, Australia: "Put into Corregidor, very cautiously, and pick up a load of special passengers for Fremantle."

Along with the 25 passengers, a roster of all army, navy, and marine personnel left on the island, several foot lockers full of financial records, and the last bag of mail to leave the Rock was also brought on board. About twenty minutes under way, Dempsey was told that two of the navy men who helped load the foot lockers were stowaways.

Although the Japanese invasion was still 24 hours away, everyone on the Rock sensed it was near. That day, May 4, the Japanese opened at 7:30 A.M. with air raid number 288 and concluded with number 294 at 6:08 P.M. In between, the island was shelled incessantly until dark. Wrote General Moore, "Heaviest general bombardment yet falling on Corregidor: all calibers including 240mm. Continuous drum-fire of bursting shells."

"Delving further into the matter of the fury," wrote Wainwright in his diary that night, "Moore and I estimated that at the end of the five incredible hours of bombardment, the Japs had hit the Rock with 1,800,000 pounds of shells."

The most ominous sign that the invasion was near was noted in Moore's 1:30 P.M. entry: "Observers reported string of 15 invasion barges being towed north to south out of range beyond Hornos Point, Bataan." And later, "bulk of enemy fire was switched today to beach defenses, especially James Ravine and the beach between North and Cavalry Points on the eastern end of the island."[16]

Due to the intense shelling of the two locations, it didn't take much to guess exactly where the Japanese intended to invade. Initial enemy plans were to land on two successive nights. The first, to come just before midnight on May 5, was scheduled to land at two locations on the eastern end of the island. One was to come ashore near Cavalry Point. The second was to land at the narrow neck between Cavalry and Infantry points. The landing scheduled for the night of the sixth was aimed at the beach below James Ravine, which provided the most immediate access to Topside.

The job of defending Corregidor against an amphibious landing went to Marine colonel Samuel Howard, commander of the 4th Marine Regiment. Before Bataan fell, Howard laid out his defenses in anticipation of a seaward invasion of the three-mile-long island, with special emphasis on defending the western or Topside end. Of the 3,900 officers and men under his command, of which only 1,500 were Marines, he had assigned the bulk, some 2,000 men, to defend James, Cheney, and Ramsey ravines on the western end of the tadpole-shaped island. Outside of a 580-man reserve located west of Malinta in Government Ravine, there were just 1,075 men left to defend over 5,000 yards of Bataan-facing beaches on the eastern tail end of the island.

Of the men under his command, Howard supplemented his numbers by 1,245 escapees from Bataan, many of whom, when they arrived, were in such poor physical condition that, according to General Wainwright, "they were incapable of even light work." Lieutenant Robert Jenkins, upon seeing the contingent assigned to his 1st Battalion, said that he had never seen men in such poor physical condition. "Their clothing was ragged and stained from perspiration and dirt. Their gaunt, unshaven faces were strained and emaciated. Some were suffering from beri-beri as a result of weeks of a starvation diet of rice. We did what we could for them, and then put them to work on the beach defenses."[17]

Although the troops involved in the island's final 24 hours fought under the colors of the 4th Marine Regiment, it could not exclusively be considered a Marine Corps battle. In round figures, of the 1,600 men who would be involved in the battle for the east end of the island on May 5–6, only 440 were Marines, less than one-third. Of the 114 American officers involved, only 24 were Marines, and most of these at the command level. Outside of command, credit to those involved in the final battle must therefore be equally divided

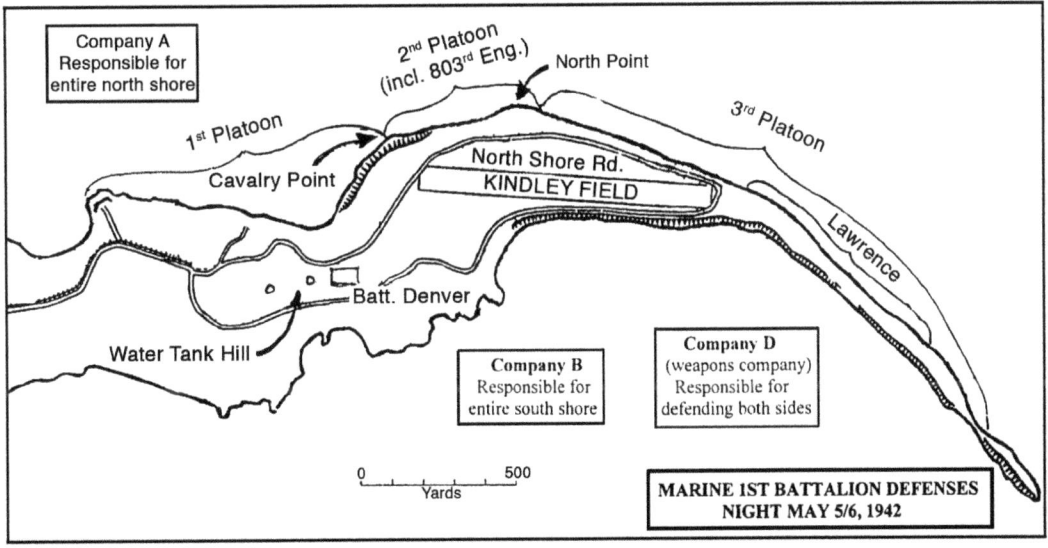

between men of the U.S. Marines, U.S. Army, U.S. Navy, Philippine Army, and Philippine Scouts.

Despite the signs after the fall of Bataan that the invasion would come from the peninsula and would be aimed at James Ravine and the eastern tip of the island, Howard made the fatal error of refusing to modify the strength and disposition of his troops until it was too late.

One only has to read General Moore's diary for May 5 to know that it was D-Day for the Japanese.

It started at 8:35 A.M.: Air Raid Alarm No. 295. Corregidor under heavy fire from Bataan.

> 0905 — Fort Drum under heavy fire.
> 0923 — Corregidor being bombed, hit Bottomside.
> 0955 — All clear.
> 1003 — Fort Frank and Corregidor received artillery fire.
> 1055 — Air Raid Alarm No. 296. Battery Craighill [Ft. Hughes 14-inch mortars] opened counter-battery fire.
> 1100 — All clear.
> 1106 — Air Raid Alarm No. 297. Five dive bombers attack Corregidor.
> 1130 — All clear.
> 1203 — Air Raid Alarm No. 298. Corregidor bombed.
> 1230 — Heavy counter-battery fire opened up at selected targets in Bataan. Several enemy batteries silenced and three ammo dumps set on fire.

[In one final defiant gesture, at 1230, dead in the middle of the heaviest and most sustained bombing and artillery attacks since the siege began, General Wainwright ordered Colonel Paul Bunker, Seaward Defense commander, to fire everything he had at known enemy gun positions on Bataan. Bunker was able to round up two 14-inch batteries, Crofton on Fort Frank, and Wilson on Fort Drum, one 12-inch mortar, Way, two 12-inch batteries, Cheney and Wheeler, and four 155mm batteries, Monja and 3 roving, Rose, Wright, and Gulick, all on Corregidor. Although many on the Rock were unable to differentiate between the sounds of friendly artillery fire and the continuous roar of exploding bombs and shells, at 1230, regardless of the results, Corregidor let the Japanese know that it could still fight back.]

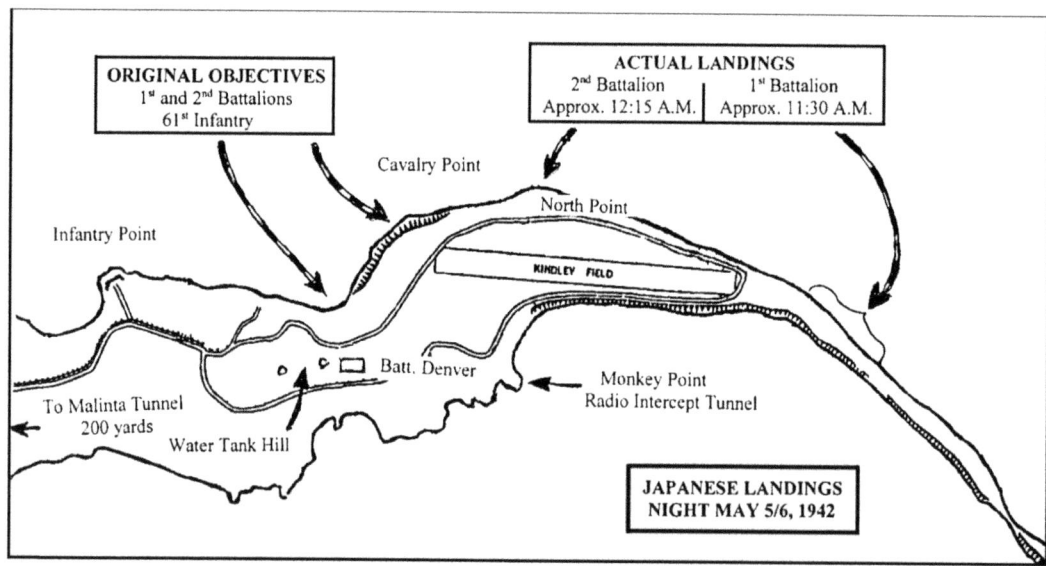

1250 — Forts Frank and Hughes under artillery fire.
1300 — All clear.
1315 — Fort Drum under fire from Cavite.
1327 — Air Raid Alarm No. 299.
1400 — All clear.
1447 — Air Raid Alarm No. 300.
1515 — Fort Hughes hit by bombs. Corregidor under intermittent artillery fire during afternoon.
1837 — All fortified islands under heavy fire. James Ravine, the North Shore, and the tail of the island pounded terribly. Communication lines cut in many places; numerous beach defense guns and searchlights put out of action; many beach defense land mines blown up by artillery fire.
2100 — Beach Defense reported manned.
2230 — Message from "H" Station [Gen. Moore's Harbor Defense Command Post] to Beach Defense Commander: "Prepare for probable landing attack." Japs cannonading of tail end of island very heavy; telephone communications out in many areas. Beach defense installations practically non-existent. Barbed wire entanglements, land mines, machine gun emplacements, personnel shelters, and most of 75mm beach defense guns have been destroyed. North side of island bare of trees and vegetation and ground powdered dust. Intelligence obtained only by use of messengers. Estimate Japanese have 350 to 400 guns varying in caliber from 75mm to 240mm in Bataan.
2350 — Runner arrived at "H" Station from North Point. Reported enemy landing.[18]

And so the stage was set for the battle of Corregidor.

A mixed bag of 7,700 U.S. Army, Marine, and naval personnel and 2,700 Philippine Scout and army troops against a force of 5,000 men of the Japanese 4th Division and 7th Tank Regiment. More specifically, it came down to 2,000 Japanese of the 61st Infantry against little more than 1,000 troops of various units in defense of the east end of the island.

For the 2,000 61st Infantry troops crossing the North Channel, things up to then had not been easy. Malaria, which had ravaged the Filipinos and Americans on Bataan, had sent 28,000 Japanese troops into the hospital in the 21-day period between April 9 and May 1. The Japanese faced the postponement of the scheduled assault; only after the emergency delivery of 300,000 quinine tablets by air was the epidemic quelled in time to meet the scheduled date for the invasion.

To meet the Japanese invasion were members of a makeshift battalion of 367 Marines, American, and Filipino army troops, a company of 803rd Engineers, 240 Philippine Scouts of the 91st and 92nd Coast Artillery, and a handful of Philippine army air corps and U.S. Navy Filipino mess boys — a total force of 1,024. Overall command of what was designated as the 1st Battalion went to Marine lieutenant colonel Curtis Beecher.

To cover the eastern end of the island, this diverse group was divided into three companies: Company A, under Marine captain Lewis Pickup, was given the assignment of defending over two and a half miles of North Shore beaches. Company B, under Lieutenant Alan Manning, was assigned defense of the South Shore. Weapons Company D, under Captain Noel Castle, was given the job of covering either side with his heavy machine guns and wooden-wheeled 37mms. Also available were eight fixed .50 caliber antiaircraft machine guns from two platoons of what was called Mobile Battery, which were in position above Kindley Field.

Despite the fact that all his north-facing defenses had been pulverized into powdered dust, Beecher's warning to Colonel Howard on May 3 — that the defensive installations in his sector were practically destroyed and that he was "very dubious as to [his] ability to withstand a landing attack in force"—still drew no reaction from the Marine commander.

Although enemy bombardment of the island since April 29 often lasted well into the night, it was sporadic. Not on the night of May 5, however. It was 11:00 P.M., the exact moment the Japanese invasion force was shoving off from Lamao on Bataan for Corregidor. At that moment, instead of diminishing, there was a sudden increase in the shelling, as enemy gunners, firing white phosphorus shells from what General Moore guessed must have been 300 guns, blasted the anticipated landing beaches. Although it was over in a few minutes, it was enough to alert General Wainwright in his living quarters in Malinta Tunnel that something was up.

"This sounds to me just like artillery preparation before an attack," he said to Lewis Beebe. "Let's go up and see what Moore thinks of it."

After discussing the situation with the two men and concluding, as Wainwright said, that they could "do nothing but wait for developments," an out-of-breath officer entered the lateral with the news that all anticipated. Diaries for that fateful moment read, "Runner arrived at 2350 at 'H' Station and reported enemy landing at North Point. As nearly as can be determined, the first wave hit the beach at 2330, 5 May, 1942."[19]

As noted earlier, the objective of the first wave of Japanese invasion boats was Cavalry Point. Was the information Moore and Wainwright received that they had come ashore at North Point correct? It was.

As the fleet of landing craft rounded the southern tip of Bataan and entered the North Channel, much to their surprise they found the anticipated east-to-west-moving current running in the opposite direction.

In the confusion, the 1st Battalion boats, with regimental commander Colonel Gempachi Sato in the lead craft, soon found themselves fighting a losing battle with the tide, which, by the time they were able to turn for shore, were over three-quarters of a mile east of their objective.

Earlier, General Wainwright, writing about the effect of Japanese artillery on the island's 75mm guns, wrote that of the 48 available at the beginning of the siege, "forty-six were knocked out by the time the Japs landed." The two that had survived had done so only because General Moore had ordered their commander, army Lieutenant Ray Lawrence, not to reveal his position during the pre-invasion bombardment. It paid off.[20]

Lawrence, who, for all practical purposes, was in command of the island from the eastern end of Kindley Field to Hooker Point, had a mixed complement of 82 men, including Marines, Philippine Scouts, and U.S. Army Bataan survivors.

Along with the two 75s, they were as well armed as any comparable unit on the island. This included two 37mms, two heavy machine guns, and eight Browning automatic rifles. To take advantage of the 50-foot bluffs that would face the enemy once they landed, each position was liberally stocked with grenades and surplus air corps 30-pound fragmentation bombs with improvised wooden chutes to drop them from.

With H-hour originally scheduled for 11:30 P.M., Japanese shelling of the eastern end of the island had all but ceased several minutes before. Evidence that the enemy was approaching was therefore detected by motor sounds from their landing craft. At that, Lt. Lawrence ordered his beach defense searchlights turned on. Although quickly shot out by fire from the boats, unknown to the Japanese, their discovery had decided their fate.

First to open up on the Japanese was Marine private Roy Hayes. Ordered to hold his fire until the barges got closer, he decided that they couldn't wait any longer and cut loose at the Japanese who, at that moment, were at near point-blank range. The initial burst from his .30 caliber machine gun was soon accompanied by small arms fire from all along the bluffs.

Illuminated by tracer fire, Lawrence's 75s then went to work on the enemy barges. His comment to the commander of one of the 75s who said he couldn't see the target through the sight was, "then use it like a shotgun, [like] you're shooting ducks on the pond." Supported by accurate .37mm fire from Scouts of the 91st Coast and .50 caliber fire from a Mobile Battery platoon on Kindley Field, few of the enemy barges ever reached shore.

For the handful of Japanese soldiers that were able to make it to the small, 30-foot-wide rocky beach, they were greeted by a fusillade of hand grenades and fragmentation bombs, and an unscalable 50-foot-high cliff. One observer said that the slaughter of the Japanese in their barges "was sickening." Lawrence said that they actually heard the enemy soldiers "crying for mercy, telling us to cease fire, that they were Filipinos."[21]

So complete was the repulse of the easternmost cluster of 1st Battalion boats that for all practical purposes, the battalion ceased to exist.

With the enemy troops who had come ashore opposite Lt. Lawrence's positions reduced to a mere handful, the remaining 1st Battalion boats who hit the rocky shoreline farther east near North Point found the going a little easier, but not much.

Defending the bluffs above North Point was the 2nd Platoon of A Company on the left and Company A of the army's 803rd Engineers on the right.

Unlike the defensive positions occupied by Lt. Lawrence's men, those occupied by the two companies above North Point had taken a terrific pounding during the pre-invasion bombardment. Before they could recover, led by Colonel Sato himself, what was left of the 1st Battalion boats slipped ashore.

One of the first to discover the Japanese was Company D army Sergeant William Dudley, who quickly propped the trails of his 37mm gun so he could depress enough to fire on the beach. Enfilading fire from Marine private Silas Barnes, operating a .30-caliber machine gun from Infantry Point, took a deadly toll on the Japanese as they disembarked from their barges opposite Cavalry Point.[22]

A few minutes after the Japanese disembarked, several were spotted coming up a ravine in front of A Company's positions. At that point, veteran Marine Gunnery Sergeant "Tex" Haynes went on a one-man crusade to stop them.

After emptying two .45s and a rifle from a dead comrade, he yanked a .30-caliber machine gun off its damaged mount, slung an extra belt of ammunition over his shoulder, and started down the ravine, firing as he went. After expending both belts, a Japanese grenade felled the gallant marine — a man whose actions under different circumstances might have earned him the Medal of Honor.[23]

Company A's 2nd Platoon, under the command of Gunnery Sergeant John Mercurio, along with the 803rd Engineers soon had their hands full. Marine corporal Edwin Franklin said that their positions were so close to the high-tide line that they could "reach out and touch the water," making it impossible to halt the enemy before they reached shore. Sgt. Mercurio killed a Japanese with his .45 the second he hit the beach.

He was "so close [when I shot him], I could have touched him," he said.

Army corporal Joseph Johnson, attached to the 2nd Platoon, said that moments after they landed, he could see enemy soldiers "fleeting [and] darting in the shadows."

Along with the enemy suddenly being upon them, the effects of what the Americans called Japanese knee mortars (actually grenade launchers) forced A Company to pull back some 200 yards across the entire North Point area to the western end of Kindley Field, leaving only the 803rd Aviation Engineers to cover the eastern end of the bluffs above North Point. With the Japanese having advanced to the edge of the airfield, the immediate fear was their crossing the field to the South Shore, thus cutting off the entire eastern end of the island.

Help came from the .50-caliber antiaircraft guns of Mobile Battery's 3rd Platoon, whose second section was in position on a little ridge on the south side of Kindley Field about halfway down the runway. Although forced to dig up the tripods of their guns to enable them to depress their barrels enough to fire on the Japanese, they were able to momentarily stop the infiltration across the little strip.

Before long, however, several enemy soldiers were spotted moving in on second section's position, forcing the abandonment of their guns. Most of the men were able to work their way to either Battery Denver, a sandbagged, 4-gun antiaircraft battery near Water Tank Hill, or to the Radio Intercept Tunnel on Monkey Point. Those who escaped to Monkey Point were soon joined by a handful of men from Mobile's first section, whose guns had been destroyed by Japanese artillery.

Unfortunately, not only had the enemy shells knocked out their guns, but in wounding several of its crew in the process, it unknowingly set off a chain of events that helped assure the struggling Japanese of success on the island.

It occurred when a truck carrying first section's wounded back toward Malinta Tunnel was interpreted by a sergeant of Mobile's 2nd Platoon that the eastern end of the island was being evacuated. At that point, according to a pre-arranged plan, the commanding officer pulled his men back to an old World War I concrete infantry trench north of Malinta's East Portal near what was called RJ (Road Junction) 43, where it remained virtually out of the fight until the end. Had 2nd Platoon remained in its position on the ridge above the east end of Kindley Field, it very well could have blocked the Japanese from making the crucial move down the airfield toward Battery Denver and Water Tank Hill.

Although unaware that the Japanese were moving west across Kindley and along the North Shore Road behind them, A Company and the small band of 803rd Engineers, along with Lt. Lawrence, were still holding out.

Within an hour of Colonel Sato's 1st Battalion boats reaching shore, the 2nd Battalion barges, which were forced to reassemble because of confusion caused by the tides, were spotted a little over a quarter mile off North Point. Spotted much farther out than the 1st Battalion and aided by the bright moon that had just come out, they would pay even a greater price for their attempted intrusion than their predecessors.

Along with those manning the North Shore guns, including Lt. Lawrence's two 75s, the most devastating results came from the mortars of Battery Way and Craighill on Fort Hughes, who were immediately ordered into action. They were soon joined by the 3-inch antiaircraft guns of Battery Idaho, whose direct fire on the Japanese from Fort Hughes added to the slaughter of the approaching Japanese.

"I doubt if any reached ... shore," remembered Lt. Lawrence. "I'm sure we sank at least a dozen."

A Japanese officer witnessing the event from three miles away at Cabcaben, Bataan, described the scene as "a spectacle that confounded the imagination, surpassing in grim horror anything we had ever seen."[24]

For those few who reached shore, one said, "Most of us just kept still ... lying against the slope — just waiting, hoping that reinforcements would arrive."

The price for helping create that spectacle was the enemy counter-battery fire that soon rained down on Battery Way.

Major Bill Massello and his made-over searchlight battery crew who had taken over Way had opened fire with the two remaining mortars, but a near direct hit soon knocked one of them out. Before long, the last of the old 1890-model mortars, which were never built to sustain firing as many rounds as it was forced to, began to fall apart. First to go were the piston rods that cushioned the recoil. They froze up, bringing Massello to pour a can of lubricating oil on the them. Amazingly, as the oil penetrated the cylinders, the barrel, stuck in the elevated position, slowly came back down.

As the chances of an accident increased with every shot, Massello, with firing-pin lanyard in hand, made his men clear the pit before firing the gun himself. Also, whenever it became impossible to traverse the gun because debris from enemy near misses had clogged the ring, he would clear and sweep the mechanism himself.

Fortunately, once the fire mission against the reeling 2nd Battalion boats ended, the intensity of Japanese counter-battery fire let up. This gave Massello and his crew time to recover and stand by for the next mission, which would come at 3:00 A.M.

By 1:00 A.M. on the sixth, of the 2,000 men the Japanese anticipated they would have on shore, it is estimated that fewer than 800 had made it.

Until daylight, the battle for Corregidor would be recorded as one of the most confusing in the history of World War II. The biggest contributing factors on the U.S. side were the total lack of all communication between command and combat units and the continuous shelling and bombing of the 1,000 yards of open ground between Water Tank Hill and Malinta's East Portal.

In anticipation of a successful Japanese invasion of the eastern end of the island, it was planned to form a line of defense along what was called Wilson Park Ridge that ran northwest across the island 1,000 yards east of Malinta. The high point, known as Water Tank Hill, sat just a few yards west of what was considered the key link to the entire line — the four-gun antiaircraft battery called Battery Denver.

Anchoring both ends of the line were A Company on the north and B Company on the south, whose primary jobs still remained defending against a seaward invasion. If the Americans were unable to hold Battery Denver, both companies would be in jeopardy of being flanked. With no line to fall back on, success or failure in keeping the Japanese out of Malinta depended on holding the center.

On April 24, 12 days prior to the Japanese invasion, Denver first sergeant Dewey Brady and another man spotting enemy fire from on top of the fresh water tank next to the battery were killed. Under most circumstances, the loss of one man wouldn't have the effect that the death of Brady had on the battery. The death of the "soldier's soldier," as one man who knew him said, devastated battery morale. Captain Paul Cornwall, who took over command of the battery from the ill Captain Benson Guyton on May 1, said that after the loss of Brady, "the Battery was never the same; the spark had died." Ironically, he was killed on the very day the order awarding him a battlefield commission came down. Cornwall says:

> On the night of May 5, a severe bombardment of the battery's position started about 7:00 P.M. Members of the battery were ordered to take cover in the two power plant tunnels on the south

side of the hill. After the shelling lifted around 10:30 P.M., a truck passed on its way to Malinta Tunnel. The occupants notified us that a landing had been made by the Japanese. Not long after that, Japanese machine gun fire alerted us from the vicinity of the water towers.[25]

Deciding that the defense of Denver itself, with its four sandbagged gun pits scattered in a half circle across the ridge, was all but impossible, Cornwall formed the hundred or so men from the battery along a line running "from Ordnance Point to the Marine positions on the Bataan side of Wilson Park Ridge." His earlier decision to bring one of the battery's two heavy .50-caliber antiaircraft guns with him would soon pay off.

About 20 yards off the North Coast Road was the entrance to a long access tunnel that led to the east end of Denver. Anticipating possible penetration by the Japanese through the tunnel, nine sharp-shooting Marines had taken position behind a barricade of railroad ties in hopes of holding the tunnel. Although it worked, once it was discovered, the Japanese were able to slip pass the entrance, moving west along the road a few yards before climbing to the top of the ridge.

When they reached the top and began to move toward the battery, they were spotted by the Denver boys, who suddenly came to life. Particularly effective was one of the .50 calibers, but not for long, as sustained fire soon forced the gun to freeze up.

At that point, both sides went at each other with small arms and grenades. "I decided that an effort be made to clear the first water tower of a Japanese machine gun," said Cornwall. "Two men, Lieutenant Perkins and PFC Cisneros, carried hand grenades forward and

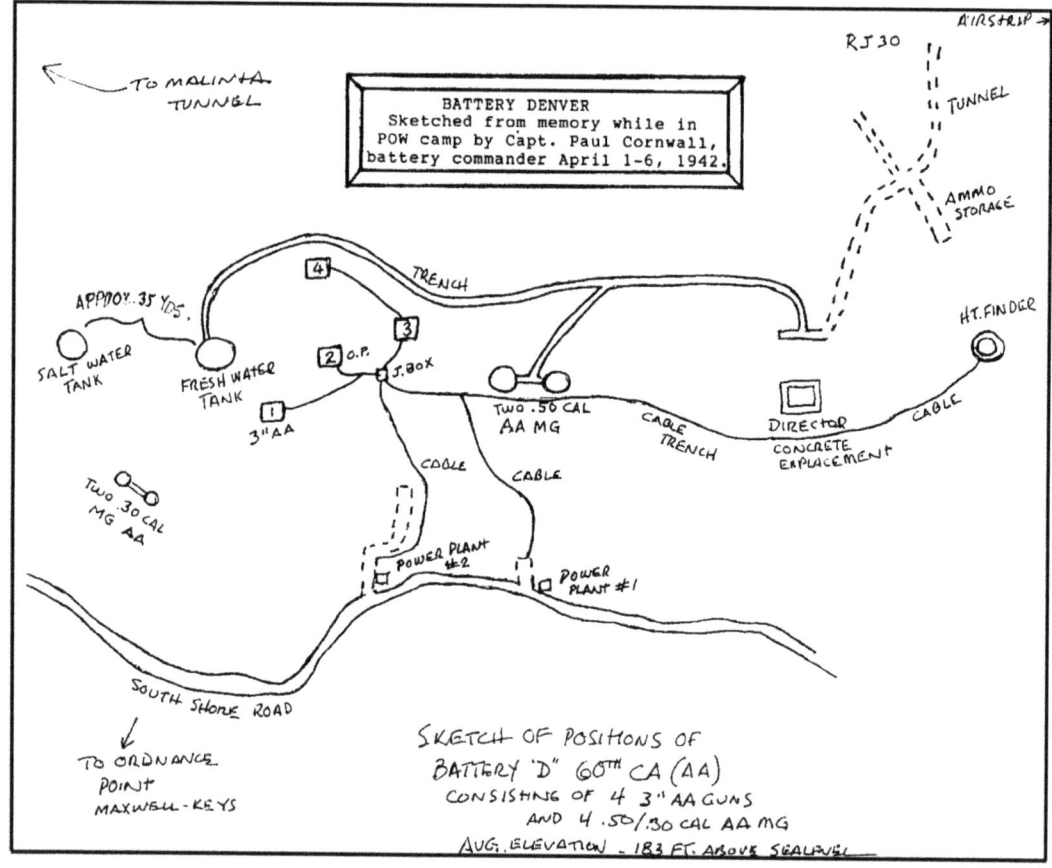

succeeded in clearing the ridge and silencing the enemy machine gun nest." However, the Japanese, led by Colonel Sato himself, soon forced the Americans back off the hill some 150 yards to RJ (road junction) 21.[26]

Despite gaining the advantage, with only a piecemeal force himself, Sato was unwilling to attempt to capitalize further on his quick success. Thus, as the Japanese commander ordered his men back to dig in across the forward slope of Denver to wait for reinforcements, the second battle for Water Tank Hill would soon be joined.

Before the Japanese could get organized in their newly won positions, a hastily formed five-man raiding party, led by army Lieutenant Robert Perkins, worked its way up to a spot behind Denver. From there they lobbed hand grenades into two of the gun pits then dashed southward across the ridge and safely into Battery Maxwell-Keys on the south side. Unfortunately, their courageous efforts did nothing to weaken the enemy's hold on the position.

Marine captain Lewis Pickup, commanding officer of A Company, whose job it was to defending the entire North Shore, because of the total absence of communications, was initially unaware of the Japanese landing until told that enemy troops had been spotted moving along the North Shore Road.

Aware that the defense plan called for establishing a line across the island anchored by Battery Denver in the center, Pickup ordered a squad, led by Gunnery Sergeant Harold Ferrell, to reconnoiter the battery to make sure it was still in U.S. hands. Of course, it wasn't.

When Ferrell got close to the battery area, he said, "I heard voices, and not American. Corporal Morris crept close enough to observe that the place seemed to have Japs all over it, digging in."

With news of the enemy's capture of Denver, Pickup, upon his return, was perplexed as to what to do. On the one hand, he couldn't afford not to go after them, nor could he pull troops off beach defense to do it.

The answer came when Captain Noel Castle, commanding officer of the Company D weapons company, volunteered to attack the Japanese with a patrol of his own men and a few stragglers. Castle, a member of the Marine Corps rifle team and who famously carried two pearl-handled .45s, moved his men into position below the hill. "Let's go up there and run the bastards off," Sergeant Ferrell heard him tell his men.

At that point Ferrell warned him of the enemy's control of the battery. Ignoring the warning, he told him that he was going to take his men up there "and shoot those people's eyes out."[27]

Marine corporal Joseph Kopacz, who survived the attack, said that they ran head on into the Japanese near the first water tower. At that point Castle picked up an abandoned .30-caliber machine gun and opened up on the advancing Japanese, almost single-handedly forcing them to fall back into one of the Denver pits. While leading his men forward, however, the young captain was killed by machine gun fire. At that point, the assault ground to a halt, the men falling back to the bottom of the hill.

With news of Castle's death and the failure to retake the hill, Captain Pickup sent a runner to 1st Battalion command post in Malinta Tunnel informing Colonel Beecher of the situation. At that moment, had the Japanese known, the U.S. line across Water Tank Hill was totally non-existent. But help, as it was, was on the way.

First to react was Lieutenant Colonel Lloyd Biggs of the 92nd Coast Artillery, who had hastily put together a makeshift group of his Scouts, stragglers from Denver and a few Marines, placing them on a line from the South Shore Road to a position just west of Water

Tank Hill. There they were joined by another hurriedly formed group who, when linked up, formed a continuous but dangerously thin line across the island.

As the night wore on, what was mentioned as the two major contributing factors to the outcome of the battle—lack of communication and relentless enemy artillery fire on U.S. positions—began to take its toll.

Relying on runners to keep Beecher and Colonel Howard informed of the progress of the battle was all but impossible. So devastating was the artillery fire on the open ground between Water Tank Hill and Malinta's east entrance that no one will ever know how many messengers were either killed, wounded, or failed to show up. Because of this, it wasn't until after 1:30 A.M. that word reached Colonel Beecher of the desperate situation and plea for reinforcements from Captain Pickup.

Despite the fact that the enemy was only 1,000 yards away from the east entrance, Beecher still had a difficult time convincing Colonel Howard that it was the main Japanese invasion effort. Still convinced that the main assault would come against the middle or western end of the island, the Marine commander was reluctant to commit his reserve forces in Government Ravine in case they were needed there.

Finally, at about 2:00 A.M., Howard acceded, ordering only the 1st Battalion, made up of companies O and P which had moved into Malinta just after midnight, to counterattack the Japanese positions on Water Tank. Had he chosen instead to commit his four 4th Battalion reserve companies at the same time, it is possible the Japanese could have been forced out of Denver and off the ridge.

First out into the now bright moonlit night was Marine lieutenant William Hogaboom's Company P. Along with Captain Robert Chambers' O Company, this reserve force was made up of 215 Marine and Navy headquarters and service company personnel, and 90 men of the fledgling Philippine army air corps who had escaped from Bataan—hardly a force to be reckoned with.

Guided by Captain Golland Clark, 1st Battalion adjutant, as the men formed into a skirmish line a few yards outside the tunnel, someone spotted some shadowy figures moving along a ridge to the left, at which a couple of men fired at with their 1917 Enfields.

Marine quartermaster clerk Frank Ferguson of Company O, whose 1st Platoon had followed them out of the tunnel, witnessed what happened. "The men who shot at the forms quickly learned of their mistake when sulfurous [four-letter] oaths came back from men on the ridge," said Ferguson.

Recognizing the booming voice as that of army Lieutenant William King, who was nearly hit by the shots, he remarked, "No Japs could cuss like that." He was right, as it seems the targets were men of Mobile Battery, who, it will be recalled, had prematurely withdrawn to the old concrete infantry trench near Malinta earlier that morning. Fortunately, no one was hit in the friendly fire episode.[28]

Moments later as Ferguson led his men forward, he spotted something that instinctively told him all hell was about to break loose. "I saw a couple of white flares go up some distance ahead of us," he remembered. "Word was passed to the men [to seek] immediate shelter for I suspected that the flares were a Jap signal for artillery support. My estimate was not wrong.... This particular barrage was the most severe and concentrated I had ever come under."

Unfortunately, the two O Company platoons that followed Ferguson out of Malinta were caught in the open when the barrage hit. Unaware of their fate and therefore still anticipating their participation, the quartermaster clerk turned company commander ordered his men to move out.

The original plan was for Ferguson's 1st and Sergeant John Haskin's 3rd Platoon to form a line from the south shore across the ridge to a point above the North Shore Road, where it would link up with Lt. Hogaboom's P Company. Together they would attack the enemy positions on Water Tank and Denver.

"I deployed my platoon straight to the front with my right resting on the road," he said. "Sergeant Haskin's 3rd Platoon was expected to deploy to my right, and I presumed the 2nd Platoon was in my rear for support."

Not waiting for Haskin to join him, Ferguson ordered his men forward. When they reached the top of the ridge behind the two water tanks, they were halted by heavy machine gun and automatic weapon fire from Battery Denver.

Although resigned to waiting for reinforcements, the resourceful Japanese, using the sandbagged Denver gun pits, had done a masterful job of establishing a defense line across the ridge.

"The Japs seemed to have a machine gun or automatic weapons every few yards or so placed to offer [interlocking] support," said Ferguson. "Three times I sent men forward, and three times they were repulsed."

Expecting 3rd Platoon support from his right during the attacks but not hearing any firing, he investigated only to find it wide open. Ordering two of his machine guns to cover the exposed area, he went to find out what happened. Unable to communicate with Ferguson as to his plight, Haskin, along with Quartermaster Clerk Herman Snellings' 2nd Platoon, had been caught out in the open in the devastating barrage that hit just as they came out of the tunnel.

"All but about five of Haskin's men had been killed or wounded when caught in the barrage," said Ferguson. "Snellings had [only] four left [out of the 50 men] in his platoon."

Realizing that both his flanks were unprotected, Ferguson sent Snellings and a handful of men to make contact with P Company on his left. "Soon word came back that P Company had been joined. My relief was great," he said, "but not for long."

Because of the effective defense the Japanese had put up, Ferguson found himself in a quandary as to what to do. With nothing heavier that a few BARs and ancient Lewis machine guns, "frontal assaults had proven foolish," he said. "Since [our] line [was] no more than 30 yards from the enemy, we ... tried to rout them with grenades, but the trees that had been felled by shell fire interfered with their use."

At that point Sergeant Harold Ferrell was ordered to have a crack at them with his old Stokes mortars that had been converted to fire 81mm ammunition. However, after firing 20 World War I vintage rounds that, at best, were considered "so unreliable as to be practically worthless from mortars for which there were no sights," it, too, was called off.[29]

Sometime during the attempt to rout the Japanese from Denver, two Marine veterans, Sergeant Major Thomas Sweeney and 3rd Platoon commander John Haskin, were able to climb to the top of one of the water tanks from where they successfully hurled grenades down on the enemy machine guns that had been holding up the advance. Haskins, however, was shot and killed while climbing up to the tower with a musette bag of full of grenades. How many times the courageous Marine made the trip is not known, nor when a Japanese sniper finally killed his buddy, Tom Sweeney. When informed of their deaths, Frank Ferguson, knowing that the two were very close friends, said that it was "almost fitting that they should go out together."[30]

When word of the successful Japanese landing on the island reached General Wainwright earlier that night, he sent a brief message to General Marshall in Washington, announcing that, "Landing attack on Corregidor in progress. Enemy landed North Point. Further details as the situation develops."

At 2:30 A.M., Lt. Colonel Johnny Pugh, Wainwright's senior aide, handed the general a handwritten message that had been scribbled on a piece of lined legal pad paper. Pugh apologized; it seemed communications had run out of official message forms. It read:

> During recent weeks we have been following with growing admiration the day-by-day accounts of your heroic stand against the mounting intensity of bombardment by enemy planes and heavy siege guns.
>
> In spite of all the handicaps of complete isolation, lack of food, and ammunition, you have given the world a shining example of patriotic fortitude and self-sacrifice.
>
> The American people ask no finer example of tenacity, resourcefulness, and steadfast courage. The calm determination of your personal leadership in a desperate situation sets a standard of duty for our soldiers throughout the world.
>
> In every camp and on every naval vessel soldiers, sailors, and Marines are inspired by the gallant struggle of their comrades in the Philippines. The workmen in our shipyards and munitions plants redouble their efforts because of you.
>
> You and your devoted followers have become the living symbols of our war aims and the guarantee of victory.
>
> Franklin D. Roosevelt[31]

Wainwright, so moved by the words, vowed to keep the message and hopefully someday pass it on to his son.

Ironically and possibly never known by the general, the president did not write the message. In fact, he may never have seen it. At General Marshall's request, Major General Dwight Eisenhower, at the time deputy director of Army War Plans in Washington, wrote it.

An hour later, Wainwright sent off a reply to the president. After expressing "gratitude and appreciation" for his "gracious and generous message" and describing the enemy landings and terrific bombardment during the past seven days, he concluded with, "As I write this at 3:30 A.M., our patrols are attempting to locate the enemy positions.... I will counterattack at dawn to drive him into the sea or destroy him."[32]

If Wainwright's message sounds as if he was unaware of what was really happening in the battle, it is true. As mentioned, because of the lack of communications, everyone from the commanding general to General Moore and Colonel Howard were in the dark as to the tactical situation.

However, both Wainwright and Moore, according to their diaries, did receive information about results of the enemy's third attempt to land. Wrote Wainwright: "A third assault wave of landing boats approaching Corregidor; broken up and practically annihilated by artillery fire from Fort Drum, Battery Way, and roving 155mm gun batteries Stockade, Wright, and Gulick."

Their targets were, as Wainwright said, boats of the enemy's third wave that were not only carrying reinforcements, but also ammunition which was expected to run out by midmorning. Few Japanese barges would make it.

Battery Way, with its high-angle fire ability, was ordered to lay fire onto the Japanese

3. Corregidor's Final Hours

beachhead in the vicinity of North Point. After a couple of 670-pound projectiles fell dangerously close to A Company defenders along the North Shore, however, Bill Massello was ordered to switch missions to the enemy barges in the channel. The counter-battery fire that would rain down on Way from the Japanese for this switch in targets, however, would mark the beginning of the end for Massello and his courageous crew.

Another battery that would reap success against the Japanese without suffering similar repercussions was Battery Gulick. In his diary, it will be recalled, General Moore made reference to the effectiveness of the four roving 155mm gun batteries on the Rock that became its "main dependence for counter-battery fire against the Japanese."

On the night of the fifth, Captain Jack Gulick, commander of his own Battery Gulick, had moved his gun to a spot on Topside between two buildings from which the flash from his gun muzzle could not be detected. When the order came to open up on the enemy's third assault wave, Gulick was ready, firing on the helpless boats with deadly accuracy. Try as they might, however, the Japanese were unable to spot the muzzle flashes from Gulick's 155, believing that it was coming from somewhere near the golf course. Although innocent Battery Globe, located near the course, got pounded, the Japanese were never able to find or stop the resourceful captain until the end.[33]

When the order to fire on the enemy boats in the North Channel was given to the commander on tiny Fort Drum, it wasn't that the battleship-shaped island's four 14-inch guns couldn't reach the target, it was, as he said, that they couldn't see it. "Just fire anywhere at that smoke between you and Cabcaben and you can't miss them," was the reply.

Effects of U.S. fire, which included machine gun and small arms fire from shore, like on the two previous attempts that night, had a devastating effect on the enemy. For the boats carrying ammunition that were well behind those with reinforcements, results of the fire from the big guns actually forced them to turn back. Recalled one Japanese officer, "[We] threw the ammunition into the nearby waters and returned to Bataan."[34]

For those carrying reinforcements, as they neared Corregidor, it was fire from machine guns and small arms more than artillery that apparently had the most effect. Wrote one boat commander who survived the attack, "American high-powered machine guns poured a stream of bullets on us from all directions. Rifle fire added to the hail of death. Men who huddled in the center of the boat were all either killed or wounded. Those who clung to the sides were hit by shells that penetrated the steel plating. The boat had sprung several leaks when we finally came within landing distance of Corregidor. Desperately, I gave the signal and led the charge against the shore defenses. I don't know how many men responded. In that mad dash for shore many drowned as they dropped into the water mortally wounded. Many were killed outright.... If it had not been for the fact that it was the dark hour before dawn, I doubt if any of us would [have made it]."[35]

If the U.S. command was in the dark about what was happening, so was General Homma at his 14th Army headquarters on Bataan. Word of the progress of the invasion had been filtering piecemeal back to him throughout the night, and none of the news was encouraging. With no clear picture of the situation other than what could be seen from the southern tip of Bataan, "every time I was disappointed [at the news]," he said.

When information reached him on what happened in the pre-dawn attempt to reinforce Colonel Sato and that only 21 of the 52 landing craft that started out that night were left, he panicked. "My God," he thought to himself, "I have failed miserably on the assault. I had plenty of troops on this side of the sea [but] could not send reinforcements with the

21 boats that were left." Unknown to the Japanese commander, the answer to his dilemma was at that moment being loaded onto three of the remaining 21 landing craft — tanks.[36]

It was a little after 4:00 A.M. when Colonel Howard got word of the plight of O and P companies in the battle to dislodge the Japanese from Battery Denver. At that point he ordered the last of his reserves into the fight.

As men of what was designated as the 4th Battalion moved out of the confines of Malinta as dawn was breaking that morning, never was a U.S. Marine unit so under-represented by Marines and non-combatants than companies Q, R, S and T of the battalion. Of the 303 men listed, only one officer, Major Francis Williams, and three NCOs were Marines. Of the remainder, 278 were naval personnel from the U.S. Navy section base on Bataan or off the scuttled sub-tender USS *Canopus*. Although equipped to match its men, with 1917 Enfields and a few Lewis machine guns, they had trained hard for the impossible task they faced as they solemnly made their way out into the open.

About 500 yards out, the brief lull in enemy artillery fire that had so devastated the area throughout the night ended. The results, along with causing many casualties, temporarily scattered and disorganized the planned attack. By 5:00 A.M., however, Major Williams had reassembled his troops, sending two companies, Q and R, to the left to help A and P Companies contain the Japanese north of Battery Denver.

It was daylight by the time the two got into position, at which the men of Company Q, on the extreme end of the line near the water, spotted two enemy barges loaded with Japanese troops that were hung up on some rocks about a hundred yards offshore. A small group of the best sharpshooting sailors in the company were sent to pick off the helpless enemy. Thirty minutes later and after several hundred rounds from their old World War I Enfield rifles, the job was done.[37]

Meanwhile, Major Williams, who had also taken over command of the decimated 1st Battalion, assigned Company T, under navy Lieutenant Bethel Otter, to help contain the Japanese in Battery Denver and brought S Company to cover the extreme right or southern flank of the line. For the first time since the Japanese were discovered in Denver, the Americans were in a position, although tenuous at best, to make a coordinated attack against them.

Scheduled for 6:15, everything went well for Q and R Companies on the left, who easily pushed the enemy back some 200 to 300 yards.

In the assault, army Captain Harold Dalness, commanding officer of Company R, and Lieutenant Otis Saalman led several men against a Japanese machine gun position at the head of a draw. Under covering fire, one of the men crawled up close enough to throw a grenade. The toss looked perfect, but to everyone's surprise, a Japanese soldier with grenade in hand, rose up to throw it back. But it was too late — his frantic effort to save himself and his comrades failed when it blew up in his hand.[38]

With news of Q and R Companies' success, Williams ordered them to pinch in toward Denver where it was hoped T Company would also have made some headway. But it hadn't happened.

It wasn't for the lack of trying, however. Six navy men, including Lieutenant Otter and Ensign James Lloyd, crawled close enough to attack one of the enemy machine gun nests — a gun that, as one man remembered, "had dealt so much misery to Company T and the rest of the battalion." Armed with grenades, when they got close enough, the six men made a suicidal charge at the enemy position. Although they knocked it out, five of the six were killed, including both officers.

At approximately the same time, a third T Company officer, army Captain Calvin Chunn, was wounded while leading a successful attack on the Japanese who were attempting to set up a 75mm mountain gun near the water towers. Chunn would survive.

On the right of the water towers, Quartermaster Clerk Frank Ferguson, commander of O Company's 3rd Platoon, and army corporal Alvin Stewart of the 803rd Engineers, had worked their way to a spot a few yards below what Ferguson recalled as a "beautiful and well-nigh impregnable position," at which they prepared to throw grenades. Apparently believing, after the first two grenades, that they'd been flanked, Japanese soldiers began to abandon the position. Silhouetted against the pre-dawn sky as they ran back, rifles were quickly substituted for grenades. "They were like ducks in a shooting gallery," said Ferguson, who, along with Stewart, estimated they shot down some twenty enemy soldiers before they were spotted.[39]

As he looked to congratulate Ferguson, Stewart saw that he had been shot in the face. Bandaging him the best he could, the two men crawled back to their own lines. With the wound, as Ferguson said, "looking like part of my face had been shot away," he worked his way back to Malinta, dodging not only enemy artillery fire on the way back, but bombs and machine gun fire from planes of the Imperial Japanese Air Force which had joined the attack at dawn.

As soon as it was light enough to see, the unmistakable sound of a .50-caliber machine was heard from the vicinity of Battery Maxwell-Keys on the U.S. right flank. It was from a machine gun emplacement near the battery that had been manned by a makeshift crew of Bataan survivors. From their position they were able to get an occasional glimpse of Japanese soldiers moving along the south side of the ridge below Denver, at which they cut loose with the big navy water-cooled .50. Until discovered and chased from their position by Japanese knee-mortar fire, they, along with the Scouts from Battery Keys who had joined in with rifles and machine guns, were, for the moment, able to discourage any idea Colonel Sato had of infiltrating the American right flank.

Upon learning of the enemy landing early that morning, General Moore had ordered the men of destroyed Batteries B, C, D, and H of the 59th Coast Artillery to form as infantry and stand by for use when needed. As things began to develop on the East Sector during the night, Moore ordered Battery B, formerly assigned to Battery Crockett, to move into Malinta as a reserve force. With men of the other three 59th batteries still being held by Colonel Howard in anticipation of a possible landing on the west end of the island, the 60 American artillerymen of Captain Herman Hauck's battery, now ordered into the fight, were the last to be sent.

The men of the battalion reflected the anxiousness and zeal of their commander. Unknown to them, however, was that with daylight Japanese artillery observers from an observation balloon on Bataan had apparently spotted them as they moved out of Malinta, bringing a rain of 240mm shells down on the small column. Fortunately, Hauck's men were able to escape the heavy losses that had been inflicted on 1st Battalion companies earlier, reporting to Major Williams around 8:30.

With the American line opposite the entrenched enemy in Denver barely but still holding, Williams sent the 59th to the south shore against several Japanese who had been spotted trying to work their way behind U.S. lines.

Ironically, as successful as Companies Q and R had been against Col. Sato's right flank, so was Hauck's effort against his left. The 59th, reinforced by a few Scouts and men from

Mobile Battery's 3rd Platoon, after disposing of the few infiltrating Japanese, launched an attack out of the vicinity of Battery Maxwell-Keys against Sato's left flank. Although successful, it would be for naught.

A little before 10:00 A.M. from his R Company position overlooking Kindley Field, Lieutenant Otis Saalman spotted the weapons that meant doom to Corregidor once they reached the island — Japanese tanks. Three of them were already moving up the slope toward the airstrip when he saw them. They had come ashore around 8:30, but for an hour and a half had struggled unsuccessfully to negotiate the steep bluffs above the beach. Ironically, if it hadn't been for one of the tanks, a captured American Stuart M-3, towing the two Japanese Type 97's up from the beach, the threat from the enemy armor might never have occurred.[40]

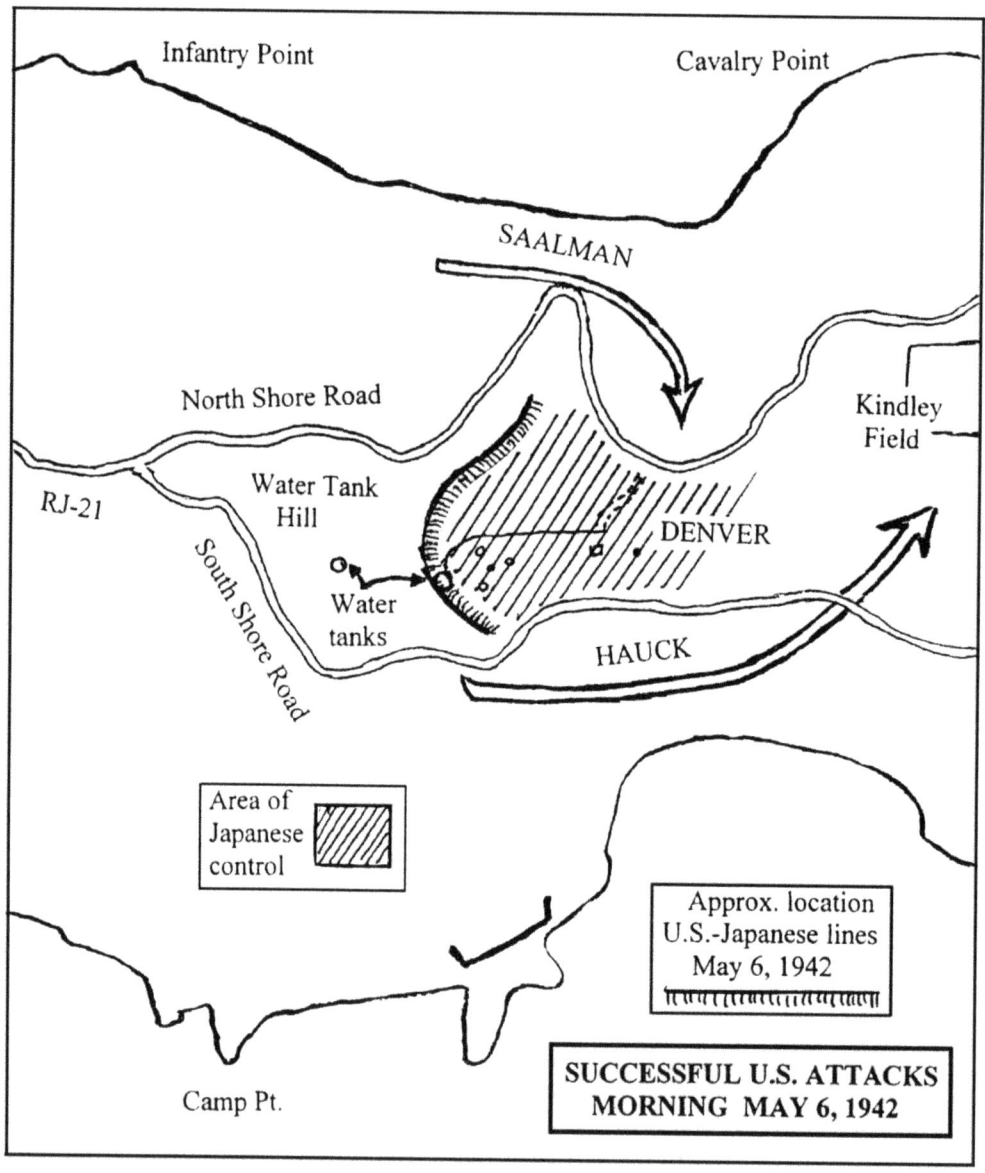

At that point, apparently prearranged with the movement of the tanks, two white flares were fired from the Japanese position in Denver, which, moments later, brought another fusillade of artillery fire down on the area between Denver and Malinta.

Moments before, Lieutenant William Hogaboom, commanding officer of P Company, in position near the North Shore Road, noticed a handful of men on his right "beginning to fall back in disorder. I detected Major Williams attempting to stop the withdrawal," he said, "and ran over to find out from him the cause. He told me that tanks had been brought into action and that there were no anti-tank weapons available to stop them."[41]

Realizing that even if it was possible to stop the retreat, it was too late to reestablish the line, Williams ordered Hogaboom to pull his men out and fall back to the old concrete trench near RJ 43, and there to prepare to make a final stand.

"I passed word down into the ravine," said Hogaboom. "Men came streaming out, and although dazed by the intense action they'd been through, indicated resentment of the unexplained order to fall back."

Getting them back to the trench wasn't easy. "We had to pass through two 240mm barrages to reach the road cut near the trench. It was each man for himself. Casualties were heavy."

When Captain Harold Dalness was ordered to pull R Company back from their position on the enemy's right flank, not only were his men resentful of the order, but, with farther to go along the more exposed north side of the island, were chewed to pieces by Japanese artillery. "Dirt, rocks, trees, bodies, and debris literally filled the air all the way back," remembered Dalness. Only a handful made it.

When Hogaboom and Williams took stock of the number and condition of the exhausted group of men who had made it safely into the trench, it was obvious that, tanks or no tanks, it was all but over.

"Those of us who reached what had been the concrete trench before the 240's worked it over prepared to set up a defense line," recalled Hogaboom. "Major Williams went to Malinta to report the situation and obtain reinforcements. Lieutenant Harris of A Company joined me in the trench I had occupied with little more than a couple dozen of my men."[42]

One battery that had tried unsuccessfully to hit one of the barges carrying the tanks across was Battery Way. For every shot fired by the old 12-incher, however, it was being hit by at least one in return.

The story of Major Bill Massello and his gun crews, who had somehow kept the gun in action steadily since 3:00 A.M., was one of both heroism and tenacity.

With three of the four guns previously knocked out, there were plenty of gun crews standing by to take over if needed. Like substitutes on the sidelines of a football game, they couldn't wait to get in. However, despite wounds and the ultimate danger of being killed at any moment, each crew was reluctant to give up or concede what they considered an earned privilege of servicing the gun.

Sergeant Walter Kulinski, who witnessed one in action, said that he had never seen men like that crew: "They were wounded, but wanted to fire the gun." One man refused to be replaced despite a severe stomach wound. "You couldn't keep them down. That's the funny thing — I couldn't understand it. They were fighting fools."[43]

With enemy counter-battery fire salvos coming in every few minutes, at 5:00 A.M. when the last trained crew went down, it was clerks, cooks, radio operators, and motor pool personnel who, without hesitation, jumped in to keep the old mortar firing.

The man behind it all was Bill Massello—a man who motivated his men by example. Together for three months on Bataan and now on Corregidor, it was his undying spirit, leadership, and courage under fire that brought Kulinski to label him "a fighting man, a real Coast Artillery officer." There were even rumors that "Wild Bill," as some of his men called him, had the telephones ripped off the walls so he couldn't be ordered to surrender.

Around 10:30, Massello, with his luck far overextended, for the umpteenth time had gone out to sweep the debris off the gun's traverse ring when shrapnel from an enemy shell that hit on the far side of the pit felled the gallant soldier. Crewmen rushed out and carried him to shelter. The wounds to both legs and one arm, although not life threatening, forced him to turn over command of the battery to Captain Fred Miller. Not long after that, the old mortar, whose life, like Massello's, was also far overextended, gave out, its breech-block finally freezing up.

Overheard as he ran out to sweep off the traverse ring for what would be the last time, he said, "If they ever get me, what a way for a soldier to go with a goddamn broom in my hand."[44]

With a casualty rate of close to 75 percent, what was left of the game men of "the last big gun on Corregidor to fire on the enemy," as Massello said, sat down to wait for the Japanese.

It was after 11:00 A.M. when Major Williams reported to Colonel Howard in his Navy Tunnel headquarters, asking him for anti-tank guns and reinforcements. The Marine commander told him that there wasn't anything he could do, that General Wainwright had decided to surrender at noon. Ironically, it was Howard who, an hour earlier, had informed the Philippine commander that the enemy had landed tanks on the island.

When informed of the tanks, "I had to make up my mind," said Wainwright. "The task of trying to find ways and means of averting the inevitable. I went over our position in my mind: shaken troops, beach defenses literally pulverized, concrete machine gun nests reduced to powder, the majority of seacoast guns destroyed, fifty-six beach defense 75mm guns knocked out, communications gone, movement of troops all but impossible because of the continued shelling, new and uncontested landings....

"But it was the terror that is vested in the tank that was the deciding factor," he said. "I thought of the havoc that even one could wreak if it nosed into the tunnel where lay helpless wounded and their brave nurses."[45]

Pacing up and down in one of the darkened laterals trying to decide what to do, "My head came up and I entered my own headquarters and called General Moore and Beebe. I had come to a decision which I never regretted. "[The two men] agreed that I had taken the only steps possible under the circumstances."

Wainwright then told Beebe to get out the previously prepared surrender message that had been readied in case of his death and to broadcast it to the Japanese over *The Voice of Freedom* transmitter at 10:30, adding that he would cease fire at noon. He then instructed Moore to have Colonel Howard initiate Plan Pontiac, the order to destroy all weapons greater than .45 caliber, by 12:00 noon.[46]

At his regimental headquarters in the Navy Tunnel, Colonel Sam Howard, with head in hands, openly wept at what he had to do. "My God," he said to his executive officer, Donald Curtis, "I had to be the first Marine officer ever to surrender a regiment."

After issuing the order, Howard wrote out a critique of the situation. "All general reserves have been committed, the enemy was making additional landings; ammunition in the East Sector was practically exhausted and it was impossible to get any into the area. Practically all of our guns were destroyed, and it became only a question or hours before our lines would be overrun." He felt better.[47]

Beebe, meanwhile, hurried to the communications lateral and at 10:30 began reading the message. Since there was no way to directly communicate with General Homma, it was hoped the Japanese, who had monitored *The Voice of Freedom* broadcasts since their inception in early January, would hear the cease fire message to notify the 14th Army commander.

To stress the importance of the message, Beebe repeated "message for General Homma or present commander-in-chief of the Imperial Japanese forces in Luzon" twice, followed by: "Anyone receiving this message, please transmit it to the commander-in-chief of the Imperial Japanese Forces in Luzon."[48]

The text, emphasizing, among other things, that a white flag would be displayed in a prominent position on Corregidor and that all firing from harbor forts would cease at 12:00, was repeated in Japanese by Japanese-American sergeant Richard Sakakida.

With no way of knowing if the message had successfully gotten through, other than to wait for Japanese reaction to the noon raising of the white flag, Beebe repeated it at 11:00 and again at 11:45.

Noon came and went, and although the few U.S. troops who had been notified of the surrender ceased firing, there was no appreciable let up in the bombing and shelling of the island. At 12:30 the message was read for the fourth and last time, and still no response. In fact, there would never be one, as General Homma neither heard nor was told of it. Quite the opposite. Believing at last report that his entire operation was in jeopardy, he had diverted the troops originally scheduled to land at James Ravine that night to reinforce Colonel Sato on the eastern end of the island.

Although it is not known what brought the Japanese to let up their attack a half hour later at 1:00, it may have been that the white flag, which had gone up at noon on the old 100-foot ship's mast flagpole on the edge of the Parade Ground, had been spotted, possibly by aircraft.

The job of replacing the American flag with a white bedsheet was given to Colonel Paul Bunker, Seaward Defense commander on Corregidor. Despite the continued enemy shelling, which at the time was still focused on the East Sector, the two-time All-American from West Point vowed the occasion would be ceremonial. Accompanied by his deputy, Lieutenant Colonel Dwight Edison, and a bugler, the three men walked out of the tunnel leading to Bunker's command post below Battery Wheeler, up the hill, and across the Parade Ground to the flagpole. There, with the two officers standing at attention, tears welling up in their eyes, the bugler played taps. Edison then lowered the flag, running up the white bedsheet in its place.[49]

When Bunker got back to his headquarters, he cut off a small corner of the flag, which he later sewed under the shoulder patch of his uniform, then solemnly burned the flag. (Although Bunker died in prison camp, the tiny corner of the flag was recovered and is on display at the museum at West Point.)

Meanwhile, back in Malinta, a touching scene occurred after General Moore was informed that the white flag had been raised over the island. Several of his staff officers had gathered in "H" Station when the word came in. Despite knowing that the most difficult part of the surrender process lay ahead, one by one they all came forward, saluted and shook hands, each congratulating Moore on the good fight he had put up.

After the last man came forward, Moore said, "Thank you for your support. With your guidance Corregidor did its job for almost five months. I don't know what history will say about the Rock and our part in the war, but from the bottom of my heart, I'm proud to have been your commander."

One of the officers there, Major Steve Mellnik, said that what followed was one of the most emotional experiences he had ever witnessed. "With tears streaming down [our] cheeks, officers and everyone in "H" Station cheered and applauded for five minutes."[50]

Assuming that the decided lull in the enemy bombardment meant that they had recognized the white flag, four men, Marine captain Golland Clark, Lieutenant Alan Manning, a Marine musician, and a flag bearer carrying a torn strip of white bed sheet tied on to a broom handle, walked out of Malinta's East Portal, hoping to be recognized as an advance surrender party.

When they passed the old concrete trench outside the tunnel entrance, realizing that the end was here, Major Williams ordered the handful of survivors to take shelter inside the tunnel. Of the many men deserving to be called heroes for their efforts that night, one was the commander of the makeshift 4th Battalion sailors, Major Francis Williams. Having taken over command of both battalions, of those survivors few hesitated to heap praise on him for his courage, leadership, and determination under the most harrowing of circumstances.

With the flag bearer holding the broom handle high over his head, the four men marched into the early afternoon sun looking for the first Japanese officer they could find.

A few anxious yards down what was left of the road, a Japanese officer, spotting the white flag, stepped out of the brush. At that point, with the bugler probably blowing "Carry On," someone in the party, most likely one of the two Chinese Marine officers, explained that they wanted to be taken to his commanding officer. They were led down the North Shore Road, across Kindley Field to Water Tank Hill, where they met with Colonel Motoo Nakayama, Homma's senior operations officer. Ironically, it was the same Colonel Nakayama that had negotiated with the surrender party on Bataan nearly a month earlier.

Nakayama, through an English-speaking lieutenant, insisted that he would talk only to General Wainwright. At that point, the four men turned and started back for Malinta.

During the three hours between General Wainwright's 10:00 A.M. decision to surrender and the initial meeting with the Japanese, a lot had been going on both inside and outside of the tunnel.

Ironically, the last to learn of the surrender that day were the Japanese. By the time they were notified of U.S. intentions to give up, the whole world knew it was over.

Once General Beebe began reading the surrender message over *The Voice of Freedom*, word spread through the tunnel like wildfire.

Army radio operator Corporal Irving Strobing, in touch with station WTJ in Honolulu, sent what was supposed to be the last message. When he was handed it, he was told to send it in the clear, and that there would be no more official messages. Simple and undramatic but omitting the word surrender, it said, "Notify any and all vessels headed toward this area to return to their home base."

Although it may have been the last official message from the Rock, Ensign Kenneth Hoeffel, over the navy's own transmitter, sent what was to be its final message to the Navy Department in Washington. Although also omitting the word surrender, it left little doubt that it was over.

3. Corregidor's Final Hours

"Our few remaining ships being sunk," it read. "Now destroying all military equipment. 172 officers and 2,126 men of the navy send last expression of loyalty and devotion to country, to families, and to friends. Going off the air."

At 11:55, Commander Melvin McCoy, the navy's communications officer, handed what was its last message to the radioman. "Beam it for Radio Honolulu," he said, "and don't bother with code."

"Going off the air now. Goodbye and good luck. Callahan and McCoy."[51]

Meanwhile, back in the army's communication lateral, Corporal Strobing, who later said that he was "afraid to let his contact [with Honolulu] go even for a second," was giving the world his own unofficial, dramatic, and sometimes rambling account of Corregidor's last hours. His words, which were also picked up by a few ham radio operators along the U.S. West Coast that happened to be listening at 3:40 A.M., would appear in newspapers and magazines all over America. Without them no one would have any idea what the last hours on Corregidor were like until after the war.

"They are not here yet," he began. "We are waiting for God only knows what.... Lots of heavy fighting going on. We've only got about an hour and twenty minutes before we may have to give up.... We don't know yet. They are throwing men and shell at us and we may not be able to stand it. They have been shelling faster than you can count."

At 11:05, after pausing for a few minutes, he came back on the air.

> We've got about 55 minutes and I feel sick at my stomach.... They are around smashing rifles. They bring in the wounded every minute.... General Wainwright is a right guy and we are willing to go on for him, but shells were dropping all night, faster than hell. Damage terrific. Too much for guys to take.... Corregidor used to be a nice place, but it's haunted now.... The jig is up. Everyone is bawling like a baby. I know how a mouse feels, caught in a trap waiting for guys to come along and finish up. My name is Irving Strobing. Get this to my mother, Mrs. Minnie Strobing, 605 Barbey Street, Brooklyn, New York. My love to Pa, Joe, Sue, Mac, Joy, and Paul. Tell Joe wherever he is to give 'em hell for us. My love to you all. Sign my name and tell my mother you heard from me." Strobing added, "ZZA, Stand by," but it was the last word from Corregidor.[52]

Although the world had heard the last from the Rock, there were two more messages out of Corregidor of official nature, sent by General Wainwright to President Roosevelt and General Douglas MacArthur. In pencil on a yellow legal pad, to Roosevelt via the chief of staff, General Marshall, he wrote,

> For the President of the United States. With broken heart and head bowed in sadness but not in shame, I report to your Excellency that today I must arrange terms for the surrender of the fortified islands of Manila Bay....
> There is a limit of human endurance and that limit had long since been past. Without prospect of relief, I feel it is my duty to my country and to my gallant troops to end this useless effusion of blood and human sacrifice. Please say to the nation that my troops and I have accomplished all that is humanly possible and that we have upheld the best traditions of the United States and its army.... With profound regret and with continued pride in my gallant troops, I go to meet the Japanese commander. Goodbye, Mr. President.[53]

The message to MacArthur was similar in content, with these exceptions:

> I feel it is my duty to the nation and my troops to end this useless slaughter.... American and Filipino troops have engaged and held the enemy for nearly five months. We have done our full duty for you and for our country. We are sad but unashamed. I have fought to the best of my ability from Linguyen Gulf to Bataan to Corregidor, always hoping relief was on the way.... Goodbye, General. My regards to you and our comrades in Australia.[54]

Although the world knew that Corregidor had surrendered, they had no idea of the difficulty that lay ahead in carrying it out.

When the execute Pontiac order was received by the 2nd and 3rd Battalion Marines defending the unchallenged Middleside and Topside beaches, it was devastating psychologically as if they'd been winning and told to surrender. Outside of the approximate 200 who had seen combat against the Japanese on Bataan in the battle for Longoskawayan Point in January, it was particularly difficult. After weeks of preparations in anticipation of finally getting their licks in against the Japanese, the order to lay down their arms without firing a shot was too much to take for all of the old Shanghai Marines. One Marine had to be corralled when he threatened to kill the messenger who had told them to surrender.

A 2nd Battalion Marine, Private William Coghlan, expressing the feelings and reactions of most at Pontiac, said, "We tore [our weapons] apart, stomped on them, cracked them across the wall, threw rifle bolts into the bay, [while] all the time giving vent to our anger with lusty curses at the Japs." With Japanese artillery still continuing to pound the Rock, after destroying his weapon, Private 1st Class Ben Lohman said, "We didn't know what to do. The word was finally passed to go into Malinta Tunnel."[55]

Battery commanders in those still-functioning coast artillery and anti-aircraft batteries ordered their guns spiked and their breeches thrown deep into the jungle or tossed into the sea. Recoil cylinders were smashed or made useless, anti-aircraft height finders were wrecked, and all records and operating manuals burned — all of this punctuated no doubt with plenty of "lusty curses" at the Japanese.

The real difficulty with the order to surrender happened in the East Sector, where because of the lack of communications, many never heard it. The continued bombing and shelling of the area by the Japanese also made it impossible to believe, even when word somehow got through, that it was over.

Although it is not known how or to whom Captain Herman Hauck's makeshift 59th Regiment reserve force surrendered, they, it will be recalled, had been successful in forcing Colonel Sato's left flank defenders back off the ridge.

Unaware of the order to surrender, led by the aggressive Hauck, they had actually driven the Japanese north over the ridge and down onto the airfield and were advancing on the lead Japanese tank when word came to give up. Hauck's men, disbelieving at first, disgustedly threw down their weapons and raised their hands in surrender.

Farther south at the Radio Intercept Tunnel on Monkey Point, a makeshift group of defenders, composed of Marines, sailors, Philippine Scouts, and army Bataan survivors, had withdrawn to the area earlier that morning when the Japanese gained control of the north side of Kindley Field.

One of the Bataan veterans, air corps Lieutenant Edgar Whitcomb, was initially assigned to B Company when he arrived and put in charge of the 37mm gun and a ten-man crew of Philippine Scouts. Unchallenged during the night, at dawn he had thrown the breech block of the old "wooden-wheeled antique," as he called it, into the sea, and proceeded with his Scouts to Monkey Point.

When they arrived, Whitcomb reported to Marine captain James Bromeyer and Lieutenant Mason Chronister, who were attempting to establish a line of defense above the entrance to the tunnel on the edge of the South Shore Road.

Whitcomb was quickly enlisted to help. Finding the men "gathered in small groups," he said, "I spent most of my time running up and down the line ordering them to scatter and take a protected position." From their position overlooking Kindley Field, the "mixed conglomeration of fighting talent," as he called them, was initially able to keep the Japanese at bay. "We had no idea of the progress of the battle," recalled the young air force officer. "All we knew was that over the hill the Japs were firing at us, and that we were firing back."

As the morning wore on, Japanese accuracy improved. Along with their machine guns, particularly effective were the enemy knee mortars. Although casualties began to mount up, it was not enough to force the Americans off the ridge.

From his position on the ridge, Whitcomb, for the first time, got a look at the precision of the Japanese artillery fire on U.S. positions between Water Tank Hill and Malinta Tunnel, leaving him with little doubt that the end was near.

"The coordination between the artillery on Bataan and the forces that had landed on the island [was surprising]," he said. "[Whenever] flares would go up, the artillery would shell a sector into which the Japs had not yet moved. While the shelling went on, dive bombers continued to fly in so low that we could actually see the faces of the pilots."

Around 11:00, a runner appeared with information that General Wainwright would surrender the island at noon. "With that information," said Whitcomb, "we withdrew down the South Shore road to the navy tunnel, where we could stand off any attack until that time."[56]

For Wainwright, the wait for the return of the advance surrender party was, as he said, "a torturous hour." Finally, at close to 2:00, Captain Clark entered the Headquarters lateral with news of the meeting with the Japanese.

"He won't come to see you, sir," said Clark. "He insists that you go and meet him."

Wainwright stood up, removed his pistol belt and .45, then he and his aides, Johnny Pugh and Tom Dooley, General Moore and his aid, Major Bob Brown, and Clark all climbed into Moore's battered Chevrolet and headed out of the tunnel. It was a rough ride over the cratered, torn-up road, but something that Tom Dooley, Wainwright's driver on Bataan, handled without difficulty.

Despite the white flag, which had been tied onto the front of the car, "enemy machine gunners from Denver Hill sprayed shots at us as we approached," said Wainwright. "We got out of the car at the foot of Denver Hill and, following Clark, began its ascent. As we did, Jap bombers opened up with heavy attacks on nearby Fort Hughes, more than two hours after I put up the white flag."[57]

Near the top of the hill, the six men were met by an English-speaking Japanese lieutenant, whom Wainwright sized up as being "wiry and fit and reeking with arrogance."

Identifying himself as Lieutenant Uramura, he shouted at Wainwright, who, cupping his good ear with his hand to hear over the noise, was told that they would not accept the surrender unless it included "all American and Filipino troops in the whole archipelago."

Not about to discuss the surrender with a Japanese lieutenant, Wainwright fired back, "I do not choose to discuss surrender terms with you. Take me to the senior officer present on Corregidor!"

At that moment, Colonel Motoo Nakayama, whom Homma had sent over to bring Wainwright back if he was ready to surrender all the islands, walked up. Through Uramura, Wainwright told him that he was there to "tender the surrender of the four fortified islands at the mouth of Manila Bay."

Uramura translated it to Nakayama, who "in an angry torrent of Japanese," as Wainwright remembered it, "told me without translation what I already knew — that my surrender must include all forces in the entire Philippines."

"In that case I will deal only with General Homma and with no one of less rank," replied Wainwright sternly. "I want an appointment with him."

Nakayama agreed to take him to Cabcaben to meet with the Japanese commander, at which Wainwright invited the two men to go with him to the North Dock and take his personal boat across. They agreed.

Johnny Pugh, in the meantime, had started for the tunnel and the South Dock, where Wainwright's boat was tied, to bring it around to the North Dock. He almost didn't make it. Wainwright says:

> Pugh's path back to the east entrance ... became beset with a sudden and tremendous barrage. But by crawling, crouching, and edging along, using whatever cover he could find, he made it — an act of striking heroism. But the shelling which Pugh had survived caused the Jap colonel to stop in his tracks, for the road [around Malinta Hill] to the North Dock lay through the same bombardment.

The two Japanese, fearing being killed by their own shells, insisted that they turn back. It was the chance Wainwright had been waiting for. "Why the hell don't you people stop shelling?" he shouted angrily. "I put up my white flag an hour ago."[58]

Colonel Nakayama murmured something to Uramura, who remarked, "We have not accepted any surrender from you as yet," at which the Japanese invited Wainwright and Dooley to cross in one of their barges from the safer eastern end of the island.

"He took us to Corregidor's tiny airfield in the vicinity of Cavalry Point," remembered Wainwright, "[where he] contacted Bataan by radio and ordered a boat to come over and fetch us. It was nearly four o'clock by the time it arrived. We shoved off for Bataan ... and Homma."

While the "tank barge," as General Wainwright referred to it, slowly made its way across the channel, Johnny Pugh, General Beebe, Sergeant Hubert Carrol, Wainwright's aide, his administrative assistant Major William Lawrence, and interpreter Richard Sakakida, had already arrived in Wainwright's boat. When the barge carrying Wainwright and Dooley pulled up to the long rock pier at Cabcaben, the general was surprised to see Major Lawrence there to meet him.

"I came over with General Beebe and Major Pugh," he said. "They couldn't find you at the North Dock, so they came ahead. They just took a Jap truck and went to look for you, figuring you might have landed someplace else."

Lawrence told him that he was to meet with Homma at a house outside the barrio of Cabcaben, at which the three Americans, Nakayama and Uramura got into a car and were driven to the location.

As the car pulled onto Bataan's East Road, Wainwright solemnly reflected back on what had occurred there on the horrible night of April 8. "The road down which Bataan's battered II Corps had been ruthlessly driven that final day."

The house, occupied before the war by Silvestre Castillo, was the only relatively undamaged structure in sight. Wainwright and Dooley were led to a long veranda at the back of the house and told to wait there.

Presently the truck carrying Beebe, Carrol, Pugh, and Sakakida drove up, and three of the men joined Wainwright on the porch. Richard Sakakida, who had come along as an interpreter for the Americans, however, was grabbed and beaten by a Japanese NCO. With blood running down from his face, which was cut when his eyeglasses were smashed, he was unceremoniously told that the Japanese had their own interpreter.[59]

"After [a] period of waiting, we were ... ordered to move off the porch and line up in front of the steps," said Wainwright. "This was for the benefit of Jap newsreel and still-camera men. We were still standing there when Homma arrived in a beautiful shiny Cadillac, flanked by three overdressed aides." It was now 6:00 P.M.

Meanwhile, back on Corregidor, a lot had happened in the two hours since the surrender party had left the island.

On the isolated end beyond the airstrip, Lt. Ray Lawrence and his men, who had remained virtually unchallenged since daylight, were left somewhat bewildered by what they observed as a let-up in the intensity of the battle. Although Japanese artillery had continued firing and planes had been working over Topside, the rattle of small arms fire had practically diminished. Finally around 5:00 P.M., the men realizing that regardless of what was happening they had been cut off behind enemy lines, the decision was made to surrender.

After throwing the breech blocks of the two 75s into the sea, Lawrence led his men toward the airfield, where they surrendered to the first Japanese they saw.

Interestingly, it was not a downtrodden group of men who had gone forward to meet their conquerors. Quite the opposite. Throughout the day they had been able to observe the results of their efforts against the Japanese that night. Of the 24 derelict, half-sunken Japanese landing craft they counted drifting offshore, four still had their full complement of enemy troops on board, all dead. And among them, hundreds of bodies in orange-colored life jackets were seen floating in and out with the tide. "We of course were in good spirits," said Lawrence. "I had only one dead Philippine Scout and one man wounded."

Other men in small groups or individually, also unaware of the surrender, continued to fight on throughout the day. A group of Marines and Philippine Scouts from Maxwell-Keys, who had holed up in a tunnel below the battery, had fought on until close to 5:00 P.M. Confused by the continuing sounds of small arms fire despite having seen several white flags, they were picked up by the Japanese as they made their way to Malinta.

Marine sergeant Lloyd Catlow, one of the last to surrender, had slugged it out with the Japanese for over an hour from behind some rocks on the south shore before spotting a white flag. Two other Marines held a off a dozen or so Japanese from their position in a small cave until 3:30 that afternoon. Days later, the body of a lone American was found amongst seven dead enemy soldiers, appearing as if he had personally killed all seven from his foxhole position.

Much more precarious since Wainwright's surrender party left for Bataan was the situation inside Malinta Tunnel. When Wainwright and Moore drove out to meet the Japanese with the white flag tied onto the front of the car, everyone knew it was to surrender the island. The only question was would the Japanese accept it, and how would they react when they did?

Not counting hospital personnel and wounded, according to conservative estimates there were some 4,000 men in the tunnel. It seemed as if all 4,000, believing no doubt in safety in numbers, had crowded into the 1,400-foot-long main tunnel by the time General Moore re-entered from his and General Wainwright's meeting with the Japanese. Wainwright had sent Moore back to Malinta to take over for him while he went to see Homma.

About the time Wainwright and Dooley were shoving off for Bataan at 4:00, the sound of battle immediately outside the East Portal had those inside not knowing exactly what to do. It was obvious that "the enemy was at the gate," as someone said. Expecting, since the Japanese now knew that Corregidor had surrendered, that the fighting would stop, many feared that Wainwright had either failed or been killed.

At this point, Quartermaster General Charles Drake took over the role General Moore, who remained in "H" Station, had been asked by Wainwright to assume.

Not bothering to consult with Moore, Drake discussed the matter with his executive officer, Lt. Colonel Theodore Kalakuka, as to what to do. Kalakuka, a West Pointer of Russian decent, volunteered to meet with the Japanese, believing, as he said, that he would be able to "[find] some Japanese officer [who] will be able to speak my language. I will explain the conditions and tell him we are prepared to surrender."

The first order of business was to get the jam-packed crowd of fearful, sweating humanity back from the entrance in order to avoid a situation that might appear as confrontational to the first Japanese into the tunnel. A rope was found, and the milling mass was physically pushed back even with the entrance to the third lateral.

At that point, Drake mounted a wooden box, raised his arms, and yelled over the noise of gunfire still coming from outside the temporary, timber-reinforced, galvanized steel gate:

> Men, listen to me. We are going to try to contact the nearest Japanese troops outside this entrance. We are going to tell them ... that we have laid down our arms and ask that all firing stop so we can get out of here properly and as soon as possible. If we show [them] that we offer no resistance, they will come in. If they do, I want every one of you to stand still. Don't move an inch, and keep absolutely still. Any demonstration, any last-minute heroics will mean the end of every one of us.... If you want to live, don't move![60]

With a piece of white cloth tied to a bamboo pole, Kalakuka, with all eyes on him, slowly opened the heavy steel door. Poking the white flag out ahead of him from the slightly opened gate, he paused a moment, then stepped outside.

With his disappearance, perhaps the most apprehensive moment of the entire siege was at hand. In the 28-day pounding the Rock had endured since Bataan, including 300 air raids and the more devastating 240mm barrages, it was this moment, preponderant with unknowns, that was the most frightening. Stories of the 1937 Rape of Nanking — the butchering of thousands of Chinese soldiers and civilians and rape of hundreds of women by Japanese soldiers — were known to most of the over 4,000 men and nurses waiting their fate in the tunnel. Would Corregidor be another Nanking?

Moments later all sounds of firing stopped. With the silence outside came silence inside, until the big door creaked open and Kalakuka came in with two Japanese officers, a major and a lieutenant. The Japanese, through Kalakuka, told Drake that they wanted everyone out of the western entrance of the tunnel in 10 minutes.

"You tell them there are close to 4,000 men in this tunnel," replied Drake, and as long as there is firing going on outside that entrance, "it must be stopped before I will place [us] in a position where they cannot protect themselves and be shot down."

Kalakuka relayed Drake's answer, and after a brief conversation between the two, they agreed to send their own soldiers out to stop the shooting. At that point the two officers and Kalakuka walked back out of the tunnel, leaving the big gate open behind them.

Outside, three Japanese tanks with troops following cautiously behind, had lumbered up the road to about 100 yards from the entrance, from where they drew abreast of each other and started forward.

Back inside, Drake and several officers had begun moving the milling pack of humanity back to create a corridor for the Japanese. "Open an aisle as wide as possible clear to the west entrance," ordered Drake, "[and] remember what I said about absolute silence.... Don't even move a finger. [The] Japs will be suspicious and jittery as hell."

A few minutes later the two officers and Kalakuka returned, followed by several soldiers, some in asbestos suits with flamethrowers strapped on their backs. Drake was told that as soon as the firing stopped, everyone except medical staff and wounded were to follow them outside.

Another officer, Major Steve Mellnik, who had stepped out of Moore's "H" Station lateral when someone shouted, "The Japs are coming!" had kept his eyes on the tanks. "They stopped ten yards from the entrance," he said, "the turreted machine guns pointing down the length of the tunnel. Seconds later [the] hatch clanked open and [an] officer leaped to the ground and strode toward the entrance."[61]

With soldiers posted at the entrance, two long files of infantry came in, and with the sounds of firing outside the tunnel gone, the "prisoners of war," as Mellnik now referred to everyone, began to filter out of the West Portal. "A soldier then planted himself at "H" Station, waved his flamethrower, and motioned us to go inside," said Mellnik. "Looks to me like they intend to take over lateral by lateral," remarked one of the officers, bringing a smile of relief to the face of General Moore.

"Wainwright and the commander must have worked an agreement," said Moore. "I was worried about this phase."

In another part of the tunnel, however, 75 American and 26 Filipino nurses were also worrying about their fate.

In anticipation of perhaps the worst, 69 of the Americans had signed their names on a white muslin bedsheet below the crudely printed heading: "Members of the Army Nurse Corps and Civilian Women who were in Malinta Tunnel when Corregidor fell."[62] "[With] no idea what was going to happen to us," said one of them, "we wanted to leave a record in case we disappeared."

Back in "H" Station, meanwhile, four submachine gun-wielding Japanese soldiers had burst into the lateral, "crouched in positions of readiness," remembered Mellnik. "Reassured by the sight of unarmed men and a pile of dismantled pistols on the floor," they began ransacking the desks and filing cabinets, "stuffing mechanical pencils, fountain pens and cigarette lighters into their shirts." Gesturing next that they wanted everyone to remove their watches, the situation was settled when two Japanese officers came in. Recognizing the situation, they, according to Mellnik, "slapped the looters and sent them scurrying out of the lateral."

"Ye gods!" said one of the officers. "Scavengers and looters. What kind of a war is this?"

It was a question that would be asked by prisoners all over the island. It was a practice for Japanese soldiers to loot, but in most cases they could count on being severely reprimanded by officers and non-coms if they were caught.

When the Japanese entered the Navy Tunnel located on the south side of Malinta Hill, it was much the same.

"When the first Japs came in ... they were ready with bayonets and grenades," said navy Commander Melvin McCoy. "When they saw no sign of opposition, they lowered their rifles and got down to the business of looting."

Prizing above all "our wrist watches, I saw one burly Jap with watches all the way up to one elbow, halfway up the other," remembered McCoy. "As a Jap was searching me, he was caught by a Japanese sergeant, who, with the soldier standing rigidly at attention, was slapped and cuffed brutally for his invasion."[63]

After the tunnel had been cleared, Japanese officers began inspecting every lateral in Malinta. Accompanied by American officers, when they walked into the hospital tunnel, they were surprised to see it staffed by nurses. Counting the Filipino nurses and civilian volunteers, there were 101 women lining the corridor of the main hospital lateral when the Japanese officers came through to inspect. Shocked at not only the numbers, but for the fact that they were there at all, as they walked away everyone could hear them chatting back and forth amongst themselves. At that point, everyone relaxed and went back to work.

Later that evening, an American officer told head nurse Maude Davison that the Japanese wanted ten nurses to pose for newsreel cameras the next day outside the West Portal. As they were led out of the tunnel the next morning, an English-speaking Japanese officer told them that they were going to send the pictures to General MacArthur "to show that you are alive and that we are looking after you."[64]

Meanwhile, outside Malinta's west entrance, the Japanese had herded everyone out of the tunnel into an open area near the north dock. Steve Mellnik and another soldier, PFC Robert Spielman, were among them.

"Bob and I [were in] a column that marched to the dock area," said Mellnik, "stopping in a semicircle formed by the Japanese soldiers. When [our] number passed the thousand mark, they showed alarm and fired over our heads, [ordering] us to kneel and raise our hands." When the flow of prisoners finally stopped, the Japanese relaxed and allowed everyone to lower their hands.

"A few minutes later, a flight of six aircraft zoomed over the dock area. Alarmed Japanese frantically uncovered signal flags and waved at them ferociously. The planes dropped bombs on Topside. I wondered why?"[65]

The answer to that could probably be traced across the North Channel to what had transpired on the veranda of the Castillo house near Cabcaben. For a man who, before leaving Corregidor, had acknowledged to himself that he would have to surrender all of the Philippines, General Wainwright's initial reluctance to do just that nearly blew up in his face.

With both parties sitting facing each other at a long table, Wainwright handed his "formally signed surrender document" to Homma. Although he could read and speak English, Homma passed it to his interpreter, Lieutenant Nakamura, who read it aloud in Japanese. The document stated that he only had the authority to surrender the four island forts in Manila Bay, and nothing else.

"With a look or two at me," said Wainwright, "[Homma] spoke sharply to Nakamura." In a stern voice, Nakamura said that no surrender would be considered unless it included all American and Filipino troops in the archipelago.

"I can only surrender my men on Corregidor and the three other fortified islands," replied Wainwright. "The troops in the Visayan Islands and Mindanao are no longer under my command. They are commanded by General Sharp, who in turn is under General MacArthur's command."

Nakamura said that Homma didn't believe him. "It has been reported many times by the United States radio that you command all troops in the Philippines. He will not accept any surrender unless it includes all forces." When did he release General Sharp from his command, he was asked.

Although he had done it earlier that day, playing his trump card, Wainwright replied, "Several days ago. Besides, even if I did command General Sharp's troops, I have no means left for communicating with them. I have destroyed my radio equipment."

"Send a staff officer to Sharp," Homma replied through Nakamura. "I will furnish the plane."

Wainwright refused, still insisting he no longer had authority over Sharp. The two men bantered back and forth for a few minutes.

Then Homma, after conferring with the other officers at the table, turned, banged on the table with his fist, and said without an interpreter, "At the time of General King's surrender in Bataan, I did not see you. Neither have I any reason to see you if you are only the commander of a unit of the American forces. I wish only to negotiate with my equal. Since you are not in supreme command, I see no further necessity for my presence here." At that point all the Japanese stood up.

All the while the four Americans, Beebe, Dooley, Johnny Pugh, and Ray Lawrence, had been nervously listening to Wainwright's puzzling attempt to bluff his way out of the inevitable. Realizing that the entire surrender process was in jeopardy, Pugh, who was sitting next to him said, "Wait!"

After a quick conference between the five men, Wainwright, nodding his head in compliance, said, "In face of the fact that further bloodshed ... is unnecessary and futile, I will assume command of the entire American forces in the Philippines at the risk of serious reprimand by my government following the war."[66]

Homma wasn't convinced. Through Nakamura he responded that Wainwright had denied his authority. "Your momentary decision may be regretted by your men. He advises you to return to Corregidor and think this matter over. If you see fit to surrender, then surrender to the commander of the regiment on Corregidor. He in turn will bring you to General Homma in Manila. This meeting is over. Good day." At that point Homma and another officer walked down the veranda steps, got into the Cadillac, and drove away.

The Americans were dumbfounded. With the words "your decision may be regretted by your men" foremost in their minds, Dooley turned to Wainwright and, in a panicked voice, said, "General, you'll have to arrange something. Corregidor and the other harbor islands disarmed this afternoon. The Japs will slaughter our unarmed people."

The five Americans officers and Sergeant Carrol walked off the porch. Wainwright, seeing Colonel Nakayama, who had been detailed to take them back to Corregidor, walked over and asked, "What do you want us to do now?"

Through Lt. Uramura, Nakayama tersely replied, "We will take you and your party to Corregidor, and you can do what you damn please!"

Fortunately, Beebe and Johnny Pugh had cornered a sharp looking young Japanese lieutenant who spoke English. They told him it wasn't clear exactly what Homma wanted them to do.

"Wainwright should return to Corregidor," he said, "and either resume fighting or surrender to the Japanese commander there."

The two men hurried over to Wainwright, who, pacing up and down in the yard, appeared more upset at the way he had just been treated than at the precarious situation he had put them in. The biggest concern being stopping the fighting on Corregidor, Pugh told Wainwright that Homma said that he could surrender the island to the commander of the Japanese forces there. The three men then walked over to Nakayama.

"General Wainwright will surrender all American forces to General Homma unconditionally," said Pugh. "Take us to General Homma, and General Wainwright will dispatch me to Mindanao to instruct General Sharp to comply with his demands."

Having overheard the conversation, a Japanese newspaper reporter walked up. It was Kuzumaro Uno, a native of Salt Lake City, Utah, who had left the country for Japan in the late 1930s because of continual prejudice against Japanese-Americans. Introducing himself, he asked the Americans if he could translate for them. They agreed.

After hearing Uno's explanation, Nakayama said that he would take them to Corregidor and safely turn them over to the commanding officer there and that the next morning they would "go to General Homma with a new surrender and an understanding to contact the other American forces in the Philippines."

At that point the seven Americans, Nakayama, Uremura, and Uno were taken by car and beer truck back to the Cabcaben dock.

Although it was out of his hands now, Wainwright, as he said later, continued to "strongly hope that some way would still be found to avert the surrender of all forces. But each time I thought of continued organized resistance on Mindanao, I thought, too, of the perilous position of close to 11,000 men, nurses, and wounded on Corregidor."

Finding Wainwright's boat in "sinking condition" when they reached the dock, everyone was loaded back into the tank barge that had brought four of them across earlier. "It was a black night," remembered Wainwright, "full of blows and the waters of Manila Bay wild."

Although the ending of perhaps the most perilous day in the lives of the Americans on board the barge appeared near as they approached the island, it was not over yet.

"We landed back at North Point," said Wainwright. "The shore is very rocky there ... prohibiting our getting close enough to step ashore. Sergeant Carroll and another soldier jumped in ... and attempted to carry me to shore, but they tripped and I went in. I waded the rest of the way. General Beebe, who had become very seasick on the rough trip [across], was similarly carried, but dunked much worse."

After waiting a few minutes for Beebe to recover, the party climbed a steep bank to the battered North Shore Road, where, with Uno leading with a flashlight, they were marched toward Malinta.

"When I reached the high ground," said Wainwright, "I saw with shock that there were little lights all over Corregidor — little campfires of Jap troops. They were so widespread that I knew a heavy additional landing must have taken place while I was on Bataan."

It was 7:30 P.M. — seven and a half hours since the white flags had gone up on Corregidor. Yet, as the forlorn party headed up the road, Japanese artillery from that end of the island was still firing on Topside.

"Take me to your commander," demanded Wainwright.

Nakayama agreed, and led them south around Malinta Hill to the demolished barrio of San Jose. There, in a partially destroyed Filipino market being used as a command post, Wainwright was introduced to Colonel Gempachi Sato, the embattled commander of the two battalions that had struggled ashore earlier that morning.

"The Jap colonel was in the midst of an order to his troops to attack Topside," said Wainwright. "From him I learned that a second large complement of Japs had landed at Bottomside and were in full charge of the area between the west entrance and Morrison Hill...." He was also told that Malinta Tunnel had been occupied and cleared of everyone except wounded and hospital staff.

Sato conferred with Nakayama, after which the two worked together to draw up the surrender document following the terms laid down by Homma. It took almost two hours to work out the details of the surrender, which wasn't signed by Wainwright until midnight, exactly 24 hours since the first Japanese assault boats hit the beach below North Point. The document, which was "typed in the stiff Japanese version of English," as Wainwright put it, in part read:

> Imperial Japanese Army and Navy are only prepared to accept surrender [of] all forces under your command.
> To troops operating in other parts of the Philippine Islands, the order shall be given to disarm voluntarily and to take the under-stipulated steps....
> The order shall be carried out within four days.
> Japanese Army and Navy will not cease their operations until they recognize faithfulness in executing the above mentioned orders.
> If and when such faithfulness is recognized, the commander in chief of Japanese Forces in the Philippines will order "cease fire" after taking all circumstances under consideration.[67]

After signing, Wainwright and Pugh, who had remained with him, were then taken under guard to Malinta Tunnel.

"On the way I passed through hundreds of my men, herded in a place near the west end of the tunnel," said their somber commander. "As I passed through them, many of those gallant fellows reached out and took my hand or patted me on the shoulder and said, 'It's all right, General, you did your best.' My eyes had filled with tears by the time I reached the tunnel."[68]

After stopping to tell General Moore of the details of the surrender, which he agreed was the only thing to do, Wainwright started out of the tunnel. Pausing at the entrance, he turned to Moore and said that he felt that he had just taken "a dreadful step." "I went back to my room with Pugh," he remembered, "[and we] threw ourselves on our cots and closed our eyes for the first time since two nights before."

Not to be overlooked in the story of Corregidor's last 24 hours was what had taken place on nearby Fort Hughes and on tiny Fort Drum.

In response to Battery Craighill's accurate fire from Hughes on the invasion boats that night, it was pounded incessantly throughout most of the night and into the morning. Moments after the white flag was spotted on Corregidor at noon, Hughes got a coded message to destroy all papers, codes and secret documents. Five minutes later, lookouts on the island reported white flags on Fort Drum and Fort Frank on the other side of the bay.

Colonel Val Foster, commander on Hughes, turned to his fire control sergeant and said, "We haven't got any white flags, have we, Jones?" "No sir," was the reply, "we haven't. We've never made any up." "We're not going to ... unless we get orders to," said Foster.[69]

Judging by the way the Japanese continued to bomb and blast Corregidor after white flags had sprung up all over the island, it is probable that they would have done the same had Hughes found one to hoist to the top of its flagpole. Caballo, like Corregidor, also had its tunnel. Sloping upwards from its mouth some 400 feet, unlike Malinta, it had no temporary steel doors protecting either entrance. Somewhat like the tunnel rats on Corregidor, the ceaseless pounding of the island since the pre-invasion bombardment started several days before had sent men into the safe confines of the tunnel by droves.

Lieutenant Commander John Morrill, who had come across with his crew from Corregidor that morning, described what he saw on his way to find Colonel Foster.

"The floor," he said, "was covered with blurred figures lying down or sitting.... Their heads hung down and they stared at the floor. It was hard not to step on them or bump into them. Each man had a dusty rag wrapped around his face. The dust was ten times worse than it had been on Corregidor. The uniforms of the men were filthy, faded, and grease stained. Their insignia of rank was virtually indistinguishable. It was hard to tell a private from a sergeant or a sergeant from a colonel. Their eyes were bloodshot from lack of sleep and from whirling, penetrating clouds of dust. And shaving had long since gone out. When a bomb landed topside ... I had a fleeting moment of fear that the whole place was going to cave in on us."[70]

Although they had been sent over to scuttle their subchaser, USS *Quail*, anchored near the island, Colonel Foster put them to work sandbagging an opening in the tunnel.

While hauling sandbags from a nearby mortar pit, Morrill heard someone yell, "*Luzon* crew, man your mortar!" Like the crew of the old China gunboat *Mindanao*, men of the *Luzon* had also been drafted for mortar duty on Hughes.

"Up from nowhere came a single file of ghosts," said Morrill. "Dog-trotting along, half staggering, dragging their feet after them, heads down.... They went about the business of getting the mortar ready like zombies. I never again in my lifetime want to see men so utterly used up as they were. It haunts you afterwards."

For a while that afternoon things on the island quieted down. That is until five o'clock, when all hell broke loose again. Unfortunately, the lull, along with news of the surrender, had allowed men to let down their guard. Some had wandered outside the tunnel when the shelling stopped.

"Then about five o'clock," said Morrill, "[the Japs] really let go on Caballo and smothered her, attacking with waves of heavy bombers in formations of nine."

Morrill's pharmacist's mate, John Head, who had volunteered to help in the hospital, said that "during the all-out concentration of fire power around five o'clock, the casualties were so heavy the hospital was filled to overflowing.... The floor was slippery from blood and the two doctors operated continuously. There was too little time for the proper giving of anesthetics, but most of the wounded were so shocked they were insensible to pain."

Ironically, the very last entry General Wainwright penned in his diary for that day was, "Japs landed and took over Fort Hughes at 2330."

Over on Fort Drum, the concrete battleship some four miles across the bay from Caballo, a message was received at 11:40 A.M. to, according to the executive officer, Captain Ben King, "demolish the armament and surrender at 1200."

Remarkably, despite having taken 593 direct hits, of which at least half were judged to have been 240mm, neither 14-inch battery was knocked out of action. The four-turreted 14-inchers of Batteries Wilson and Marshall continued to wreak havoc on enemy targets until the very end. Also amazing was that not a single man of the 200-man battery was killed, and only five were wounded.

So methodical had Colonel Lewis Kirkpatrick been in preparing his men for this eventuality that when the demolish order came, it was carried out with drill-team precision. The recoil cylinders of the guns were drained and obstructions placed in their muzzles," said King. "Then they were loaded with a round and fired. Breeches were thrown over the side, as was all communications material. Plotting room equipment was smashed with an axe and records thrown in. Buckets of salt water were poured into the six—and 14-inch powder cans, making the powder useless."[71]

The Japanese did not occupy Drum until the next afternoon.

Earlier that same morning back on Corregidor as General Wainwright was dressing, a Japanese officer "strode into the room accompanied by the same insolent Nakamura who had interpreted for Homma." Introducing himself as Colonel Haba, he said he had come to discuss the details of the surrender.

Realizing the urgency of notifying General Sharp that he was resuming command of his troops and to prepare to surrender, he sent for Colonel Jesse Traywick, his assistant chief of staff.

Wainwright told him that to avoid any misunderstanding, he was going to send him to Mindanao to deliver a written copy of the surrender. With the general dictating and Traywick writing it down on the familiar yellow legal pad, it said, in part:

> Subject: Surrender.
> To: Major General William F. Sharp, Jr., Commanding Visayan-Mindanao Force:
>
> To put a stop to further useless sacrifice of human life on the fortified islands, yesterday I tendered to Lieutenant General Homma the surrender of the four harbor forts in Manila Bay. General Homma declined to accept my surrender unless it included the forces under your command.... After leaving General Homma with no agreement between us, I decided to accept in the name of humanity his proposal.... You will, repeat, will surrender all troops under your command ... to the proper Japanese officer. This decision on my part, you will realize, was forced upon me by means beyond my control.
> You are hereby ordered by me as the senior American Army officer in the Philippine Islands to ... carry out the provisions of this letter.... There must be on your part no thought of disregarding these instructions. Failure to fully ... carry them out can only have the most disastrous results.

When Traywick returned with the typed copy, Haba told Wainwright that he was taking him to Manila to broadcast the instructions to Sharp over the radio. Balking at first, but after thinking that the 24 hours between the broadcast and Traywick's arrival would give Sharp time to "inform General MacArthur of the existing situation and obtain his approval of the proposed surrender," Wainwright agreed to go.

At five o'clock that afternoon, he was led out of Malinta Tunnel for the last time. As they walked down the road toward the north dock, again he passed through the same throng of American prisoners that had saluted him the night before. "They were standing there in the blazing sun," he said, "where I had seen them the night before. Obviously they had not been fed or given any water.... They were in very bad shape. But as I walked through them, they got to their feet. Some stood at attention and saluted as I passed.... Others took off their hats and held them across their chests."[72]

With tears again welling up in his eyes, Wainwright raised his hand to his "old sun helmet," in silent tribute to them and to Corregidor, the Rock, the fortress that he would never see again.

At 11:43 that night, sitting at a small bamboo table at Manila radio station KZRH, Wainwright began reading virtually the same message Colonel Traywick would be delivering to General Sharp the next day. Emphasizing again and again that he had resumed "direct command of Sharp and of all troops under his command," he warned him that "the Japanese army and navy will not cease their operations until they recognize the faithfulness of execution of these orders. [They] must be carried out faithfully and accurately, otherwise, the Imperial Japanese Army and Navy [will] continue their operations. If and when such faithfulness ... is recognized, the commander-in-chief of the Japanese forces ... will order that all firing be ceased."

At that point Wainwright paused, was heard to cough, then, after saying, "Taking all circumstances into consideration, and ... " there was another long pause. Realizing he could say no more, the Filipino station announcer broke in with the announcement that the broadcast was over and signed off. It was 12:30 A.M., May 8, 1942, and it was over.[73]

When General MacArthur received word of Wainwright's surrender from General Sharp, he initially messaged General Marshall in Washington that he had "no credence in the alleged broadcast by Wainwright." This was followed with information that Wainwright had reassumed command of all forces in the Philippines and directed their surrender. "I believe," he said in an incisive overtone, "[that he] has temporarily become unbalanced and his condition renders him susceptible of enemy use."

Whether this comment in any way indicated MacArthur's resentment or disapproval of his handling of both the surrender of the Philippines and Bataan is best illustrated in his response to General Marshall's request to endorse General Wainwright for the Medal of Honor. In part it read, "I do not, repeat, not recommend him for the Medal of Honor.... [To] award it to General Wainwright would be a grave injustice to a number of other general officers of practically equally responsible positions who ... exhibited powers of leadership and inspiration to a degree greatly superior to that of General Wainwright.... It would be a grave mistake which later on might well lead to an embarrassing repercussion to make this award."

The number of dead and wounded on the U.S. side in the last 24 hours would never be known. For days after the battle, American prisoners were forced to collect the dead from both sides. Although the Japanese kept a record of the number of their dead, they did not allow the Americans to keep count.

Although the Japanese never made public the number of bodies that were collected and ceremoniously cremated after the battle, they did admit that 903 men had been killed in the 24-day period between April 14 and May 7, 1942. While most of the American and Filipino dead were cremated—but without ceremony—an unknown number were also buried, often times near where they had fallen.

In the end, were U.S. efforts in the Philippines in vain? Corregidor, along with Bataan, had thrown Japanese hopes for a quick capture of the Philippines for a loop. The Americans and Filipinos, by forcing them to bring in units from Japan and other active theaters, perhaps saved Australia from invasion. As for General Homma, since Japan had calculated a mid–February victory in the Philippines, the battle, lasting an additional 3 months, cost him his career.

Immediately after things were wrapped up in the Islands, the Imperial General Headquarters ordered him back to Tokyo, where he was relieved of command. He spent the rest of the war as a reserve officer.

CHAPTER 4

Hong Kong's Final Hours

In December 1940, the newly appointed British Far East commander, Sir Robert Brooke-Popham, referring to possible war with Japan, commented that Hong Kong—specifically the island of Hong Kong—with adequate reinforcements, could hold out for at least six months.

On January 7, 1941, British prime minister Winston Churchill, in answer to Brooke-Popham's suggestion, wrote that in the event of a war with Japan, there wasn't the slightest chance of holding the island, and it would be therefore unwise to increase the inevitable losses they would incur by reinforcing the garrison. "Whether there are two or six battalions at Hong Kong," he wrote, "will make no difference to [the outcome]."[1]

At the time there were four battalions stationed at Hong Kong: two British—the 1st Middlesex and 2nd Royal Scots—and two East Indian—the 2/14 Punjabis and 5/7 Rajputs—amounting to close to 10,000 men.

In September 1941, with urgings from the British Chiefs of Staff, and in the belief that a reinforced Hong Kong garrison might give the Japanese pause before going after the British in the Far East, Churchill changed his mind.

With the British home army stretched thin in Africa at the time, however, Canada was requested to send two battalions to Hong Kong. The two selected were the Winnipeg Grenadiers and the Royal Rifles of Canada, totaling close to 2,000 men. Placed in command was Colonel John K. Lawson, who, prior to his assignment, was Canada's director of military training.

Back in 1934, the island of Hong Kong, unfortified and without a regular garrison, organized its own defense force. Called the Hong Kong Volunteer Defense Corps, and patterned much like the U.S. National Guard, it was made up of some 1,800 English, Eurasian, Chinese, and Portuguese men from every walk of island life—engineers, clerks, businessmen, educators, and the like. Their equipment was of World War I vintage, and the general physical condition of the "Old Boys" or "playboy soldiers," as they were called, most of whom were over 55 and had never done anything physical in their lives, was as poor as their well-worn equipment was old. Mobilized on December 6, 1941, their numbers would be added to the 10,000 or so British, Indian, and Canadian troops which had withdrawn to the island from the New Territories on December 13.[2]

In command of the Hong Kong garrison was 50-year-old Major General Christopher Maltby, who had taken over in July 1941. Suspecting, as the British had at Singapore, that the main threat, if it came, would come from the sea and not from the New Territories across Victoria Harbor, Maltby placed eight 9.2-inch coastal defense guns at three prominent locations on the southern shore of the island.

Not totally ignoring the possibility of an invasion from the Territories, he had six 18 and four 2-pounder guns located at ten fixed-position sites across the north, New Territories-facing coast. To further discourage an invasion attempt from there, a string of two-dozen concrete pillboxes were built along the shoreline that ran from North Point to Victoria. In addition, he had a total of 42 mobile field artillery guns of various caliber at his disposal, although many were obsolete and short of ammunition.

Unknown to the defenders of Hong Kong and the New Territories, by the night of December 7 (December 6 at Pearl Harbor), 60,000 Japanese troops of the 38th Division had moved into position along the northwestern edge of the China–New Territories border. Their attack, which was launched before dawn the next morning, within six days forced the British defenders to evacuate Kowloon and the New Territories for the island. On December 13, what would be the first of the eleven-day siege of Hong Kong Island began.

Before the shooting started, however, a launch flying a white flag was spotted crossing Victoria Harbor. In it were three high-ranking Japanese officers and an interpreter. Also with them were two female hostages, brought along to insure the delegation's safe return to the mainland.

The Japanese were met by Major Charles Boxer. Colonel Tokuchi Tada, the officer in charge of the mission, in good English, said, "I have a letter for your governor. We wish you to surrender. I will wait for your answer."

The governor of Hong Kong was 55-year-old Sir Mark Young, who, like General Maltby, was also relatively new on the job. It took Young, a career civil servant and former rugby

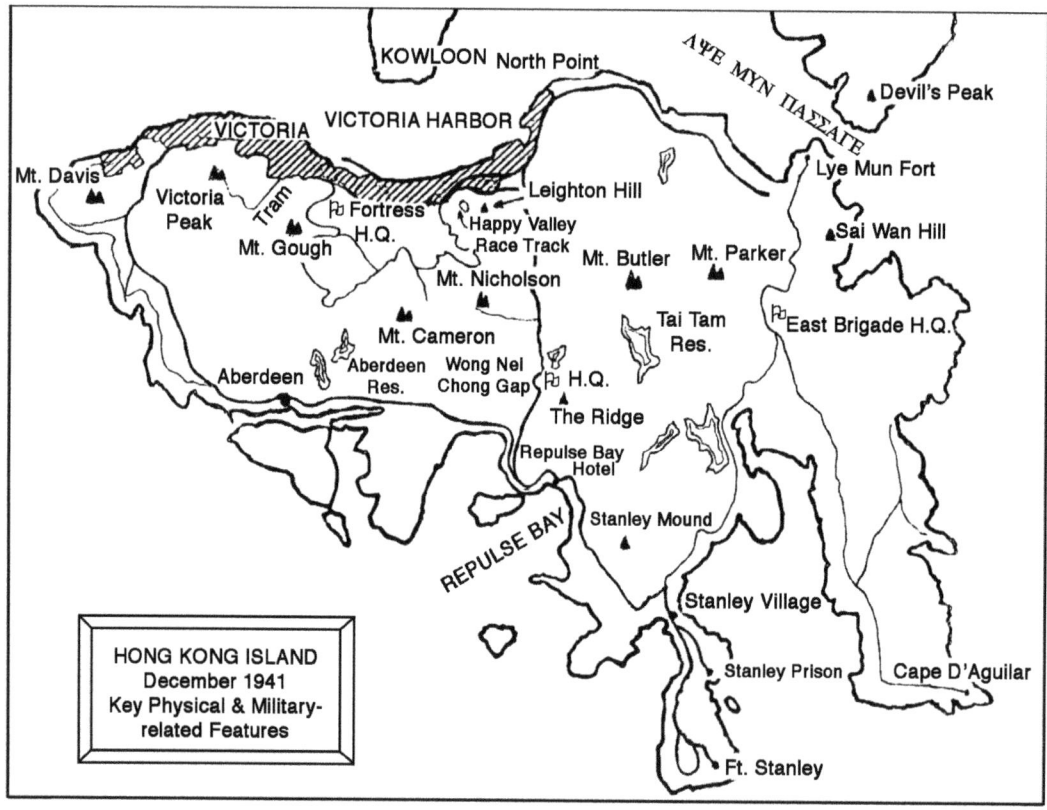

player from Cambridge, less than one minute to reply to the surrender demand. It was one word, "No!"

In less than 20 minutes Boxer was back with Young's reply. The Japanese appeared surprised. "It will be a pity if we have to level this beautiful city," said the interpreter as the party turned to leave.[3]

To understand the battle for Hong Kong, it is necessary to first describe the island. First and foremost it is mountainous, with no less than ten identified and named mountains within its 55-square-mile area. Important to both the defenders and attackers, therefore, were the network of roads that criss-crossed and roughly followed the shoreline of the 5-by 11-mile-wide island. The most prominent of these, and one that virtually split the island in half, was the north-south road that ran from Victoria to Repulse Bay and Stanley Peninsula on the southern coast. Key to existence on the island, which was totally without a natural water source, were four manmade reservoirs, three on the eastern half of the island and one, Aberdeen, on the western side.

In preparing for the inevitable invasion of the island, General Maltby remained convinced clear up to the last minute that because of his north coast defenses, the assault would still come from the sea. In anticipation of this, he sent his two Canadian battalions, the Royal Rifles and Winnipeg Grenadiers, to cover the southern coast.

He then split his command, placing the Rifles and the 5/7 Rajput East Indians under Brigadier Charles Wallis and assigned them to the eastern sector. The Granadiers, 2/14 Punjabis, and part of the 1st Middlesex were put under now Brigadier John Lawson and assigned to the west. Maltby, at Fortress Headquarters, or Battle Box as it was also called, an underground concrete structure dug into the hillside above Victoria, held a reserve force of the 2nd Royal Scots, a contingent of the 1st Middlesex and the 1,800-strong civilian Volunteer Defense Force.

Believing that if the enemy gained a foothold its ultimate objective would be to capture the city, Maltby convinced Lawson that the key to holding the island rested with his ability to successfully defend the narrow, what was called Wong Nei Chong Gap near the center of the prominent north-south road. A breakthrough there, if it came from the south, would allow the Japanese relatively easy access to Victoria.

But what of the other possibility: an invasion across the narrow, half-mile wide Lye Mun Passage on the northeastern corner of the island? Although this was somewhat discounted, along with the 18-pounder guns at Ly Mun Fort, Maltby allocated a third of his mobile guns and three platoons of Volunteers to Wallis' East Sector.

December 13: On the afternoon of Saturday the thirteenth, with the withdrawal of the last British troops from the New Territories completed, Japanese artillery opened up on what would be the first of eleven straight days of bombardment of the island, with Victoria, the North Point waterfront, and the mansions on the Peak the primary targets.

The area known as the Peak (actually Victoria Peak), which rose sharply above Victoria, for years had been settled by the more affluent Englishmen in Hong Kong. Known as the Peakites, many lived in giant hillside mansions with tennis courts, lush gardens, and as many as a dozen servants.

Looking down on everyone from their lofty mansions sadly carried over in their social dealings and affairs with the rest of the colony. "Snobs from the nob," as an American traveler once put it, pretty well summed up how they were viewed by most of those not fortunate enough to reside on the Peak.

December 14: Before the shelling resumed on the first Sunday morning of the war, Victoria residents and soldiers in positions along the waterfront were serenaded by music from a loudspeaker set up by the Japanese on a Kowloon wharf. Popular songs sung by Vera Lynn, Bing Crosby, and others were heard, interrupted by propaganda messages trying to convince those listening of the futility of trying to defend their island. By mid-morning the artillery barrage and attacks by planes of the Imperial Japanese Air Force resumed.

On the enemy side, contrary to Maltby's beliefs, the Japanese had no plans to invade the island from the south. Instead of barging troops all the way around the island to strike from the sea, they chose to attack from across narrow Ly Mun Passage, which, outside of Ly Mun Fort, the 2-gun coast artillery battery on the northeast tip on the point, and a few field artillery pieces, was the most lightly defended sector on the northern coast.

The initial assault, scheduled for early Monday morning, was disrupted, however, when the British destroyer *Thracian* late Sunday night found and sank two river steamers jammed with Japanese troops. The job of the 300 or so man enemy assault force was to gain a foothold on the island and help pinpoint the location of the British defenses for the main landing scheduled for the next night.

December 15: Fortress Headquarters was awakened Monday morning with a call from Government House informing them of a message from Winston Churchill. Addressed to Governor Young and "the defenders of Hong Kong," but careful not to arouse their hopes of reinforcements, it read: "We are all watching day by day and hour by hour your stubborn defense of the port and fortress of Hong Kong. You guard a link between the Far East and Europe long famous in world civilization. We are sure that the defense of Hong Kong against barbarous and unprovoked attack will add a glorious page to British annals. All our hearts are with you and your ordeal. Every day of your resistance brings nearer our certain final victory."[4]

While the Japanese spent the day scrounging up boats for another try at crossing the Ly Mun that night, Governor Young, reacting to the growing problem of robbery and looting being carried out by gangs of armed Chinese hoodlums, imposed a strict curfew on the city. From then on, anyone walking the street between 7:30 P.M. and 6:30 A.M., unless carrying a special permit, would be arrested.

The order also helped curtail activities of the surprisingly large number of Chinese fifth columnist who had also surfaced when the siege began. A mass roundup of a known number of them was also carried out by the Hong Kong police that same day. Despite this, sniping and sabotage activities would continue to plague the defenders, growing bolder and more damaging each day until the end.

The fact that the Japanese, as the day wore on, were preparing to make another attempt to cross the Ly Mun that night was easily predicted by observers on the British side. Across the narrow half-mile-wide channel, it was difficult to hide the buildup of boats that had been steadily increasing throughout the late afternoon.

In response, Brigadier Wallis ordered units from the Rajput's and Canadian Rifles to the area. He also got Fortress Headquarters to release three platoons of Volunteers and two searchlights.

Their predictions soon proved right, as around 1:00 A.M. motor noises were heard, prompting the searchlights to come on. For the defenders it was what the Americans would call a turkey shoot. While Volunteer-manned artillery poured fire into a large sampan, small-arms fire from the Canadians and East Indians sank or scattered many of the smaller boats, forcing those that were left to scurry back to the mainland.

4. Hong Kong's Final Hours

Although fire from Japanese artillery on Devil's Peak across the passage had knocked out one of the searchlights, around 3:00 A.M. the remaining light picked up boats making another try at crossing. Like the first, of those not sunk, the remainder again turned and fled.[5]

December 16–17: Outside of continuing to bombard North Shore fortifications, of which close to 50 percent had already been badly damaged, the Japanese made plans for a second attempt at convincing the British to surrender the island. Around 10:30 the next morning, artillery fire against Victoria and the north shore fortifications suddenly stopped. It would be the first and last time the guns would remain silent for the next nine days.

At 11:00 A.M. the reason for the cease-fire was explained when a boat with a white flag prominently flying from its masthead pulled out from the Kowloon docks for Victoria. On board was the same surrender party that four days earlier had tried and failed to convince the British to give up.

This time the letter to Governor Young, signed by both army and navy commander Takashi Sakai and Masaichi Niimi, demanded that Hong Kong surrender unconditionally.

Major Charles Boxer, who had carried the first demand to Young, was there to accept the second. Instead of having the Japanese wait for the reply, Boxer told them to return to Kowloon and that he would have an answer for them at 2:30.

Like he had with the first surrender offer, Young was adamant in declining the second. Maltby, too, agreed, holding out hope that Japanese fear of the rumored attack by the Chinese army against the New Territories' northern frontier was behind the surrender ultimatum. If they could hold out until it came, the British commander felt victory was still possible. Also, although still convinced that the main enemy attack against the island would come from the sea, results of their failures to cross the Ly Mun channel the night before, if that was where the main assault would come from, also boosted his confidence.

At two-thirty, Boxer handed Colonel Tada the British response. Written by Mark Young himself, it read: "The Governor and the Commander-in-Chief, Hong Kong, declines most absolutely to enter into any negotiations for the surrender of Hong Kong, and he takes this opportunity of saying he is not prepared to receive any further communications on this subject."[6]

When news of Young's response reached Britain, the *London Times* wrote that his reply to the Japanese "should be read in every public place and school throughout the Empire." In typical *London Daily News* style, their interpretation of his reply to their ultimatum was for the Japanese to "Go to Hell."[7]

On the Japanese side, and unknown to the British, the reason for the second surrender offer at this time and within four days of the first was that pre-war estimates concluded that Hong Kong could be taken in 10 days.

December 17 marked the tenth day. Because of the strong British response and of the anticipated difficulty in taking the island, Tokyo gave Sakai an additional 15 days—until January 1—to get the job done. He would need only eight.

December 18: Thursday the eighteenth turned out to be not only a bad luck but fatal day for the British. Had not the entire coast been pelted with heavy rain and winds, and had Japanese artillery not set fire to a North Point oil refinery whose dense smoke, combined with the storm, cut visibility to practically zero, the main enemy invasion scheduled for that night might have been broken up.

At 10:00 P.M., with the defenders' only source of detection—searchlights—completely neutralized, 3,500 men of the Japanese 228th and 229th Infantries struck out from across the Ly Mun Passage in a mélange of boats, from junks and sampans to commandeered Chris-Craft speedboats. In most cases they landed silently and without opposition.

Even when Fortress Headquarters was told that Japanese soldiers were landing near North Point, the caller, in one case, was told to go back to sleep, that his report would be tended to in the morning. Response to a similar call a few minutes later was, "Impossible. The Japs would never cross the harbor in the rain. The water's too choppy. They'd get seasick." In fact, so silent and efficient were they that the first the Ly Mun Fort knew of the invasion was when someone shouted, "We Japanese have captured Sai Wan Hill! It is useless to resist!"[8]

Seasick or not, and despite General Maltby's belief that they would be driven off, by 1:00 A.M. over 7,000 Japanese troops were on the island. On lightly defended Ly Mun Peninsula, with help from well-organized fifth columnists, the Japanese easily overran the defenders before daylight, forcing the bulk of Volunteers, Rajputs, and Canadian Rifles to pull back a mile and a half to Mt. Parker.

In two instances, the harbinger of things to come when falling into the hands of the Japanese occurred that night on the peninsula. Twenty-six Volunteers surrendered when the Japanese overran an artillery position on Sai Wan Hill, a mile inland from the coast. Six officers were immediately separated from the group and bayoneted. The remaining men were put into a small room, where, one by one, they were led out into the compound and used for bayonet practice; their bodies then tossed into a nearby gravel pit. Two men who feigned death survived to tell of the atrocity.

At an aid station not far from the coast that was overrun by Japanese 229th troops, of the six doctors at the hospital, four were immediately shot. A fifth, who was also shot, feigned death and lived to tell of the murders, as did an enlisted member of the medical team who survived bayonet practice. The man, Corporal Norman Heath, also witnessed two Japanese officers behead several of the captives. The fate of the 15 nurses, which, given what happened to female prisoners later, was surprising. They were taken away and confined in a separate building until the end of the battle, after which they were sent to a POW compound set up at Bowen Road Hospital.[9]

One the most heroic and least likely defensive stands made that night involved a detachment of 22 Volunteers who were originally assigned to prevent fifth columnists from sabotaging the city's electrical plant.

Around 11:00 P.M., Major J.J. Patterson, 61-year-old commanding officer of the Old Boys, phoned Fortress Headquarters with information that the Japanese were landing. After being politely told, "Thank you for the information," the call was ignored, no one at headquarters actually believing it.

Minutes passed. Patterson called again, his report again falling on disbelieving ears. At midnight a third call was made, telling them that they were under attack.

This time headquarters, with information of enemy landings coming in from other locations along the coast reacted, sending a machine gun platoon from a nearby Middlesex camp in two trucks and an armored car to reinforce the Volunteers.

A quarter of a mile from the plant, the small convoy was ambushed, resulting in the loss of all three vehicles and all but seven men, who were able to fight their way through to the Volunteers at the powerhouse.

No sooner had they reached the building than enemy attacks began in earnest. The Volunteers, whose oldest members were 67-year-old Thomas Pearce and 70-year-old Edward de Voeux, secretary of the prestigious Hong Kong Club, together with the seven

Middlesex survivors, two Lewis machine guns, and a box of grenades, held off everything the Japanese could throw at them.

At dawn the end came when, after a mortar barrage, the Japanese overran the building, scattering the defenders. Six men took refuge in a double-decker bus that was parked in the compound, where they were all eventually killed. The remaining 12 men, including nine Old Boys who had retreated to the plant's office building, held out for another 4 hours, surrendering only after they ran out of ammunition.

If the playboy soldiers were made light of in the NAFI houses before the battle, their stand at the power station forever placed them alongside the most courageous of their British, Canadian, and East Indian counterparts.

Obviously, with the reports that had been coming in to Fortress Headquarters throughout the day, Maltby's belief that the major invasion would still come from the south was over. In fact, realizing that night that the entire East Sector was in jeopardy of falling to the Japanese, he ordered the commander of the 9.2-inch battery on distant Cape D'Aguilar to spike the guns and report to Stanley Peninsula.

December 19: By 9:00 A.M., less than 10 hours since their initial landing, the Japanese had all but achieved their primary objective of driving a wedge down the center of the island to cut off those forces in the east from contact with Victoria and the west.

In fact, so desperate was the situation with Wallis' East Brigade, which had taken the brunt of the attacks that night, that it was ordered to pull back all the way to Stanley Peninsula on the southern coast. From there, according to an optimistic Maltby, a counterattack would be launched the next morning to retake what was lost the day before.

The situation at West Brigade Headquarters at the Wong Nei Chong Gap was also desperate. Standing between Lawson's headquarters and the marauding Japanese were a few Winnipeg Grenadiers. Despite warning from the Canadians that it was time to initiate his pre-arranged plan to pull back to Mt. Nicholson, Lawson refused to be hurried. Why he personally waited until it was too late is not known.

At 10:00 A.M., with the Japanese having completely surrounded the headquarters building, Lawson calmly phoned Maltby, telling him that he had ordered the Grenadiers to pull back to Nicholson, and that he was "going outside to fight it out."[10]

What followed is not officially documented. All that is known is that Lawson and six of his staff officers were shot down in their attempt to make a fight of it with the Japanese.

The only British counterattack that day involved a detachment of Grenadiers, who, after being driven from Mt. Butler, a mile northeast of Lawson's Gap headquarters, were ordered to retake the mountain. Although initially successful, an enemy counterattack drove them off again, scattering the Grenadiers and resulting in isolated firefights with the Japanese and the eventual capture of most of the survivors.

One small group of 20 or so Canadians was ambushed as it was attempting to pull back from the mountain. Sgt. Major John Osborn, in command of the group, spotting an enemy grenade land among his men, dove on it, using his body to shield them from its deadly blast. His heroic act resulted in his being posthumously awarded the Victoria Cross, the equivalent to the American Medal of Honor.

Again, as it had with units that had surrendered or been overrun, the Japanese continued to murder their helpless captives. Two men in Osborn's unit who had given up were killed, one as he waved a white flag of surrender.

Japanese soldiers then helped themselves to the watches, rings, and wallets of the captives. This less-threatening but widespread practice by Japanese enlisted soldiers here and throughout the Pacific war to come could lead to a severe beating or, in some cases, death if the captive showed any reluctance to give up his personal possessions.

December 20: By the morning of the second day, the Japanese had captured all three reservoirs on the eastern side of the island, leaving only Aberdeen on the west to supply water to Victoria. Enemy patrols had already infiltrated as far south as Repulse Bay, shattering Maltby's plan for an effective counterattack that day.

Although not in total control of the area east of the road down the center of the island, at least 70 percent could be considered in enemy hands. Of the area still held by the British, part was made up of units that had been cut off or isolated in the rugged area around Mt. Butler and Mt. Parker. Given their circumstances, however, they could not be considered as a viable part of any attempt to mount an attack in the East Sector.

Led by the 230th Infantry, the Japanese had also made moderate gains along the North Point waterfront. It did not come easy, particularly in the battle for the series of pillboxes held by 100 D Company Rajputs. In a fight involving bloody hand-to-hand combat, the East Indians held out for over 5 hours against the Japanese before succumbing to the ten-to-one odds against them.[11]

By daylight of the twentieth, Colonel H.B. Rose, newly appointed commander of the West Sector, red-penciled a line on his map running from the North Shore, over Leighton Hill and Mt. Nicholson, across the island to Aberdeen on the south coast, indicating how far the Japanese had already penetrated. Examining his map and those showing how far south the East Sector had been pushed within the first 36 hours, would, one might think, give the commanding general cause to worry.

Not so for the ever-optimistic Maltby.

Along with truly believing that the Japanese could still be driven off, Fortress Headquarters that morning had received the message they'd been waiting for. It was from the Chinese, who said an army of 60,000 men was preparing to strike the northern border of the New Territories.

With this information in hand, Maltby sent the following message to units throughout his command: "There are indications that Chinese forces are advancing toward the frontier to our aid. All ranks must therefore hold their positions at all costs and look forward to only a few more days of strain."

As it has with soldiers throughout history, the rumor that help was on the way quickly changed the feelings of men from hopelessness to one of optimism. Many, after hearing the message, made bets that with Chinese help the battle would be over by Christmas Day. They were right, only it would be without the Chinese, whose promised attack never came. It would instead be the Japanese, not the British, who would celebrate victory on Christmas Day.

Unknown to the British, back on December 15, a fairy-tale Chinese communiqué to the U.S. reported that the two armies it had dispatched to attack the Japanese who were attacking Hong Kong had engaged the enemy and inflicted 15,000 casualties.

December 21: A late Saturday night meeting between Maltby and Colonel Rose at Fortress Headquarters led the two men to agree that, before a major counterattack out of the south was possible, an attempt had to be made to push the Japanese back from the center of the island. A call went out to the Grenadier commander at Fort Stanley to order his companies B and D, along with as many stragglers from other units as could be put together, to prepare for a counterattack the next day.

At 7:00 A.M., the two companies and a composite force of Punjabis, Volunteers, Royal Scots, and Royal Navy sailors, amounting to some 500 men in all, jumped off in an attempt to clear the enemy from the hills around the Gap. Although it was doubtful that Fortress Headquarters realized this attack would be their best and last chance to hold the island, it was. Sending a makeshift force of just 500 men against over 1,500 Japanese holding a commanding high-ground position, the battle was, for all practical purposes, over before it started.

The game attackers, with little or no artillery support, for over 10 hours pushed the futile assault until they were either wiped out or forced to retreat. Fragmented reports that filtered into the Battle Box throughout the day indicated that not only had the attack to dislodge the enemy from their positions in the Gap failed, so had Grenadier efforts to hold Mt. Nicholson.

Hoping to save as many of his troops as possible, Rose ordered those units who could to withdraw west to Mount Cameron or south towards Repulse Bay. Because of the loss of communications with some units, however, many failed to receive the order, which eventually led to their falling into enemy hands.

At Mt. Nicholson, to help cover the Grenadiers' withdrawal, a 12-man Volunteer force, under the command of public school headmaster Evan Stewart, held their position on Jardine's Lookout, the high point on the 1,420-foot mountain, for 16 hours before being forced to pull back to Cameron. It could be said that the courage and tenacity of the dozen Old Boys equally matched that of their comrades at the power plant two days earlier.

Of the fighting that day, outside of the Volunteers' stand at the Lookout, the only other positive result came when the British made a successful defensive stand at Leighton Hill, a mile and a half east of downtown Victoria.

Following the successful Japanese landings at North Point, General Maltby dispatched a 42-man force to Leighton Hill, the only high ground between Victoria and the invading Japanese. Located a half mile east of the Happy Valley Race Track, the densely wooded hill offered the British the best chance of keeping the enemy from breaking through to Happy Valley and Victoria itself.

The small British force, made up of thirty-five Middlesex troops and seven Volunteers, were dug in along the steep north-south ridgeline across the hill when the enemy struck. Fighting without mortar or artillery support, with rifles and just six machine guns, they held off every Japanese attempt to take the hill that day.

On a small treeless hill a half mile south of the Gap, a bitter firefight had erupted between the Japanese and an outnumbered force of 150 or so British army and Canadian Royal Rifles. Unable to hold what was called The Ridge against the overwhelming number of enemy troops, they were ordered to disengage and pull back farther south.

One small group of British soldiers, many of whom were wounded, were overrun and captured before they could withdraw. What followed was a continuation of what appeared to be Japanese policy toward prisoners, particularly wounded prisoners. To the man, the entire unit of some 30 men were executed.[12]

Farther south at Repulse Bay, the battle and siege of the famous cliffside Repulse Bay Hotel, which had been going on for a day and a half, ended on Sunday morning when the Japanese, without opposition, occupied the building.

When they entered the hotel, they were surprised to find that the 200 or so British soldiers who had kept them at bay for over 36 hours had gone. Realizing that holding the hotel against the ever-increasing number of Japanese was impossible, Fortress Headquarters had ordered them to slip out in the middle of the night for Fort Stanley.

Although none of the trapped hotel guests were bothered by the Japanese, perhaps the frustration of finding that the British soldiers had escaped brought them to take it out on a group of prisoners who had been captured earlier during the retreat from the Gap. Fifty-three Canadian Royal Rifles and Middlesex prisoners were herded to the edge of a cliff not far from the hotel where they were shot, bayoneted, or beheaded, their bodies then pushed over the cliff. One man, a Middlesex sergeant, survived to tell of the atrocity. Sadly, the worst was yet to come.

Late that night at the Battle Box, after shifting through reports of the day's actions and staring at the map, the ever-changing red lines of which reflected how dire the situation had become, General Maltby picked up a copy of a message he had received earlier that morning. It was from Winston Churchill. After re-reading his uplifting 134-word message, he focused back on the words "there must be ... no thought of surrender." To the still-optimistic commander, there wasn't. After all, the Japanese had not yet set foot in Happy Valley, and if Mt. Cameron could be held, there was still a chance for a successful counterattack out of the south.[13]

December 22: Little did the British commander know that the continuous sound of

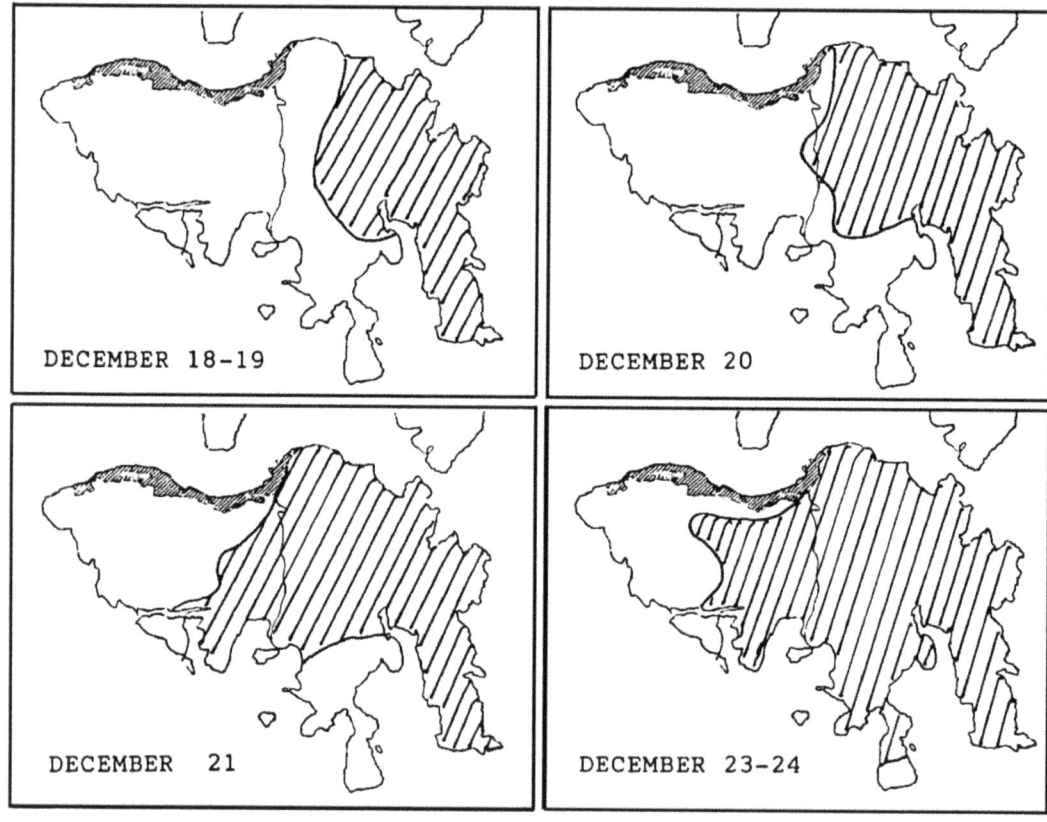

AREA UNDER JAPANESE CONTROL
DECEMBER 18-24, 1941

DECEMBER 18-19

DECEMBER 20

DECEMBER 21

DECEMBER 23-24

artillery he had been hearing since 10:00 P.M. was preliminary to the Japanese capture of Mt. Cameron.

Ironically, it was the first time in the siege that artillery was used in a night assault. The Japanese, using mules left on the mainland by the British in their haste to withdraw, had used the faithful animals to haul disassembled field pieces to their forward units. By daylight, the Grenadiers and Royal Scots defending the mountain, pounded by artillery and facing odds of ten to one against them, had pulled back to Mt. Gough, a mile to the northwest, from whose heights they could look directly down on the main Japanese objective — Victoria.

With the Japanese having dashed Maltby's hope of holding Mt. Cameron, it was the same in the south. With the capture of the Repulse Bay Hotel, and with it control of the main road leading to Stanley Peninsula, by late afternoon on the twenty-second, 2,500 Volunteers, Canadian Rifles, Middlesex, and Royal Scot troops were hopelessly bottled up on the peninsula.

Their withdrawal to there had not been voluntary, however. Throughout most of the day, the game but exhausted and outnumbered troops had unsuccessfully slugged it out with the Japanese over a series of hills northeast of the hotel.

The battle for a hill known as Stanley Mound was the scene of perhaps the most determined effort by the Royal Rifles since the siege began. Three different times in the six-hour battle for the 1,265-foot mound, the Japanese routed the Canadians only to be pushed back off themselves by the determined Rifles. Finally, with darkness and a casualty rate of close to 50 percent, Brigadier Wallis ordered them to pull back to the peninsula.[14]

In the north, meanwhile, outside of infiltration by small groups of Japanese along the waterfront, the British line across Leighton Hill was still intact. In Victoria itself, results of the seven straight days of bombing and shelling had not only taken its toll on its commercial and industrial buildings, but, as Maltby was informed that morning, the water supply to the city had been cut off. According to a memo from the director of waterworks, Japanese bombing of the pumping station at Aberdeen, the only reservoir not in enemy hands, had left close to 1,700,000 civilians with no water whatsoever.

Despite the grim outlook, as long as the city was in British hands, looting by groups of Chinese, which had become widespread because so many city dwellers had fled or gone into hiding, would not go unpunished. Police response, which earlier had been to arrest looters, had changed to shoot to kill, as was the policy of leaving the bodies where they fell as a warning to others.

December 23: Outside of the continued attempts by the Japanese to take Leighton Hill, December 23 was the quietest day since the battle began. It was, of course, dictated by the Japanese, who used the day to bring up tanks, armored vehicles, and reinforcements in preparation for the final assault on Stanley.

Outside of Victoria and Aberdeen, Stanley Peninsula was the heaviest populated area on the island. At the 230-yard-wide northern or isthmus end of the peninsula was the village of Stanley. About a hundred yards south of the town was St. Stephen's College, located on a rocky ridge overlooking the road. A private boys school before the battle, it had been converted into an emergency hospital. A quarter of a mile south of the college, the road forked, one leading to Stanley Prison and the other to Fort Stanley, one mile away on the tip of the peninsula.

December 24: Not waiting for daylight, at 2:30 A.M. on Christmas Eve, the Japanese led their attack against the British roadblock above the village with a column of tanks. The easily distinguishable sound of them coming down the road brought the Volunteers to wheel a 2-pounder anti-tank gun out onto the road.

Probing blindly in the early morning darkness, the lead tank never saw what was in store for it until it was too late. Firing at point-blank range, within seconds accurate fire from the gun knocked out the two lead tanks. The third, which was also hit, was able to escape.

The British didn't have to wait long for the Japanese to come again. With their armor all but destroyed, it was the infantry's turn. The house-to-house battle for the village that followed was fierce. Focused on the post office and police station, in the end the outnumbered defenders were forced to fall back. Chased out of the village, they went in both directions.

Most of the Scot and Rifles survivors took the road to Fort Stanley. About 75 Volunteers and Middlesex troops took refuge amongst a row of fishing shacks on a ridge above the Prison Road. Unknown to those involved, the bitter house-to-house, hand-to-hand fight that followed there would be the last battle in the 11-day siege of Hong Kong.

The Japanese, compelled to use banzai attacks and flamethrowers to flush out the stubborn defenders, paid a heavy price for their efforts. According to the 45 men who managed to escape to Fort Stanley, the enemy's loss ratio from the mass attacks was at least three-to-one in favor of the defenders.[15]

December 25: With what was left of the British defenders hopelessly bottled up at Fort Stanley, the Japanese decided to give the survivors a chance to give up. Two civilians, Major Charles Manners, a retired army officer, and a civilian named Andrew Shields, captured at the Repulse Bay Hotel, were selected to carry the offer to General Maltby at Fortress Headquarters.

At 9:00 A.M. near the Happy Valley Race Track, two men were seen walking toward British lines carrying a white flag. Telling a British officer that they had a message from the Japanese for General Maltby, they were driven to Fortress Headquarters.

Manners, identifying himself as a retired major, told the British commander that he was carrying a surrender offer from the Japanese. He told him that they were giving him a 3-hour cease-fire period to make up his mind. By noon, if there was no response, attacks would resume.

It was not an easy decision nor one made without input from his staff. First, with all lines of communication with Fort Stanley out and the two messengers also ignorant of the developments there, Maltby's decision was based primarily on the local situation and of comments made by Manners of the large number of Japanese troops they'd seen lining the road from Repulse Bay.

East of the city, word had come in that Leighton Hill had been overrun during the night, which, although opening the way for the enemy to move against the city, was not serious enough to convince Maltby's staff to give up. At twelve o'clock the two civilians were escorted back to the Japanese command post at North Point, where they reported that the surrender proposal had been rejected.

Despite having conceded to the urgings of his staff, the British commander remained skeptical as to their chances. His greatest fear was that it might lead to a prolonged, bloody, and in the end, hopeless street-to-street battle for the city.

At 2:00 P.M. he phoned the commander of the battered string of North Shore pillboxes, that when last heard from were still in friendly hands. The answer as to the situation there, he decided, would be the deciding factor.

"How long can you hang on?" he asked Lt. Colonel Leslie Stewart, commander of the beleaguered bunkers.

4. Hong Kong's Final Hours

"We're in a bad way," said Stewart. "I'd say an hour at most."

His mind made up, at three o'clock Maltby was driven to Government House, where he hoped to convince Governor Mark Young that, given the information he had, further resistance was impossible.

That morning, the island's one-page *South China Morning Post*, in its last issue, had run the governor's Christmas message to the colony, which read: "In pride and admiration I send my greetings this Christmas Day to all those who are working so nobly and so well to sustain Hong Kong against the assault of the enemy. God bless you all in this, your finest hour."[16]

Having read it, the British commander knew he would have a tough sell. "It's a hopeless situation," he told Young. "Once the pillboxes are gone, the enemy will flood into Victoria. We haven't the strength to stop them."[17]

Despite arguing that the battle, as Churchill had said in his December 21 message to him, should be fought "if need be, from house to house," Young called a meeting with the two civilian members of the Defense Council, Maltby, and naval commander A.C. Collinson. Succumbing to the obvious after a round of discussion, he authorized a cease-fire, which, until it would become formalized later that night, would take place immediately.

Back at Fortress Headquarters, Maltby sent word to those still fighting to surrender to the nearest Japanese troops. In his official dispatch to London regarding the surrender, he wrote that he had capitulated because "further fighting [not only] meant the useless slaughter of the remainder of the garrison, [but] risked severe retaliation on the large civilian population, and could not affect the final outcome."[18]

Although the surrender of the island had taken place, with no communication with either side in the unresolved situation at Stanley Peninsula, the outcome had the word trouble written all over it.

Sandwiched between the village and the Prison Road, where the battle had raged throughout the day, was St. Stephen's College. Because of its isolated location above the road, it had been ignored during the night and was thought of only after the battle had moved past.

Inside the 30-year-old school were close to 100 wounded British and Canadian soldiers. In charge was 72-year-old Hong Kong physician Dr. George Black and Medical Corps captain John Whitney.

That night several patients, not wanting to face capture by the Japanese, said that they wanted to be evacuated to Fort Stanley. Dr. Black, knowing that the wounded at Repulse Bay Hotel had not been molested, said that with the Red Cross flag on the roof, he was sure they had nothing to worry about.

"Frankly," he said, "I'd sooner be here than with the soldiers at Fort Stanley."

A little before 7:00 A.M., Private T.J. Cruz, a Portuguese stretcher-bearer with the Volunteers, looking out of a first floor window, spotted a large group of bayonet-wielding Japanese soldiers moving up the driveway toward the front entrance. Dr. Black also saw them. Rushing into a converted classroom, moments later he returned with a torn piece of white bed sheet. As he walked toward the front door, he said to the wounded men that lined the hallway, "The Japanese are here. Don't be afraid. There's a Red Cross flag on the roof. I'll tell them to leave us alone."

With Captain Whitney standing close behind him, Black opened the door. Holding up the bedsheet, he said, "This is a hospital." Then, placing his arm across the doorway, he told them that they couldn't come in. "Please leave us in peace."

Two shots rang out. Both men fell dead where they stood. Moments later a horde of enemy soldiers, repeatedly stabbing the two doctors and the wounded men in the hallway, burst into the main room. Its walls were lined with wounded. In a killing frenzy, they began bayoneting the helpless patients, murdering every one of the 56 men in the room.

Others broke into the classroom next door. Yelling "Banzai!" as they entered, everyone in the room except one man was bayoneted to death. That one man, Private Sidney Skelton, who had rolled under a cot when the Japanese entered, survived by playing dead. Spotting him under the bed, an enemy soldier dragged him out by his feet. The Japanese kicked him in the head, then tore off his bandages. Skelton, somehow spared the bayonet, did not move. Apparently thinking he was already dead, the man moved on.

Private Cruz, who had witnessed the murder of Black and Whitney, had run upstairs when the Japanese burst through the front door. Hiding in a classroom with five other men, he remembered hearing the screams and cries of wounded men as they were bayoneted.

Suddenly the door was kicked open, and a soldier with a submachine gun came in. The six men raised their hands and stepped forward. The Japanese hit Cruz in the face with the butt of his gun, then motioned them into the storeroom next door. Cruz found the small, dark, 10 by 20-foot room jammed with what he guessed was close to 40 prisoners. For the men crowded in the standing-room-only room, the question of what was going to happen to them grew minute by minute.

One time a Japanese officer opened the door and in English said, "You were stupid; you should have surrendered. You will be slowly killed four at a time."[19]

Although they could hear cries of torture coming from the next room, not all the screams were from men. Along with the two doctors, the hospital was staffed by four Chinese and seven British nurses.

Sometime after noon, Japanese combat soldiers returned to the hospital. Many appeared drunk, having broken into the local bar. Breaking into the room where Japanese officers had locked up the nurses, they took the Chinese and the three youngest English girls into the room, where they were held down and gang-raped on mattresses brought in from the dormitory. After they were finished, the Japanese bayoneted all seven women, took their bodies downstairs and dumped them into the yard.

The four older nurses, whose lives were spared, throughout the afternoon and into the night were taken back and forth to the room, where they were raped, returned, then taken and raped again.

Meanwhile, back in the storeroom, a Japanese officer opened the door again. Fearing the end was near, Cruz was relieved when this time he heard the words, "You boys very lucky. Hong Kong has surrendered. Now we will no longer have to kill you."

Most of the men were ordered downstairs. About ten were sent to clean out the room next door. What they saw when they entered, as Cruz remembered, made many of them retch. Blood-soaked mattresses and cushions were scattered around the room. The floor was also covered with blood, many men slipping as they carried out the mattresses.

Although unaware up to that time of what had gone on throughout the building, as they looked around the yard where they were told to stack the mattresses, they were horrified at the number of bodies that had been and were still being carried out from the building.

Cruz remembered that all had been bayoneted and that some had ears, fingers, and noses chopped off; eyes were poked out, tongues cut out. Little did he suspect that one of the bodies with missing ears and another whose tongue had been cut out were indirectly responsible for saving his life and those of the men in the storeroom.[20]

Around the middle of the afternoon, with no response from Fort Stanley on their surrender demands, the Japanese picked four Royal Rifle prisoners to carry a message to the fort. To make sure the British commander knew of the repercussions should he refuse, the Canadians were made to watch while they cut one man's tongue out and chopped off the ears of another.

"Go to Fort Stanley and tell your commanding officer what you have seen," said the Japanese officer. "[He] must surrender or else all prisoners will be killed in this manner."

An hour later the four returned with word that the British would offer no further resistance. Whether Brigadier Wallis' decision was based on threat or in reaction to the two officers sent by Maltby about that same time is not known. What is known is that the East Brigade commander, although promising no opposition, did not consider his surrender as official until he received written orders from Victoria, which arrived shortly after midnight.

Back at St. Stephens, although the murder and rape had ended, the Japanese forced the prisoners to burn the evidence. A huge funeral pyre, fueled by blood-stained blankets, sheets, and mattresses was started. Although an accurate count was not made, an estimate by James Barrett, a Canadian army chaplain who tried unsuccessfully to allow the men to be buried, claimed that the bodies of as many as 170 men along with the four Chinese nurses were cremated that night. Of that number, it was estimated that at least 90 were wounded men who had been murdered in their beds.[21]

December 26: Boxing Day for the British and Canadians. Like Christmas, it, too, was a dark day for the vanquished defenders.

It started when rumors of the rapes at St. Stephens somehow reached a company of Royal Scots, who, although aware of the surrender, had not yet been taken prisoner.

Taking a lorry, Sergeant Bill Stoker and two volunteers drove unmolested to Stanley Peninsula, parked and walked into the school. After asking about the whereabouts of the nurses, they were led to the room where the four older women were being kept. They, as Chaplain Barrett said when he saw them, walked and talked like zombies, "for they had experienced dreadful things during the night." When asked about the other nurses, one mumbled that she didn't know what happened to them, but that they might be dead.

As the men led them out of the building, a man in a group of prisoners, recognizing the nurses, yelled, "Have you seen my wife?" Before they could respond, a sympathetic Japanese captain named Kawai, who overheard him, led the soldier outside. In the corner of the yard near some bushes, under a coat the soldier recognized the brutalized bodies of the three English nurses. One was his wife.[22]

In most cases to avoid any misunderstanding, units that had been in contact with Fortress Headquarters waited for the Japanese to come before surrendering. Possibly because of this policy, there were very few instances of prisoner mistreatment.

In one defiant but well-earned gesture, one Volunteer outfit which decided not to wait marched smartly into an enemy camp whistling *Tipperary*.

As other units, some organized and some scattered among the hills in the center of the island, surrendered throughout the day, Victoria residents prepared for the occupation.

For the victors, it is not known if they had a handy supply of sake for their victory celebration, but by the time they entered the city the next day, Victoria was drier than Chicago during Prohibition.

In anticipation of the celebration and occupation, someone in one of the luxury hotels suggested that the liquor supply should by dumped to keep it out of the hands of the Japanese. Although the idea soon spread to all of the hotels and bars, with the water supply to the city cut off, most of the drains and toilets had been clogged up.

Before long, along with the smell of alcohol that soon permeated the air, people found themselves literally wading through Scotch, bourbon, gin, and even champagne that had overflowed into some of the hotel lobbies and bars, and in one case, into the street. How much was poured into the drains in relation to how much was consumed would never be known, however.

December 27: By 11:30 A.M., Des Voeux Road in downtown Victoria was lined with clean-uniformed Japanese troops and hundreds of Chinese holding tiny Japanese flags that had been passed out by unabashed fifth columnist and soldiers. Promptly at twelve noon, a long line of officer-mounted horses rounded Queen Victoria Street onto the road, with Lt. General Takashi Sakai, Japanese 23rd Army commander, and naval Admiral Masaichi Niimi leading the parade.

The cheers of the flag-waving Chinese as their conquerors passed by led a Japanese correspondent to happily write that he had witnessed a "never-to-be-forgotten ceremony."

For the few British, most of whom witnessed it from hotel windows, it wouldn't be forgotten either, particularly when an open convertible occupied by a Japanese general passed by. To the onlookers' amusement, a bright sticker in the car's window said, "Holland will rise again."

Hong Kong would rise again, too. On September 16, 1945 — three years, seven months, and 22 days later, the Japanese would formally surrender the island back to the British.

And what would the history books say of the British, Canadian, East Indian, and Volunteer forces at Hong Kong, who, unlike their counterparts at Singapore, never had a chance to win? They would say that they did themselves proud. Or, as Winston Churchill put it, their prolonged resistance with no hope of victory indeed won them the lasting honor of their countries.

CHAPTER 5

Singapore's Final Hours

In this chapter, because of the circumstances leading to the fall of Singapore, the story of its final hours go back 7 days to the initial Japanese invasion of the island.

When the British failed to launch their pre-war planned Operation Matador in time to break up the Japanese invasion of the east coast of Thailand on December 8, 1941, for all practical purposes, the fall of Malaya was foreordained.

Operation Matador, originally designed to have the British Army in position at the two well-anticipated invasion locations when the Japanese landed, needed at least 36 hours' advance notice to be effective. Delayed by a confusing political situation with the Thai government and a response from London authorizing the launching of Matador, the operation was not initiated in time.

Despite British efforts to halt the relentless Japanese drive down the Malay Peninsula, by February 8, just 31 days since their initial landings, the Imperial Japanese Army had gobbled up over 50,000 square miles of Malaya, with nothing left but the 14-by-26-mile-wide island of Singapore.

The dominating physical feature of the island on which the battle would be fought could be summed up in one word: flat. Its highest point at the village of Bukit Timah (Hill of Tin), located 6 miles northwest of Singapore city, was a mere 581 feet. Outside of a lower hill at Bukit Panjang, 3 miles north of Bukit Timah, the island was generally low lying and intermittently covered with rubber plantations.

A factor that particularly affected the Occidental soldier was the weather. Sitting one degree north of the equator, daily temperatures on the island averaged 90 degrees, with humidity levels not far behind at between 75 and 85 percent.

A little after 8:00 A.M. on February 1, 1942, on the heels of the last British forces to withdraw across the 1,100-yard-long causeway connecting Singapore to the Malayan mainland, charges were detonated that opened a 70-yard-wide gap across the Strait of Johore, cutting the only direct access to the island.

Preparing to face the British in the battle to come was a Japanese force of nearly 30,000 men. They would be facing a British, Australian, Malay, and Indian army of close to 90,000, of whom 15,000 were non-combatants. Of the remaining 75,000, however, barely half were considered front-line quality.

Despite the fact that the Japanese had complete control of the air, not only were they outnumbered three to one, but they would be attacking what was officially and historically known as Fortress Singapore. Although the word fortress denotes a degree of impregnability, it was far from being so in this case.

The island got its label primarily because of its world-famous fixed-position coast

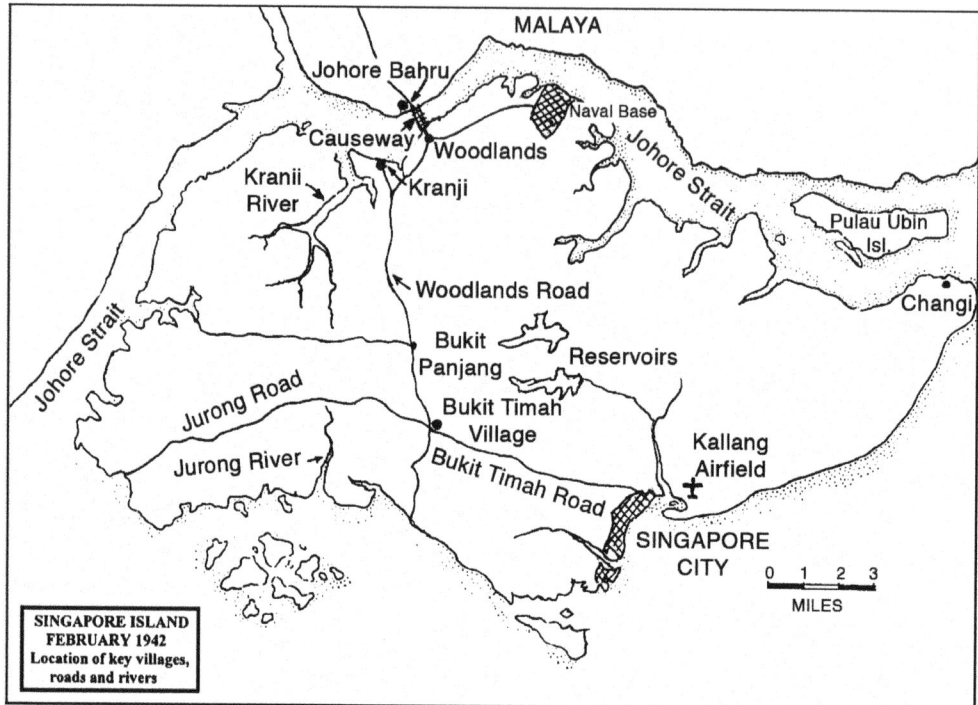

SINGAPORE ISLAND
FEBRUARY 1942
Location of key villages, roads and rivers

artillery batteries, which included five giant 15-inch guns, six 9.2 and eighteen 6-inch guns. They were originally built to defend against an assault on the Royal Navy Base, which was anticipated to come from the seaward side of the island. Outside of a single isolated 6-inch battery on the southwestern coast, there was not one gun between it and Fort Changi on the very eastern tip of the island.

As far as beach defenses, like its fixed gun positions, they, too, were built to defend against an invasion from the sea. Extending to protect 20 miles of the island's southeastern coast, they included concrete pill boxes, a number of 18-pounder mobile guns, barbed wire, casemated searchlights, and offshore obstacles—all of which, like its big guns, would go untested throughout the brief battle.

On the British side, the man who would make the ultimate decisions on where and how to defend the island against the anticipated Japanese invasion was Lt. General Arthur E. Percival. His decisions could be overruled or modified only by the supreme commander of what was designated as ABDA (American, British, Dutch, and Australian), General Sir Archibald Wavell, whose headquarters at the time was near Batavia, Java.

British chances obviously hinged on their ability to repel the Japanese invasion. The most important factor in achieving this was determining where the enemy would strike and how fast the defenders could react.

In defending the island, three factors came into play, all having a significant role in the outcome. First, the initial plan itself; second, the reaction to the attack; and third, communications.

General Wavell, who placed General Percival in charge of preparing the defense of the island, suggested that with the information he had, he believed the enemy attack would be launched across the narrow Strait of Johore on the northwestern side of the island.

5. Singapore's Final Hours

Everything pointed to it. Brigadier General Ivan Simson, commander of the Royal Engineers, having personally reconnoitered both possible enemy launching sites before the withdrawal, said that "owing to the good embarkation facilities available" it would come against the northwest coast. Because of this he took it upon himself to move barbed wire, mines, and beach searchlights, originally assigned to the northeast, to likely landing points on the northwest. Once Percival found out about it, however, he ordered everything moved back to where he was convinced the enemy would strike.

"[The order] was incredible," said Simson, noting how difficult it was to "follow the minds of the leaders ... on the subject of defense."

Despite Simson's and his own feelings, Wavell agreed not to interfere "since Percival ... seemed convinced of the probable direction of the enemy attack."[1]

Given his freedom to decide how to best defend the island, Percival outlined his plan. First, he said, we will "endeavor to prevent the enemy landing or, if he succeed[s], to stop him near the beaches and drive him out by counterattack." In defending his decision and sounding as if one of his major concerns was morale, he said that "the moral effect of [allowing the Japanese to land without a fight] would be bad both on the troops and on the civilian population."[2]

Application of his endeavor to prevent the Japanese from landing, however, meant that troops would be on guard to defend the entire 72 miles of Singapore coastline and that units on the far side of where the enemy chose to strike could play no role in the defense until it was too late. More importantly, for all practical purposes, it left the defenders without a significant or immediate reserve force to "drive him out by counterattack."

Despite the weakness of Percival's plan, there was still a chance that the Japanese would attack at his strength, which was defined by the freshest, best-equipped unit on the island — the British 18th Division. Landing between the 13th and 29th of January, although untested by combat and originally destined for North Africa, it was the only complete division in Singapore. In fact, so confident was General Wavell that the 18th offered the best chance to stop the Japanese, he strongly suggested that it be placed to defend the northwest sector of the island. Percival, still clinging to his theory, however, ordered the division into position on the northeast coast, where it would remain virtually untested throughout the crucial first days of the battle.

Assigned to defend the important northwest was the A.I.F.'s (Australian Imperial Forces) 8th Division under the command of Major General Gordon Bennett and composed of two infantry brigades, the 22nd and 27th, plus the newly arrived and untested 44th Indian Brigade. Unlike the British 18th, the tired and battle-worn 8th had been involved in fighting on the Malayan mainland since the first days of the war. Although reinforced on January 22 by 1,900 men, Bennett, after an inspection tour, said that they were "so raw and incomplete [that] they cannot be counted on. Untrained men, most of whom have not even fired a rifle, should not [have been] sent to fight [the] well-trained Japanese."

As predicted by everybody except Percival, the focal point of the Japanese attack was the area northwest of the causeway. On line to defend it, Bennett assigned his 27th Brigade to what was called the Kranji-Woodlands Road sector, running 800 yards from the demolished causeway to the mouth of the Kranji River. To its left, the 22nd Brigade was given the nearly impossible task of defending 8 miles of coastline, extending from the Kranji south to the Berih River.

Of his division's position, Bennett wrote that the "area is the most uninhabited part of the island. To hold the Australian front, I have only four reliable infantry battalions and two companies of well-trained machine gun battalions." Specific to the area occupied by the 22nd, he noted that "this part of the island is thickly covered by timber, mostly rubber, with thick mangrove growing right down to the water's edge. The posts, which are many hundreds of yards apart, have a field of fire of only 200 yards."[3]

With each battalion forced to defend close to 3 miles of beach, the gaps between posts, according to 22nd Brigade commander Brigadier General H.B. Taylor, could not be defended because they had been assigned to too wide a front. "The coastline, broken here and there by indentations, creeks, and thick mangroves, denied the men from seeing any more than 50 yards on either flank."

Although Percival could be blamed for failing to acknowledge the northwest as the most likely landing site, Gordon Bennett, in the assignment of his two brigades, must also bear some of the responsibility for what was to come.

Along with assigning the 22nd to a nearly impossible task, as mentioned, the Strait of Johore fronting their positions was just 600 yards wide. Compared to the 1,000 yards opposite the 27th's half-mile-wide front, there seemed little doubt as to where the main Japanese effort would come.

In anticipation of the attack coming against his Australians, General Bennett, on February 6, urged General Taylor to send patrols across the Strait to reconnoiter for any Japanese buildup. That night three boats shoved off for the eastern shore. Although one was caught and destroyed, the other two, after successfully avoiding detection, returned the next night with word of heavy concentrations of Japanese troops along the immediate coast and on roads as far inland as two miles. In addition, in some spots they found the coastline jammed with inflatable landing craft with powerful outboard motors. Larger barges capable of hauling tanks and vehicles were also reported.

Not that it made any difference, but their report did not reach Percival until 3:30 that afternoon — less than 7 hours from the attack. Although by his actions it is not known if Bennett received the message, it must be assumed that he did.

The response of the two generals when given this information was far from what might be expected. Even after the Japanese opened up on 22nd Brigade positions at 10:30 A.M. on the eighth with an artillery barrage that would last until their assault boats shoved off some 12 hours later, both determined that it was the first of what would be several days of pre-invasion bombardments. Percival, in fact, judged that there would be 8 days of preliminary shelling prior to the attack. As a result, no orders were issued to either prepare for an immediate attack or, because of an acute shortage of artillery ammunition, to fire on possible enemy embarkation points.[4]

Of their error in judgment, Colonel Masanobu Tsugi, 25th Army Operations Officer, wrote that their barrage "covered the whole shore in order to make it difficult for the enemy to judge the points at which our main attack would be launched. Four hundred and forty guns were in action, and the field guns fired two hundred rounds per gun during the night and heavy guns one hundred rounds.

"The troops of both divisions in the first wave — roughly 4,000 men — went aboard 300 boats at [11:00 P.M.]."[5]

In fact, Bennett, at division headquarters that evening in Bukit Timah Village located 10 miles southeast of the threatened coast, had actually gone to bed. At nine o'clock, aroused by the ever-increasing sound of enemy artillery fire, he phoned his operations room. "Ask

22nd Brigade Headquarters if it's had any reports from forward positions," he told his duty officer. "Tell them to switch on their beach lights."

A few minutes later he got his answer. 22nd Headquarters reported that the telephone lines between General Taylor's headquarters, located three miles from the coast, had been severed by the bombardment.

Despite this information, Bennett still chose not to find out more about what was going on until two hours later, when at 11:00 P.M., still unable to sleep, he drove to his operations room at Bukit Panjang Village. It was not until eleven-thirty, an hour after the assault had begun, that the commanding general of the division discovered what had happened.

It is ironic that the two men, whose decisions could have perhaps led to the repulse of the invasion or at least made the enemy pay a heavy price for their efforts, did virtually nothing until it was too late. It was later claimed that on the night of February 5, three days before the invasion, General Percival was told of the heavy Japanese troop buildup opposite the northwest coast. Perhaps realizing that he may have miscalculated enemy intentions to hit the east coast, he ordered General Simson to rush the already once removed coastal defense equipment back to that coast. Obviously, it was not to be done in time.

As planned, at 10:30 P.M. the first 4,000 Japanese troops of General Tomoyoki Yamashita's 25th Army shoved off for the island. The focal point of his 5th and 18th Divisions, which would initially outnumber their enemy by six to one, would be the Australian 22nd Brigade.

When the first wave of collapsibles neared the shore, Australian sentries, alerted by the sudden halt of enemy artillery fire and the sound of outboard motors, sounded the alarm. According to a Japanese 18th Division officer, despite the fact that the enemy had been alarmed, "during the first landing, it appeared that our bombardments kept the enemy troops well down in the bottom of their trenches. But during the second and third landings, manning their parapets they resisted splendidly.... They broke through and attacked a pillbox we had occupied, and Staff Officer Ito lost both legs in a hand grenade explosion. The division commander was wounded and another staff officer [was also hit]. It was a desperate fight while it lasted." Another said that "while we suffered no damage during the first landing, during the second and third landings the enemy kept on firing even as they were retreating."[6]

But the opportunity to perhaps effectively beat off the invasion was lost when the beach lights, which would have illuminated much of the enemy's pre-selected landing beaches and allowed the Australians to be as effective against the first wave as they had against the second and third, failed to come on. Although ordered from the top, whether there was a breakdown in communications at 22nd Headquarters or severed phone lines prevented the order from getting through, it was never discovered.

By 1:00 A.M., without beach lights and overwhelmed by sheer weight of numbers, the Australians began to fall back. It was reported that on some of the isolated beaches, often defended by a single company of 120 to 140 men, as many as 40 to 50 landing craft came ashore in front of their positions.

Once on shore the resourceful Japanese, taking advantage of the broken shoreline, quickly moved inland, avoiding frontal attacks by the tactic they had become famous for in the battle for the Malayan mainland — infiltration. One 1,000-man strong Australian battalion that ran into the left wing of the Japanese 5th Division lost over 500 men, 334 of which were killed. Not counting 66 of its men who were captured, a forward company of that battalion was wiped out to the last man.

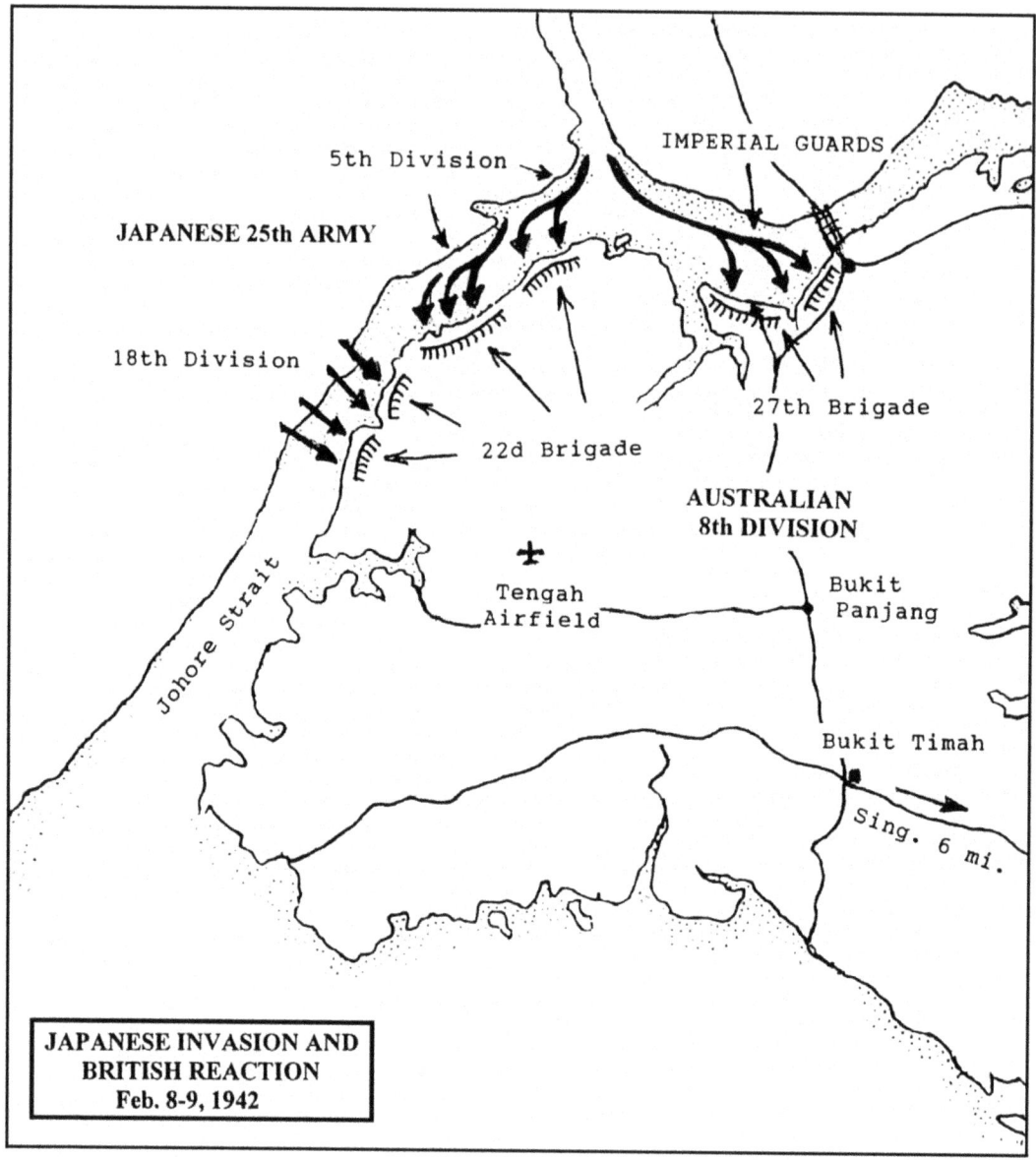

JAPANESE INVASION AND
BRITISH REACTION
Feb. 8-9, 1942

Before long many Australian units found themselves cut off and surrounded. Those who were able, pulled back. But because of the dark night, confusing rubber plantations, mangrove swamps, and patches of jungle behind the front, for all practical purposes they ceased to exist as organized fighting units.

An Australian soldier, Kenneth Attwill, who lived through the nightmarish ordeal, said, "Groups of men became separated from their comrades in the bewildering darkness. Others lost their way. Many died.... By ten o'clock in the morning of the 9th, less than 12 hours after the [enemy landing], the 22nd Brigade ... was no longer a cohesive fighting force."[7]

During the night, Bennett, with information that his entire division had been routed back to within 2 miles of Tengah Airfield, ordered his reserve battalion to General Taylor with orders to counterattack the Japanese at dawn. However, by the time it arrived and was forming up for the attack, the Japanese struck. Using infiltration again as the primary tactic against the confused and disorganized Australians, by 10:00 A.M. they had pushed the division perimeter back to within just yards of the airstrip.

The 22nd Division front, that 12 hours earlier encompassed some 8 miles of coastline, by midmorning of the ninth had been squeezed into a mere two-and-a-half-mile-wide perimeter.

General Percival, meanwhile, before releasing his two command reserve battalions to Bennett, had continued to hold them until he was sure that the attack on the 22nd was not a feint. Waiting until 8:30 A.M., by the time they arrived at the front, it was too late.

When Bennett got through to General Taylor to find out how the attack had gone, he was told that the Japanese had already captured the airfield. "Just as the advance was to commence," said Taylor, "the enemy attacked in strength and the line had fallen back behind the aerodrome."

At that point, the Japanese, who, in less than 12 hours, had captured over 14 square miles of the island, were forced to halt operations to allow reinforcements, ammunition, and armor to catch up. When Colonel Masanobu Tsugi, 25th Army operations officer, arrived at the field, he said that when they entered the British barracks, they found "fresh bread and soup were on the dining tables and clothing and suitcases belonging to the troops lying around. From this we knew that our successful forcing of the Strait ... had not been expected by the enemy and had come as a complete surprise to them."[8]

During the lull in the fighting, decisions were made on the British side that would already have a direct effect on the outcome of the battle.

It was planned before the attack that if the current situation presented itself, defense of a pre-determined position called the Jurong Line would be made to block the Japanese from reaching the important Bukit Timah Village, junction of the main and only road leading directly to the city, and location of the largest army supply dump on the island.

The line, some 3 miles in length, was anchored and somewhat protected on its flanks by the swampy headwaters of the Jurong River on the south and the Kranji on the north. In addition, two good roads connecting to the Woodlands Road and Bukit Timah provided easy access to the front. Key to holding the Japanese here rested with two things: first, Percival's willingness to release the bulk of the 18th Division to its defense, and second, to hold what was called the Kranji-Woodlands Road sector defended by the Australian 27th Brigade. However, if the Japanese were as successful in their invasion of that area as they had been against the 22nd, the Jurong Line, in jeopardy of being flanked or cut off from behind, would have to be abandoned.

On February 7, the night before the invasion, something occurred that, as much as anything, influenced the outcome of the battle — the Japanese's uncontested capture of the island of Pulau Ubin. Located in the center of the westernmost entrance of the Strait of Johore, it was its occupation that convinced Percival that the enemy took it to use as a jumping off point for his anticipated invasion of the northeast coast.

Despite what had transpired that night against the 22nd Brigade and the importance of holding the Jurong Line, it was because of Pulau Ubin that Percival lost his last and only opportunity to strip the 18th's defenses in order to suitably reinforce Bennett's shaky front.

In the meantime, on the 27th's Kranji-Woodlands front, after a rather quiet afternoon, dive-bombing attacks and an artillery bombardment similar in intensity to the pre-invasion assault on the 22nd hit that brigade's positions all across its 800-yard front.

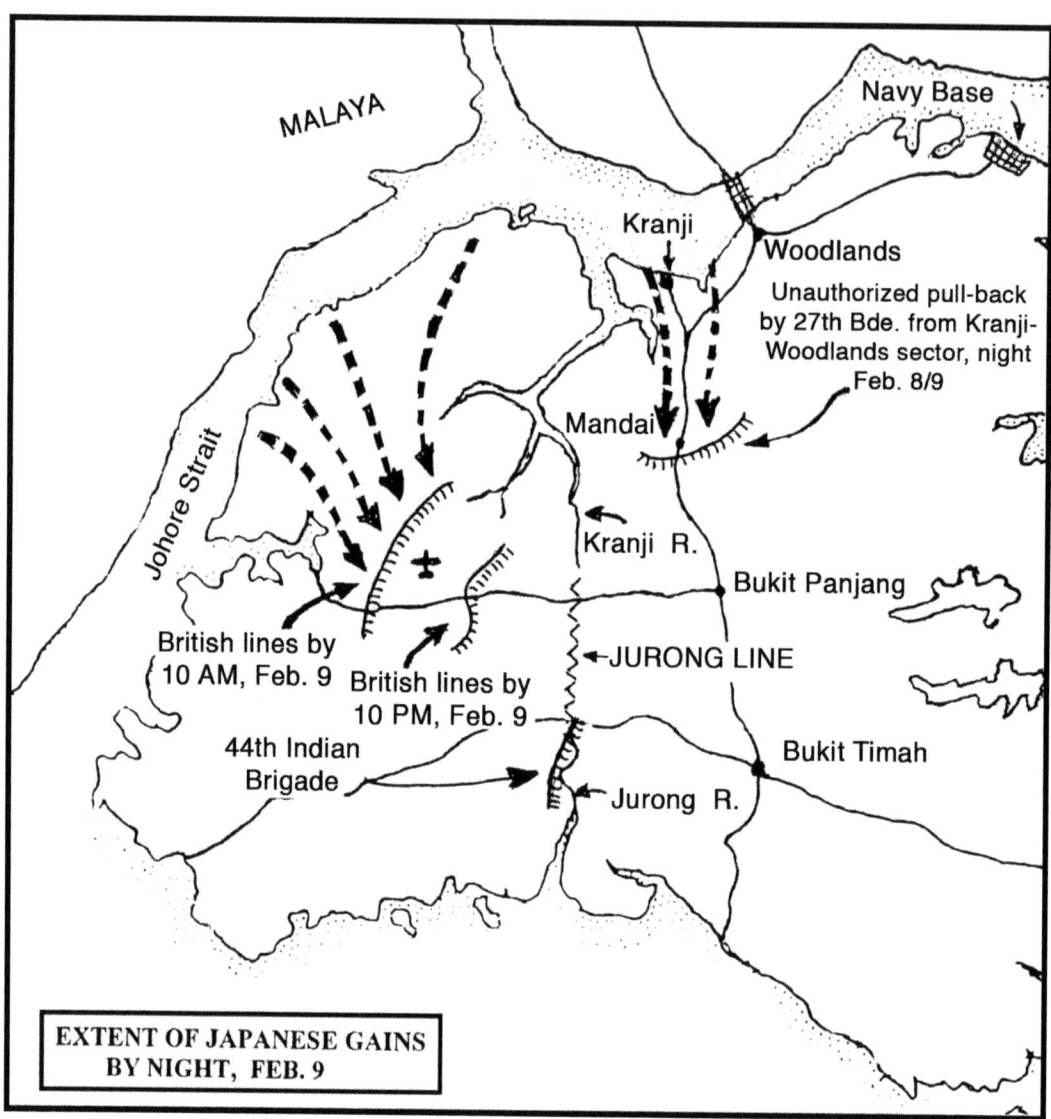

Reacting to what he correctly surmised was the enemy's pre-invasion bombardment and apparently to what had happened earlier to the 22nd Brigade, Brigadier General D.S. Maxwell, 27th commander, requested permission to pull back from the area and reform on a west-facing, north-south line along the Kranji River — a move he apparently felt would block a Japanese attempt to flank the northern end of the Jurong Line. Shocked by the request, Bennett sternly refused, telling him to stay put and fight it out on the beach.

Surprisingly, that is initially what happened. Around 9:00 P.M. Japanese invasion craft were spotted approaching the westernmost beach opposite the 27th's 26th Battalion.

The enemy force, made up of the Imperial Guards Division, was stopped cold on the edge of the muddy banks of the Kranji River delta by the Australians. Firing from well-concealed positions some 500 yards from the marshy shoreline, they were able to effectively beat off the enemy attack to the degree that Colonel Kobayashi, commander of the regiment, requested the attack be called off. In fact, so effective was the defense put up by the 26th that, according to Japanese sources, for all practical purposes, the regiment had been wiped out. Although unreported by the Australians, Japanese survivors of the attack said that the defenders had also flooded the waters along the immediate coastline with gasoline, which they set ablaze as troops disembarked.

So incensed was the Japanese high command of the regiment's failure that, according to Colonel Tsugi when asked later how the division was to be used subsequently in the battle, he replied that they didn't need the Imperial Guards. "We can take Singapore with the 5th and 18th Divisions. The incident," he said later, "was the only mistake throughout the Malayan campaign."[9]

Despite the 26th's success against Kobayashi, another major command blunder on the British side allowed the remaining two Imperial Guard regiments an hour later to literally walk ashore in front of what then were freshly abandoned 27th Brigade positions. So surprised was General Yamashita when told early the next morning that "all resistance had melted away [during the night]," he refused to believe it. Nevertheless, it was true. Without firing a shot, the Japanese had inherited direct access to Woodlands Road, the main north-south highway leading directly to Bukit Timah and Singapore city.

The circumstances behind this were never fully explained. It was reported that in the early morning hours of the tenth, the 27th Brigade received orders to pull back. That they were issued by General Maxwell is not debated. What was debated is who initiated the order. Maxwell, who was not at the front, claimed it was Gordon Bennett. Bennett insisted that he had not issued the order, which seems likely after having just received the only good news of the day—his 26th Battalion's repulse of the Japanese. At any rate, the first of several crucial communication breakdowns that would mar the battle to come had occurred.[10]

As if that was not bad enough, another unexpected blunder of even greater magnitude quickly followed. On the night of the tenth, General Percival drew up a plan for the defense of Singapore city. Although the battle for the island was barely 24 hours old, should it happen that the Japanese could not be stopped, troops, he wrote, should fall back to a perimeter around the city that he specified would encompass two of its reservoirs. He then asked two of his three division commanders, Generals Lay and Lewis Heath, to report to him. The third, Gordon Bennett, tied up because of the serious situation facing his command, could not get away.[11]

After verbally explaining his plan, the two men left. Within an hour motorcycle couriers had hand-delivered typed copies of what Percival referred to as "secret and personal instructions" to the three division commanders, who in turn, distributed copies to the senior officers under their command.

Obviously, under the shaky and uncertain circumstances of the first 24 hours, Percival did not stop to think of how his secret instructions might be interpreted. General Taylor's interpretation, perhaps like others but far more costly, was that the command must have decided that holding the still-untested Jurong Line was hopeless, bringing him to abandon it without a shot being fired. Again communications, or in this case the lack of, could be blamed for the blunder. For this Bennett got the blame for failing to define for his subordinate commander the real intention of Percival's instructions.

Arriving at this time in what could be called the middle of it was General Wavell, who had flown in from Java. His visit had been partially inspired by a cable he had received from Winston Churchill that morning.

After acknowledging the fact that the Japanese had successfully "crossed the straits" but that the defenders "greatly outnumbered the Japanese and in a well-contested battle should destroy them," the prime minister said that there must be no thought of saving the troops or sparing the population. "The battle," he said, "must be fought to the bitter end at all costs.... Commanders and senior officers should die with their troops. The honor of the British Empire and the British Army is at stake.... It is expected that every unit will be brought into close contact with the enemy and fight it out."[12]

After meeting with Percival, the two men drove to General Bennett's bungalow headquarters at Bukit Timah. Unfortunately, they arrived in the middle of an air raid. As the sound of falling bombs drew closer, the three men dove for cover under the nearest table. Percival, as he stood up and brushed himself off after it was over, was told by an aide that his car had been blown up. That wasn't the only direct hit. It was discovered that an unexploded Japanese bomb had landed in the middle of Bennett's next room office.

What was said or discussed at the meeting that followed is not recorded, except at one point an obviously agitated Wavell was overheard yelling at Bennett to "get the hell out" and take his "bloody Aussies" with him.[13]

Not long after that, and with Bennett not yet fully apprised of the situation with the Jurong Line, Wavell and Percival decided to find out for themselves what was going on in the Kranji-Woodlands sector.

Nearing the village of Mandai, some two miles inland from the coast, they were surprised not only to find it occupied by the enemy, but by the withdrawal that night of the 27th Brigade as well. Percival, who apparently did not question what had led to the 27th's pull-back, ordered them to recapture Mandai Village to prevent the Japanese from moving any farther down the Woodlands Road. At the same time he at last ordered units from the British 18th Division, albeit just two battalions, released to Bennett.

When the two men returned to 8th Division headquarters early in the afternoon, they got the full story of what had happened on the Jurong Line. Shocked by news of the unauthorized withdrawal, Wavell, for the first and probably only time in the battle, gave Percival a direct order. He told him to "counterattack with all troops possible" and "recapture the abandoned line."

Leaving Bennett to work out the details of the attack, the two men were driven back to Fort Canning. Before he left that night, Wavell ordered what was left of the remaining serviceable aircraft and all the ground personnel that could be taken to take off for the Dutch East Indies. Kallang Field outside the city, he was told, was "so pitted with bomb craters that as a functioning air base it was no longer usable." A pilot of one of the three patched-up Hurricanes and the single Brewster Buffalo fighter that took off the next morning was Flight Lieutenant Arthur Donahue, an American who had volunteered to fly with the RAF. Of that last flight he later wrote:

> We made one circuit of the airdrome after we took off and were followed by Japanese anti-aircraft fire—the first time I was ever shot at by [the] enemy ... over my own field.
> I had my camera in my pocket, and while we were making the circuit, I took a snapshot of the north part of the city where a huge ugly fire was raging among a lot of buildings. When we were out two or three miles, I took another photo—presumably the last air picture of Singapore.
> My final memory of Singapore looking back for the last time is of a bright green little country resting on the edge of the bluest sea I'd ever seen. Lovely ... except where the dark tragic mantle of smoke ran across its middle ... darkening the city on the seashore.

5. Singapore's Final Hours

The city itself, with huge leaping fires ... appeared to rest on the floor of a vast cavern formed by a curtain of black smoke which towered over it, prophetically, like a great over-hanging cloak of doom.[14]

As supreme commander, Wavell, before leaving, issued what he called the Order of the Day to be read throughout the command. In it, in Churchillian style, he wrote, in part:

> It is certain that our troops ... greatly outnumber any Japanese that have crossed the Straits. We must defeat them. Our whole fighting reputation and the Honor of the British Empire is at stake.... There must be no thought of sparing troops or the civil population.... There must be no question or thought of surrender. Every unit must fight it out to the end.... I look to you to fight to prove that the fighting spirit what won our Empire still exists.[15]

Whether it was read or heard by those it was intended for is not known. What is known is that it made no difference. By the time his plane set down back at Batavia late that night, it was already too late.

In the north, efforts by the 27th to recapture Mandai Village and attempts by the 11th Indian Division to drive the Japanese off the Kranji-Woodlands beachhead had both failed.

In the most important 22nd Brigade area, General Bennett's plan to reoccupy and make a stand at the Jurong Line was too little too late. By the time the attacking forces, amounting to some 4,000 men, moved out, the Japanese had already moved six infantry regiments and a single tank regiment into position opposite the line. Using the two access roads connecting Bukit Panjang and Bukit Timah to the line, the Japanese were able to pincer Bennett's forces before they could get into position (see map).

The Japanese 5th Division struck first on the northernmost road that led directly to Bukit Panjang Village. Spearheaded by tanks, after fighting their way through the town and overwhelming a hastily improvised roadblock on the Woodlands Road, by 11:00 P.M. they were heading virtually unchallenged toward Bukit Timah.

Further south along the Jurong Road leading to Bukit Timah, at 2:30 A.M. enemy 18th Division troops surprised a unit of 22nd Brigade soldiers as they were moving to their jumping-off point. Although the attack was halted with help from the 15th Indian Brigade, it became obvious at that time that the planned reoccupation of the line was impossible. Regrouping, five hours later the Japanese struck again.

An unnamed Australian 22nd Brigade officer described the American Indian-style fighting used by the enemy. Different than the infiltration tactics used at night, he said they "pushed up to our line firing around and dodging behind trees, crawling along drains, and using every fold in the ground. Many had cut a bush and used this to push in front of themselves as they crawled forward while others smeared mud and clay over their faces and clothing."

The resulting hand-to-hand fighting that followed fortunately slowed the Japanese attack enough to allow the bulk of the 22nd defenders to disengage. With word that Bukit Timah was all but in enemy hands and with it any hope of retreating down the Jurong Road, they fell back cross country some three miles to the vicinity of Reformatory Road, moving in next to the 44th Indian Brigade.

While the withdrawal of the main body was taking place, a mile or so west of Bukit Timah on the Jurong Road, word had come to the temporary command post of the 15th Indian Brigade of the Japanese tanks that were heading down Woodlands Road from Bukit Panjang. Convinced by the sounds of small arms and artillery fire coming from Bukit Timah that it, too, could be in enemy hands, Major Charles Moses, brigade liaison officer, volunteered to get word to headquarters of the situation there.

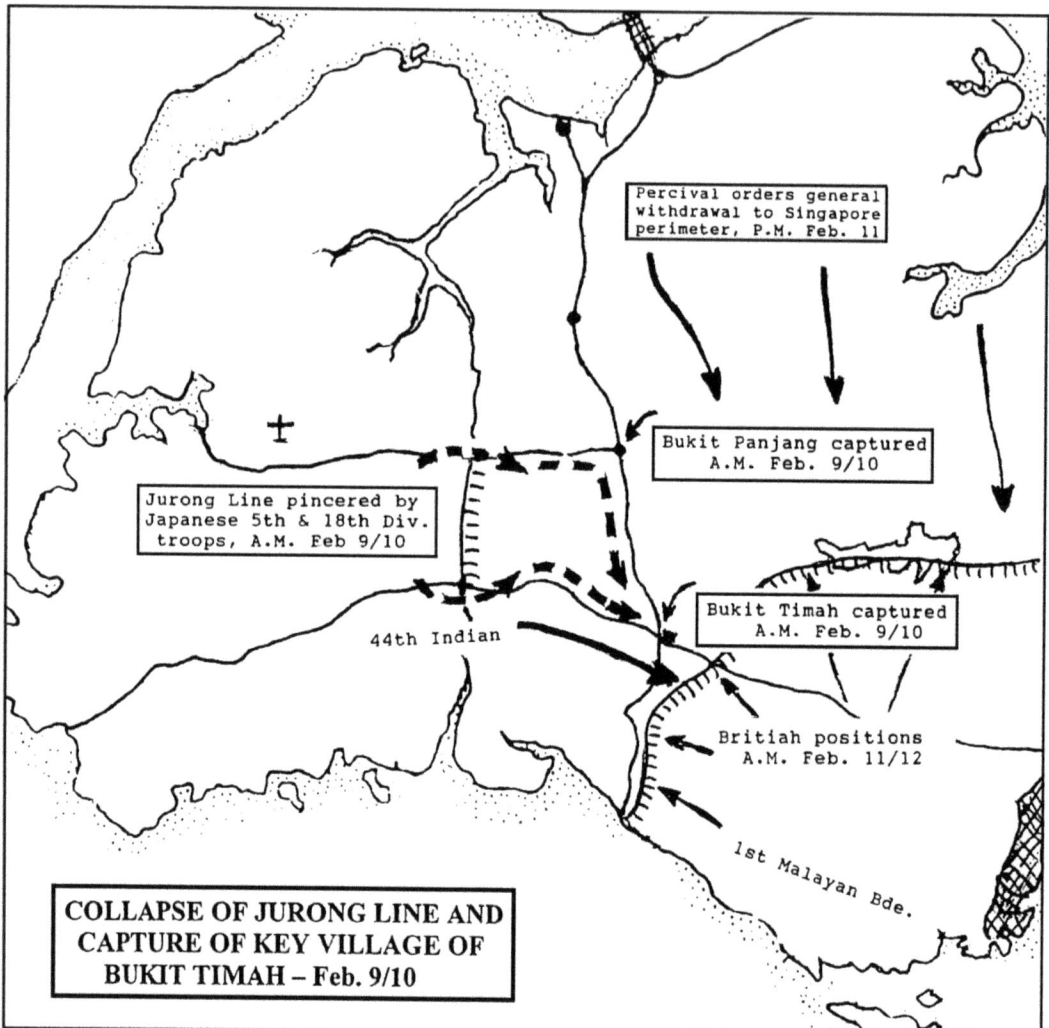

At 2:00 A.M. Moses decided, as he wrote later, "to try to rush [his] car through [Bukit Timah] and chance it." The following excerpts from his diary of what followed, among other things, convey the confusion that existed throughout the command that night. After writing of his decision to "chance it" by car, he continued:

Start off as quietly as possible down lane then speed up on Jurong Road and rush for the village. In front dark solid objects across road. Have to stop. Lights show Japs standing, sitting, lying, scores of them. Objects are two tanks astride road. Tommy gun opens up from 10–15 ft. away into radiator, everyone shooting. Tank guns smash into my car, four shells. My army boots clatter on road and I'm [running] over 200 yards to last house, across small stream, scramble up bank and rush up hill. Take stock. What to do? Temptation to strike S.E. to safety of mangroves and sampan to Sumatra, or go back to brigade headquarters.

Tempted to stay put but know must go on and try to get to headquarters. Decide to detour to south of village ... going over hill through rubber [plantation] and trying to reach main road near Reformatory Rd. Sound of motor vehicle coming down Jurong Road. Obviously 15th Brigade officers. Poor devils.

Can do nothing. Ten seconds of silence then rattle of firearms, three shots from tank guns and it's over. Force myself to my feet and hurry to darkness of trees. A branch scratches noisily across my helmet. Nearby I hear Jap voices call out. I've been heard. Decide to remove my helmet and shoes. Silently I move forward in stocking feet. I find myself near some native houses. All is quiet, then a dog barks.... I feel that every Jap in [village] will be drawn to me.

I pick up a couple of pebbles and throw them at the dog. I could strangle it if I could get hold of it. A few more yelps as I get away ... then all quiet again.... Now I'm in a rubber plantation and the darkness is intense. I can just avoid running into trees.... Slipped over the edge of a sandpit and dropped 10 or 12 feet. I'm all right. I must be ½ mile south of Bukit Timah now. Out of rubber trees. More houses. Round the first house then the next and nearly into the arms of a Jap patrol — half a dozen of them — one standing, the others sitting. I could almost touch the man standing.

Thank goodness I was moving silently. I drew back and darted around the other side. I want to run ... like a madman.

There seemed to be Japs everywhere. It must be three hours since I left [the brigade CP]. Why couldn't I have been killed cleanly ... stead of being saved to be tortured like this. I kept on — through some scrub and out into an open field. It was a big Chinese cemetery. After about 300 yards I came to Reformatory Road and now the first light of dawn was streaking across the eastern sky. I was about 200 yards from Bukit Timah Road.

British troops going up [the road]. Jap machine gun fire. Troops pulling back. [Catch] young officer [running away] — threaten to shoot him. Back he goes to his troops.

Meet Bren carrier which takes me to Malaya Command HQ. See General Percival and tell him what I know. He looks tired, says 'What do you think we should do, Major?' Back to HQ. Report to general.[16]

With information of the capture of Bukit Timah Village and its key supply dumps, General Yamashita, on the morning of the eleventh, decided to give the British an opportunity to surrender. Typed in English by his English-speaking intelligence officer, Lt. Colonel Ichiji Sugita, 29 rolled-up copies of the document placed in 18-inch-long wooden tubes with red and white streamers were dropped over the city by a low-flying reconnaissance plane. Addressed "To the High Command of the British Army, Singapore," in part it read:

> My sincere respect ... to your army which, true to the traditional spirit of Great Britain, is bravely defending Singapore, which now stands isolated and unaided.
>
> But the development of the ... war situation has already sealed the fate of Singapore, and the continuation of ... resistance would only serve to inflict direct harm to thousands of noncombatants living in the city [and] would add nothing to the honor of your army.[17]

Despite the offer there was no let-up by the Japanese while waiting for Percival's answer, which never came.

The capture of Bukit Timah Village was a staggering loss for the British, not only because it provided immediate highway access to the city itself, but for the loss of the most important army supply dump outside Singapore and the visual command Japanese artillery would have of the city's two reservoirs. Gordon Bennett, when told of it, wrote that with its loss, "all dumps of food and petrol had been lost, [leaving] only 14 days' supply of food in the depots still outside Japanese control."[18]

Despite game but failing efforts to retake Bukit's Timah and Panjang and a stout defense put up by the 22nd Brigade of a position described as "a line of gaps ... between formations of dispersed and isolated detachments in an area ill suited [for defense]," British lines, by the end of the day, looked like Percival's secret instructions to form a defensive perimeter around the city were in process of being carried out.

Of the few positives that day, a sound not heard during the first three days was identified as rounds from a British 15-inch gun battery located somewhere on the island. Battery Johore on the eastern end of Singapore, firing blindly in the direction of Tangah Airfield and Bukit Timah, although only marginally effective, did give a morale boost to troops who so far had nothing to celebrate about. The only recorded incident involving the effect of the 15-inchers came from Colonel Masanobu Tsugi, who, forced into a roadside ditch east of Tangah, wrote that the shells "tore holes in the ground [50 feet] in diameter, and [15 feet] deep." Their blast, he said, "shattered our eardrums and jarred our spines."[19]

Before the day was over, Battery Connaught, a 9.2-inch battery on Blakang Mati Island, a mile off Singapore's southern coast, like Johore, also got some licks in against the advancing enemy before both were pounded by Japanese planes. Although minor in their contributions, the vaunted guns of Fortress Singapore were at last put to use.

On the morning of the twelfth, General Percival made an inspection tour of the front. Although there had been no formal orders to withdraw back into his planned Singapore perimeter, by the time he had personally met with Gordon Bennett and General Lewis Heath, commander of the northeastern sector, including the British 18th Division, his mind was made up. In his meeting with Heath, both agreed that the only possible chance to save the city was for him to fall back inside the perimeter positions he outlined. At the same time units assigned to defensive positions along the still-untested southern coast were ordered to withdraw and reform on a north-south line east of the city.

The line in Bennett's sector, although also in jeopardy, was still holding, particularly because of the fight being put up by his 22nd Brigade. In fact, of it Percival, in his official report of that day wrote, "Throughout the day the 22nd ... continued to hold its advanced position in the Pandan-Holland Road area in spite of all attempts by the enemy to dislodge it. Towards the evening, however, the enemy effected a deep penetration south of the position.... The brigade was withdrawn under cover of darkness to the Holland Village area. It had fought a gallant action for 48 hours and done much to hold up the enemy's advance in this area."[20]

General H.B. Taylor, whose 22nd Brigade had been continuously involved in the battle since the night of the invasion and who himself had gone non-stop for four straight days and nights, after supervising the withdrawal, collapsed and was taken to the hospital at Fort Canning.

General Bennett, meanwhile, commenting on the situation he found himself confronted with upon moving into the new position, wrote that it was evident that "every man was needed in the line: signal company, the engineer companies, the service company, a mixed force of stragglers—everyone that could be found was sent forward to fill gaps in the perimeter. I recognized," he said, "that the end was near." Although it was still three days away, he was right.[21]

The situation within the city itself, that in five days had gone through the transition of being confident in the army's ability to hold the island to the realization that its fall was imminent, on the night of the twelfth looked like London during the blitz.

At the outbreak of war on December 8, everyone seemed confident that the British Army would soon "shove the little men off," as Governor Shenton Thomas had said to General Percival when informed of the invasion that day. On that fateful Monday, there were over 30 members of the press on the island representing some 22 newspaper, radio and press information services. There were also four local newspapers. On the night of February 12, there was only one correspondent left, Yates McDaniel of the Associated Press, and one newspaper, the *Straits Times*, whose publication had been taken over by the governor himself. Everyone else had left.

In the 67 days since the outbreak of hostilities on the eighth, Singapore had gone through the gradual transition of believing in the impregnable theory to realizing, as Gordon Bennett said on the night of the twelfth, that "the end was near." The city, of course, had been bombed on and off up to the army's withdrawal across Johore Straits on February 1. From that time on, life changed.

Along with stepped-up bombing raids, unmolested enemy fighters began strafing the streets. Perhaps more frightening was when Japanese long-range artillery, firing from high-ground positions on the mainland and directed by an observation balloon, began lobbing shells on the city. By the end of the first week of what had become a siege, not counting the bodies that were never found, an average of 200 civilians a day were being killed.

That Singapore was under siege was not in doubt. However, those newspaper correspondents still in the city were told by the War Council, who controlled what information was allowed to be reported, that the word siege could not be used in their cables or in local press columns. Bad for morale, they were told.

Despite the siege, things were going on in parts of the city that defied the reality of the situation. As desperate as the situation at the front was, a surprising number of leaderless soldiers could be seen aimlessly walking the streets, some drunk, many AWOL, but nothing being done to round them up and return them to their units. People still frequented the department stores and shops. Robinson's reported sales were as brisk as ever. Soldiers were still buying souvenirs to take home. During the day the Raffles Hotel bar was crowded with army officers with nothing to do but drink and commiserate. At night you could not get a table without a reservation. It was the same for the Cricket Club, whose tennis courts and bowling greens still saw occasional participants.

Movies were still a popular attraction. At the Cathay Theater inside the city's only skyscraper, despite the bombing people still lined up to see Cary Grant in *The Philadelphia Story*. A comment by Flight Lieutenant Arthur Donahue after seeing *Ziegfeld Girl* at the Alhambra Theater perhaps explains why people continued to risk being killed by a bomb while standing in line to get in. "We got completely lost in the lovely atmosphere of American girls and song and gaiety and peace."[22]

On the darker side, because of the damage to many buildings and businesses, looting soon became a problem, with little apparently done to stop it.

American AP correspondent Yates McDaniel, on his way to the cable office to file his last story, saw yet another side to what was going on in the city. Seeing British, Chinese, and Malayans working together pulling dead and wounded from a bombed out building was actually uplifting.

"Although it took a war to do it," he thought to himself, "democracy has finally come to Singapore." In contrast, further on he saw the words "England for the English, Australia for the Australians, but Malaya for any son of a bitch who wants it" scrawled on a wall no doubt by some disgruntled soldier.[23]

Governor Shenton Thomas, who had taken over publication of the *Straits Times* newspaper, delivered the first edition on the morning of the twelfth. Interestingly, of the six news items crammed on what had been reduced to a single page paper, only one pertained to the war. Its small, bold print headlines read: Fighting Continues on West Front — Ack-Ack Guns Destroy Three Jap Planes. Follow-up stories, once the censors got through with them, unfortunately left much to the imagination.

Yates McDaniel's experience with the censor, which involved what information was released to the outside world, was quite different. When he reached his office to get his last story cleared, he found the man packing. "How can I do my job without a censor?" he asked.

"Write anything you want. Send anything you want. I'm leaving," he said, as he stamped "Cleared by Censor" on the cover page of his story.

A few minutes later McDaniel entered the cable office and laid the story on the desk in front of the operator. Pointing to the censor's stamp on the front, he asked that it be sent as an "official dispatch." Correctly prefaced by the words, "This will probably be my last message from this crumbling fortress," in the story that was sent to the outside world, he wrote, in part:

> The sky over Singapore is black with smoke from a dozen huge fires as I write my last message this morning from this once beautiful, prosperous, and peaceful city. The war ... of cannonade and bursting bombs which are shaking my typewriter ... tell me that the war which started nine weeks ago 400 miles away is now in the outskirts of this shaken bastion of Empire....
>
> [From my window in the Cathay building] I see relay after relay of Japanese planes circling, then going into murderous dives on our soldiers who are fighting back in the hell over which there is no screen of our own fighter planes....
>
> There are many brave men in Singapore today. Not far away are A.A. Batteries. They are in open spaces because they must have a clear field of fire. But those gun crews keep on fighting and peppering the smoke-filled ceiling every time Japanese planes come near, which is almost constantly.
>
> My colleagues left last night by ship, and the military spokesman gave his daily talk to an audience of three representatives of two local papers and myself.
>
> [I] have less than a 50 percent chance of getting [out].... Please inform my wife, Mrs. McDaniel, Hotel Preanger, Bandoeng, Java that I have left this land of the living and dying.[24]

The positions which the 18th Division had taken up on the night of the twelfth was where Gordon Bennett had decided to "make our final stand." To support this decision, the entire division plus the British 2nd Gordon Highlanders, who had been attached to his command, was organized to defend not only its front but both flanks as well.

The move paid off, as enemy pressure throughout the thirteenth forced the Malay 1st Brigade and Indian 44th back nearly 2 miles. Although totally exposing the 18th's left flank by this, the Japanese decided not to challenge the well-dug-in Australians.

Back at Fort Canning, meanwhile, a special 9:00 A.M. meeting was held between, among others, British Naval commander Rear Admiral E.J. Spooner, Air Vice Marshal C.W.H. Pulford, and Army chief engineer General Ivan Simons.

Admiral Spooner, who had called the meeting believing the collapse of Singapore was imminent, had decided that night was the last opportunity for organized parties to leave the island. Having already ordered the roundup of all remaining ships and naval patrol vessels, it was estimated that there would be room for about 3,000 key military and civilian personnel. The only requirement was that they be chosen for their potential contributions to the coming war effort. Evacuees were to report at the waterfront at four o'clock that afternoon.

As they were leaving, Spooner told Simson that if, because of the short notice, he was unable to fill the 300 places he'd been allotted, he could use women and children.

People, both military and civilian, had begun arriving at the dock as early as three o'clock. By four, after the military personnel had been taken on board, civilians who had not been allowed through the gate because passes issued by different authorities had created a near-riotous situation. Even a bomb from a Japanese plane that landed in the middle of the crowd killing several people did not deter the clamor to get through. In fact, not until General Simson arrived at five-thirty to help iron out the problem did things quiet down.

A particularly sad scene occurred when shrapnel from a bomb killed a woman as she and her husband were about to board their ship. The man, who was holding their infant baby when it happened, with little choice, was forced to leave the lifeless body of his wife on the dock as he was physically herded onto the boat.

By 6:30 P.M., after three hours of panic and confusion, the last passenger had been loaded. At dark, one by one the armada of 44 strange-looking ships began their 700-mile voyage to Java and freedom.

Air Marshal Pulford, on one of the navy patrol craft with Admiral Spooner, before he left said goodbye to General Percival. "I suppose you and I will be blamed for this," he said as he turned to walk away. "But God knows we've done our best with what we'd been given."

Sadly, few of those who left that night ever reached freedom. Of the 44 ships, over 20 were sunk when they ran into a Japanese invasion convoy heading for Sumatra. Traveling through what was called the 1,000 Island chain, many attempted to hide among the myriad of tiny islands, only to be caught or die of exposure. Both Admiral Spooner and Air Marshal Pulford were among those who failed to make it. General Simson had remained in Singapore.

That afternoon another meeting was held at Fort Canning between General Percival and his entire command staff, including Generals Bennett, Heath, and Key and Governor Shenton Thomas.

Although realizing that all reserves had been committed, he asked if there was a chance a counterattack could be launched across a front that was now only some 20 miles long. On paper the figures appeared to favor the British. A force of some 65,000 against just three Japanese divisions of probably 20,000 who, like themselves, had had little rest, few replacements, and were probably low on ammunition.

Going around the room, all three division commanders said the situation was hopeless, each suggesting that it was time to surrender. Gordon Bennett remembered that "it was unanimously considered that new enemy attacks would succeed, and that sooner or later the Japanese would reach the streets of the city" and that "it was decided to send a message to General Wavell urging him to agree to immediate capitulation."

At that point Percival held up a copy of a second Japanese offer to surrender that had been dropped that morning. Only in this one he said that Yamashita advised him "to surrender the whole force in Malaya" or he would order his army to "make annihilating attacks on Singapore." Below the signature he directed that the surrender party should "proceed to the Bukit Timah Road ... bearing a white flag and the Union Jack."[25]

Aware of Wavell's Order of the Day of February 10, that "there must be no question or thought of surrender" and that every unit "must fight it out to the end," Percival messaged the ABDA commander of his subordinates' views on their chances.

Along with a copy of Yamashita's latest ultimatum and that he had no thought of answering it, he wrote that "there must come a stage when in the interest of the troops and civil population, further bloodshed will serve no useful purpose. Your orders to 'fight it out to the end' are being carried out, but under the circumstances would you consider giving me wider discretionary powers to end it if and when I see fit?"

Wavell, under similar pressure from Churchill to "fight to the bitter end ... at all costs," agonized over what he no doubt knew would be a fruitless response. His message, which did not arrive until the next morning, disappointedly offered more of the same. It said in part: "You must continue to inflict maximum damage on enemy as long as possible by house-to-house fighting if necessary.... [I] fully appreciate your situation, but continued action essential."[26]

On his way out of the city to his new headquarters at Tanglin Barracks, Bennett, for the first time, got a look at what was happening throughout the city. Having been in the field for the past 15 days, he was shocked. "There was devastation everywhere," he wrote in his diary. "There were holes in the road, churned-up rubble lying in great clods all around, tangled masses of telephone and electric cables strewn across the street, here and there smashed cars, trucks, and buses ... shops shuttered and deserted.

"Bombs were falling in a nearby street. On reaching the spot, I saw that the side of the building had fallen on an air raid shelter. A group of Chinese, Malays, Europeans, and Australian soldiers were already at work shoveling and dragging debris away."

At that point he stopped and got out of the car to observe what happened.

"At last," he said," the top of the shelter was uncovered. Beneath it lay a crushed mass of men, women, and young children, some still living, others dead. This was going on hour after hour, day after day in the city; and the same stolidity and steadfastness remained evident in every quarter of the town."[27]

It is not known if Bennett happened to see a copy of the governor's *Straits Times* for that day. Outside of the fairy-tale headlines that said, "Singapore Must Stand; It SHALL Stand" and "Japanese Suffer Huge Casualties," again there was nothing in the accompanying five news items about what was really going on.

Throughout February 13, the battles on both flanks of the A.I.F.'s defensive perimeter continued. On the 22nd Brigade's right, Japanese attacks against the 18th Division's 55th Brigade forced a deep salient in their line, forcing them to give up any chance of holding MacRitchie Reservoir, the last major water source for the city. By the end of the day, the position the 55th occupied, like the Australians on its left, was where it would be when the end came.

On the A.I.F.'s extreme left along the coastal corridor, the 1st Malay Brigade, a unit made up of Malayans and led by native-speaking British officers, had turned out to be as tough a fighting force as there was on the island. For 2 days the "Malayans fighting for Malaya," as one of its officers put it, held the Japanese until forced to commit the entire 18th Division to the battle. By mid-morning of the fourteenth, isolated units of the brigade which, according to Percival, had "held their ground until wiped out almost to the man," gave way. By 12:30 P.M., lead elements of the Japanese 55th Regiment, having covered nearly two miles in less than three hours, were spotted approaching the Alexandra Barracks Hospital.

The following story of what occurred there was compiled from eyewitness accounts of the small handful of survivors who lived through or happened to escape from the bloody ordeal that followed.

Colonel Masanobu Tsugi, 25th Army's chief operations officer, earlier that day had requested permission to accompany advanced elements of the 55th Regiment as they moved south. When Japanese troops, accompanied by Tsugi, were about to enter the hospital, eyewitnesses said that "Lt. Weston went to the entrance with a white flag. The Japanese took no notice of the flag and [he] was bayoneted to death by the first Japanese to enter the hospital. The troops were excitable and jumpy, and neither Red Cross arm bands nor shouting the word "hospital" had any effect.

At this time operations were being prepared in the theater block corridors, this area being the best lighted and most sheltered part of the block. About ten Japs came into the corridor and all the medical staff personnel put up their hands. Captain Smiley pointed to his Red Cross arm band, but the enemy took no notice. The Japs then motioned them to move along the corridor, and then for no apparent reason, set upon them with bayonets. Lt. Rogers was bayoneted through the throat twice and died at once.

Captain Parkinson was bayoneted to death as also was Corporal McHewan and Private Lewis. A patient on the operating table was bayoneted to death. Captain Smiley was bayoneted but the blade hit his cigarette case. He was again lunged at and was wounded in the left groin. He then pretended to be killed and pushed Private Sutton to the floor calling to others to be quiet. The Japanese then left the corridor.

Another party of Japs went into the wards and ordered the medical officer and those patients who could walk outside the hospital. In one ward two patients were bayoneted. The Japs then went upstairs and gave similar instructions. Patients and personnel numbering about 200 were taken outside, their hands tied behind them. Some could only hobble, others had only one arm, while some were still in plaster ... one or two collapsed and had to be revived.

They were [then] marched to the old quarters, where they were herded into rooms, 50 to 70 persons per room, where they were literally jammed in. Sitting down was out of the question. During the night many died, and all suffered severely from thirst. Water was promised but none came.

Japs then lead small parties out of sight where afterwards we heard yells and screams, then a Jap [would] return wiping blood from his bayonet, [leaving] little doubt as to their fate. An artillery shell, possibly from British lines, hit the building, allowing eight men to try to escape. Five were gunned down before they could get away. Except for three that escaped, none of these parties were ever seen again.[28]

In all, 323 men were bayoneted to death, including 230 patients that were killed in their beds or on operating tables. The next day, Tsugi, who two months later claimed that Emperor Hirohito had ordered all Bataan prisoners executed, allowed several survivors to return to the city to explain what might happen to everyone in Singapore if Percival didn't surrender soon.[29]

Despite the fact that the collapse of the 1st Malay Brigade left close to 2 miles of the A.I.F.'s left flank exposed to the enemy, the Japanese still chose not to challenge the Australians. Had they, it could have been disastrous. Because of the acute shortage of 25-pounder artillery ammunition, its use was restricted to firing "only in defense, and only on specific targets." The order was particularly difficult on Australian artillerymen who could plainly see Japanese troops moving against the Malayans but could do nothing about it.

With the loss of MacRitchie Reservoir earlier that day, the only source of water to the city came from a lone pumping station at Woodleigh located just inside the southwest corner of the Singapore perimeter. Even with the station remaining in friendly hands, due to innumerable breaks in the water mains caused by the bombings, there was a chance the city's already dwindling water supply could be cut off at any time.

Fearing the intense heat and humidity would drive people to drink contaminated water resulting in a typhoid epidemic, Governor Thomas met with Percival to discuss the situation. Frustrated that nothing could be done, both men resorted to sending messages—Shenton Thomas to the Colonial Office in London and Percival to Wavell—where, after explaining the situation, he again asked that he be granted the discretionary power to surrender if and when the time came.

Wavell, no doubt aware of Singapore's fate, was himself somewhat hamstrung until he received an answer from Churchill to his latest message, which said: "Have received telegram from Percival that the enemy are close to town and that his troops are incapable of further counterattack. Have ordered him to continue. Fear however that resistance [is] not likely to be very prolonged."

With no alternative left, the prime minister signaled back: "In all places where sufficiency of water exists for troops they must go on fighting. Your gallant stand is serving purpose and must be continued to the limit of endurance."[30]

Percival, meanwhile, to help alleviate the situation, arranged for a unit of Royal Engineers, then on line as infantry, to be released to assist with repairs of the water mains.

Although there was a letup in enemy activity across much of the British front that day, bombing and shelling of the city was recorded as the heaviest it had ever been. It was estimated that close to 500 people were killed on that day alone. For the most part, it looked to some as if the whole city was on fire. Along with what seemed like the entire waterfront, the fire was particularly bad on the Singapore River. There, along with a row of fiercely burning warehouses, the incoming tide had literally pushed a huge mass of burning oil upriver from a bombed-out tanker. Before it stopped, it was estimated that over 1,000 sampans and junks, all tied up or anchored at a wide spot just inside the mouth or the river, were burned.

Mr. Jack Bennett, standing on the roof of the Mercantile Bank, commented that from that height "one got the general impression of a vast ring of fire, almost as if there were four walls of fire and Singapore burning in the middle ... whereas the city as a whole was not very badly knocked about. Outside of Chinatown, there were no vast areas of the town devastated."

The combination of fire and bombed-out buildings drew looters by the hundreds. Warehouses in particular were a popular target. People, arriving on foot, in cars, and even rickshaws loaded up and quickly dashed off in search of the next spot. It was not uncommon to see people carrying, and in some cases struggling under armloads of merchandise of all sorts: clothing, radios, lamps, bicycles, cameras, you name it. When some business owners whose undamaged stores were being looted called the police, there was usually no response. Interestingly, even when the Japanese entered the city on February 16, it was still going on. According to Colonel Tsugi, "The English storehouses and dwellings were swallowed in waves of looting Chinese and Malays. Even the women and children were all mobilized like thieves at a fire."[31]

Despite the fact that fighting was still going on, city streets were choked with hundreds of soldiers. Deserters most of them, they wandered around aimlessly waiting, like everyone else, for the inevitable end. Either too many in number for the military police to handle or the M.P.s, too, had given up, no discernible effort was made to either question or detain any of them.

A British officer, David James, who spotted a line of Indian soldiers filing into the city, asked their officer why they were going in the wrong direction. He was told that an Australian major said for them to "beat it because the Nips were coming over the hill." James told him that they were supposed to fight the Japanese, not run from them. "Quite so," he said, "but you don't remain where you are not wanted, do you?"[32]

The situation with the thousands of wounded civilians by the night of the fourteenth had literally overwhelmed the city. Not only were the various hospitals jammed with casualties, the lobbies of many of the larger hotels and even St. Andrew's Cathedral had been converted into temporary aid stations.

The scene at the overcrowded Singapore General Hospital, in particular, was nightmarish. Outside on the once lush green lawns, huge pits had been bulldozed as mass graves for the almost steady stream of bodies being stretchered out and unceremoniously dumped into one of the holes.

Inside it was even worse. Overwhelmed by the sheer weight of numbers, operating theaters looked more like butcher shops, with wounded in an almost unending line of gurneys awaiting a quick decision by an exhausted doctor in a bloodstained gown as to their fate. Without a supply of fresh water, instruments were sterilized in reused water. Because there was no time for the sophisticated operation usually performed to save a shattered arm or leg, amputations, equal in number to those seen in some American Civil War hospitals, were performed.

Wounded were everywhere, in wards, lining corridor walls, lying on beds, between beds, under beds, and even on the stairs. By the time the nurses could get to them, many were already dead.

Sunday, February 15, 1942. "Today opened with a hopeless dawn of despair," wrote Gordon Bennett in his diary that morning. "There is no hope or help on the horizon. The tropical sun is already sending its streaming heat on to the dying city which is writhing in its agony."

After writing that the flanks of the army had continued to fall back but that "enemy troops movements along the Bukit Timah Road have been shelled by our artillery, as also have enemy troops opposite our own A.I.F. front," he clarified that sentence by saying, "but the momentum of the enemy advance goes unchecked."[33]

Interestingly, had he known about the effect his artillery would actually have on the Japanese that day or been aware of the stubborn fight still being put up by the defenders, he would certainly have amended his last sentence.

The best example of that stubbornness actually came from the Japanese. That morning, Colonel Tsugi had decided to personally witness a planned attack by the 18th Division's 114th Regiment on the British left flank, which had been forced back to within a mile and a half of the city.

Attacking against the tough 1st Malayan Brigade, supported now by artillery units whose numbers had increased in direct proportion to the decreasing area they had to defend, foreshadowed a much more difficult time for the Japanese than they expected. Tsugi's narrative of the events of that afternoon offer the only glimpse of what happened that day on the enemy side of the line.

Intending to call in person at 18th Division Headquarters, he wrote:

> We instead drove straight through to the frontline command post, which overlooked the enemy position but was under enemy observation so that the movement of even one Japanese soldier brought down a concentration of shell fire....
> [We] were in the midst of preparations for an attack at 12:30 P.M. (Tokyo time), which had been ordered by the division....
> After roughly a week of fighting since we crossed the Johore Strait, the ammunition accumulated for the assault on Singapore Island was nearly exhausted. We had barely a hundred rounds per gun left for our field guns, and less for our heavy guns....
> With the enemy apparently resting while waiting for our assault, the Ito Battalion decided to attack, [but] as the men began to emerge from their trenches, a large number of British guns directed an intense barrage on the position....
> The division chief of staff ... came reluctantly to the conclusion that it was a sheer impossibility to proceed, owing to the fact that the troops were exhausted.... Arms and legs were flying through the air and heads scattered everywhere.

The regimental headquarters trench became shallower every time a shell exploded close to it.... At last we moved out of the trench and sought shelter behind the brick wall of a wrecked house. A soldier beside me had his head blown off and blood was scattered everywhere.

The furious enemy bombardment eased off about two-thirty (Tokyo time) in the afternoon. I started homewards thinking, "If the enemy resists in this manner, he probably contemplates fighting from house to house, and it will take more time to capture the fortress. Our artillery ammunition is almost exhausted. We will have to concentrate on a new plan."

Tired and heavy footed, my orderly and I walked back along the road by which we had come that morning. We had left our car concealed under the shade of a tree. Returning to the spot we found that it had been blown up. It was the third car I had had destroyed by shellfire. Proceeding by foot, we arrived at 18th Division Headquarters, where I explained the strategic position to the division commander.

As the day was gradually drawing to a close, I was called to answer an excited call on the telephone. Trembling with excitement the voice said, "The enemy has surrendered! They have surrendered!" Only a few moments ago we were engaged a life-and-death struggle. "Perhaps I'm dreaming," I thought. But it was no dream.

During the day on the 5th Division front (against the British 18th Division), the troops had never before been under such heavy shellfire from which the frontline trenches afforded very little shelter. The division had attacked from the main road, but the troops were finally brought to a standstill at two in the afternoon. Then suddenly, ahead of the frontline which was renewing the assault along the central highway, there appeared a large white flag.

Like lighting this was reported to Bukit Timah headquarters. Immediately on receiving the news, Staff Officer Sugita, in charge of intelligence, was taken by car to the front line, where he personally delivered to the bearer of the flag of truce documents which had been prepared in anticipation at our army headquarters.[34]

The story of what led to the delivery of the surrender documents to "the bearer of the flag of truce" had actually begun at 9:30 A.M. at Fort Canning when General Percival called a meeting of his senior commanders and appropriate civil authorities.

Unknown to the British commander, General Wavell's message to Churchill requesting authority to allow Percival to surrender been answered. It was what he hoped for. It said: "You are, of course, sole judge of the moment when no further result can be gained at Singapore and should instruct Percival accordingly."

Relieved that he was at last allowed to place the fate of island in the hands of the man who would ultimately have to make the final decision, he messaged Percival: "Whenever you are fully satisfied that [your ability to inflict losses on the enemy] is no longer possible, I give you the discretion to cease resistance."[35]

Whether Percival already had Wavell's message when the meeting started is not known. He started the meeting by asking General Ivan Simson and chief of police A.E. Dickinson to give him a rundown on the situation inside the city. Gordon Bennett's notes on what was said left little doubt as to the outcome regardless of what the military staff had to say.

"Each ... gave his pitiful story," wrote Bennett. "Food and water had almost run out; the civilian hospital had been without water for 2 days; the civilian air raid service was nonexistent; air raids continued to destroy buildings in which the injured and dying lay among the dead."

Turning to his division commanders, he said they had two choices: launch a counterattack to recapture the reservoirs and supply depots at Bukit Timah, or surrender.

It was a non-decision decision, as everyone in the room without hesitation agreed that it was over. Bennett wrote:

> It was unanimously considered that new enemy attacks would succeed and that sooner or later the enemy would reach the streets of the city, which were crowded with battle stragglers. It was

also realized that the civilian population ... which could not escape through the enemy cordon, were the main sufferers. The heavy air blitz and artillery fire were causing great havoc, killing and maiming thousands of innocent victims. It was decided to send a message to General Wavell urging him to agree to immediate capitulation.[36]

Fortunately, General Yamashita, in the second surrender message he had dropped to the British, had outlined the steps he wanted them to follow. A car flying a white flag and the Union Jack was to proceed north up Bukit Timah Road until met by the Japanese. Nothing else was mentioned.[37]

The decision finally made, Percival decided to send an advance surrender party forward to meet with the Japanese, with written instructions suggesting a 4:00 P.M. cease-fire, at which time the two commanders would meet to discuss the terms.

It was 11:30 A.M. In requesting a meeting with Yamashita four-and-a-half hours later, Percival felt that it would give both parties ample time to prepare a cease-fire. With this in mind, he notified his division commanders to destroy all weapons and secret codes. In case Japanese troops had not been notified of the cease-fire by 4:00 P.M., or if, by chance, terms of the surrender had not been agreed to by then, he told them to let their men keep their rifles and personal sidearms.

Despite General Heath's argument that 8 hours rather than four was a more realistic time for them to put the wheels of surrender in motion, Percival disagreed. Thinking of both soldiers and civilians, "the sooner the fighting stops," he said, "the fewer lives will be lost."

To carry the message to the Japanese, Percival selected his chief administration officer, General A.G. Newbiggin, and Colonial Secretary Hugh Fraser, as a representative of the civil population. Captain Cyril Wild, who spoke some Japanese, would go along as interpreter. The trip would not be an easy one, nor would the results be exactly as Percival had hoped for.

It was only 3 miles to where the British lines crossed the Bukit Timah Road, after which they could run into the Japanese any time after that. Anticipating no more than a 30-minute trip to that point, at 11:30 A.M., with flags furled, the three men left Ft. Canning for the front in an open sedan.

A mile or so outside the city, they, more than ever, became aware of the sounds and sights of the battle that was still raging in the sky and around them. Enemy planes were busy over the front lines, and among the distant clatter of machine guns, the whine of shells passing overhead, as one of them remembered, was so frequent that they "became almost monotonous."

Unexpectedly forced to detour from the road because of bomb craters, it was twelve-thirty before they reached an unmanned roadblock at the junction of Bukit Timah and Adam Road. Fortunately for the three men as they got out to remove the obstacle, they were stopped by a British patrol. After explaining their mission to the officer in charge, they were told that because the road from that point on was heavily mined, they would have to go the rest of the way on foot. Once past the roadblock marking the British front line, they would be in enemy territory.

Leaving the car and driver behind, the three men, with flags unfurled and raised prominently overhead, picked their way safely through the minefield. Expecting to be met at any minute by an enemy patrol, after covering a little over a quarter of a mile through the peaceful, serene countryside, a group of Japanese soldiers stepped out from a nearby rubber

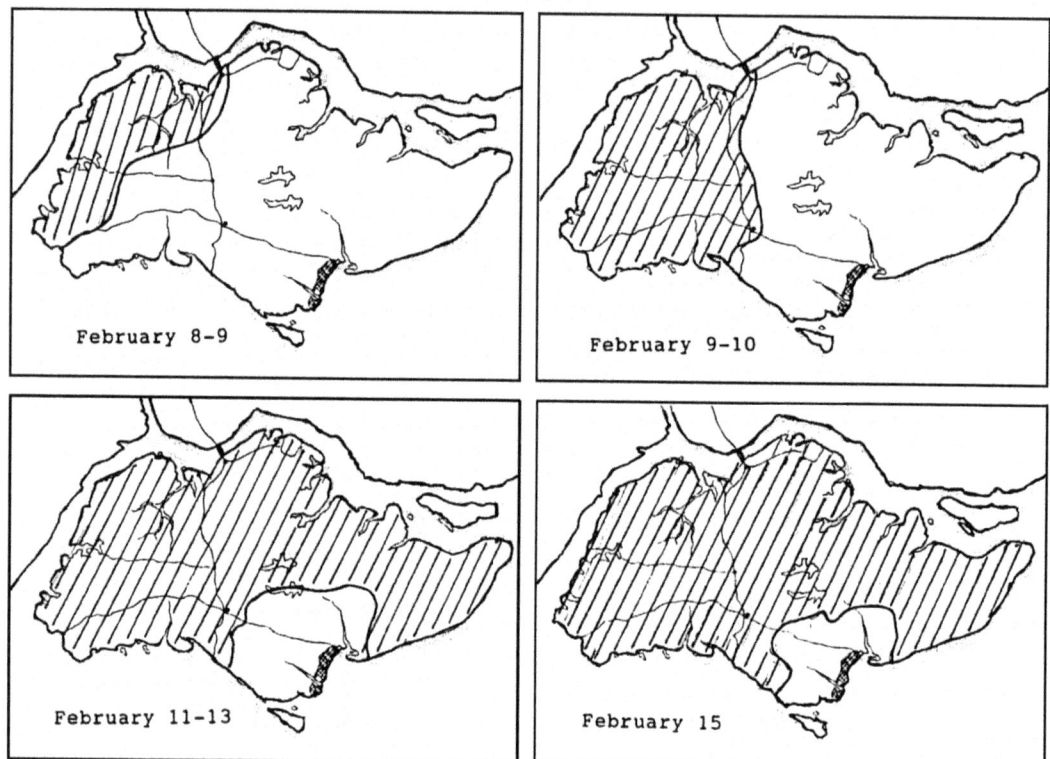

AREA UNDER JAPANESE CONTROL FEBRUARY 8–15, 1942

February 8-9

February 9-10

February 11-13

February 15

plantation. Unknown to the three men, however, the described "serene countryside," according to Colonel Tsugi, throughout the day had been the site of a violent battle which "our front line had ... never before been under such heavy shellfire.... The division had attacked, supported by the full strength of the ... tank brigade, but the troops were brought to a standstill at half past three in the afternoon. Then suddenly, ahead of the most forward troops, there appeared a large white flag."[38]

Upon seeing the Japanese soldiers, Captain Wild, pointing to the white flag, in his best Japanese explained that they wanted to be taken to their commanding officer. "Soon, soon," replied one of the soldiers in Japanese. "Take picture." Wild recalled that several had cameras. Before sending for an officer, they were made to pose together until all their film was used up.

Finally, after an hour of posing and waiting for a Japanese officer to arrive, a car pulled up. Out stepped Lt. Colonel Ichiji Sugita and another officer.

Speaking in broken English, Sugita, who had written the two surrender messages that had been dropped on February 10 and 14, said, "We will have truce if the British Army agrees to surrender. Do you wish to surrender?"

"We do," replied Wild.

At that point General Newbiggin handed Sugita the letter from Percival addressed to the Japanese High Command. Giving it little more than a quick glance, he produced one from Yamashita. Prepared in anticipation of this meeting "in order that the Japanese Army commander may accept the surrender of your army," it directed that Percival was to meet the Japanese leader at the Ford factory above Bukit Timah.

According to Wild, the time of the meeting was left blank. Assuming two and a half hours would give Percival enough time, Newbiggin penciled in "4:30 P.M."

The letter, which said that a car would be waiting at the Bukit Timah–Adam Road junction to take the British commander to the factory, directed that the British should "promptly suspend resistance all along the line and disarm." Omitted, however, were two important points: what time it should take place, and would the Japanese honor it by ceasing operations themselves?

Despite Wild and Newbiggin pressing Sugita for an answer, he refused to discuss the matter. Instead, he produced a large Japanese flag that he said should be raised from the top of the highest building in Singapore as a signal that Percival had agreed to meet with Yamashita.

The three men were then blindfolded and driven back to the edge of the minefield near Adam Road. Finding their driver still patiently waiting, they started back. A mile or so down the road at the junction Stevens Road, an obviously drunk British sergeant, with pistol in hand, waved for them to stop. Newbiggin told the driver, who had slowed down, to keep going, bringing the man to fire towards them as they passed by. At that point several soldiers jumped in front of the car, forcing it to stop.

In his drunken condition, among other things he accused them of being deserters but was thankfully restrained by two officers who, "at the point of their pistols," remembered a relieved Hugh Fraser, "persuaded the sergeant of his error."

It was after three by the time they got back to Fort Canning. Newbiggin told Wild to take the flag to the Cathay Building and, after seeing that it was hung as directed, to hurry back so he could accompany Percival to the meeting with Yamashita.

Fortunately for the British, the 4:00 P.M. cease-fire notice in Percival's letter to Yamashita had apparently not been issued to his three division commanders. Since the Japanese had also not been made aware of it, both sides continued to fire on each other throughout the afternoon.

Of that day, artilleryman Ken Marshall with the British 18th Division remembered they had:

> fired continuously from early morning till the evening. By then our guns were beginning to feel the strain. The recoil systems were beginning to leak. They were oil filled normally, [but] we ran out of oil. They were leaking so badly we filled [them] with condensed milk. It worked well enough to go on firing....
>
> For the past five days and nights we'd had continuous artillery fire and very little sleep. We were getting heavy casualties, which wasn't helping. Most ... were from shrapnel, mortar fire and antipersonnel bombs.
>
> We wondered what was going on [in the city].... [Then] we saw the Jap flag go up over the Cathay Building. We had no thought of surrender or being prisoners. We'd been told the Japs didn't take prisoners. We went on fighting.[39]

By four-thirty the surrender party, including Percival, Wild, and Brigadier Generals Newbiggin and K.A. Torrance, who had taken Fraser's place, left Fort Canning for Bukit Timah. When they reached Adam Road, Colonel Sugita was waiting, having driven down to escort them to the Ford plant.

The last time the British commander had been up the road was on the morning on February 12. Ironically, except for the circumstances, the scene was very much the same.

There were no other cars on the road then either, a road that in peacetime was usually jammed with traffic. He remembered having looked up at planes of the unopposed Japanese air force, and saying to himself, "Why does Britain, our improvident Britain, with all her great resources, allow her sons to fight without air support?"[40]

Colonel Sugita, who had seated himself next to Percival, introduced himself and said, "We fought for 2 months. Now we're coming to the end. I compliment you on the British stand." Percival made no response.

When the two cars reached the factory, Colonel Tsugi, along with several other officers, correspondents, newsreel photographers, and a line of Japanese troops, were waiting.

Of the scene, Tsugi wrote, "The streamlined motor car in front with the Union Jack and a white flag crossing each other in the back, stopped in front of the Ford Car factory.... The British Commander, Lt. General Percival, accompanied by Brigadiers Torrance and Newbiggin, carrying the two flags, and Captain Wild, were led to the place of interview by Staff Officer Sugita. General Yamashita, who was roughly five minutes behind time, entered followed by his staff officers, exchanged handshakes, and took his seat. How did the English general feel surrendering to his enemy after defeat? The faces of the four English officers were pale and their eyes bloodshot."[41]

Possibly because of the language difficulties and Percival's concern for the safety of his troops and civilians in the city, the meeting between the two leaders was not without its tense moments.

The physical difference between the two men as they faced each other across the long table was glaringly obvious. The tall, slender Percival, his fresh uniform belying the gaunt, fatigued look on his face, in contrast to Yamashita, a short man, stocky of build, with a bulldog, no-nonsense appearing face, left little doubt as to who was the victor and who was the vanquished.

Since Percival never wrote his version of the meeting, outside of comments made by witnesses, the only published account of the 50-minute conference came from the Japanese. However, since each comment or statement had to be translated back and forth from English to Japanese and from Japanese to English by a very inept official Japanese interpreter, no single version agrees completely as to what was specifically said.

Probably the most accurate summary came from notes made by Colonel Sugita and Cyril Wild, who not only helped with the translations but remained behind after the meeting to work out the details. Of everything that transpired during the 50-minute meeting, it is agreed by most that the context of what follows is reasonably accurate.

It began, according to Tsugi, when Sugita handed Percival a list of questions. Before he had a chance to go over them, however, Yamashita interrupted, "We have just received your reply [to meet to discuss surrender terms]. "Have you any Japanese prisoners of war?"

"None at all," replied Percival.

"Have you any Japanese civilians?"

"No. They have all been sent to India."

"The Japanese Army will consider nothing but surrender."

"I fear we shall not be able to submit our final reply before 10:30 P.M.," said Percival.

Worried by his shortage of artillery ammunition and that Percival, outnumbering him three to one, might use the five hours he was requesting to give him enough time to organize a counterattack, Yamashita, banging his fist on the table, sternly said, "Reply to us only whether our terms are acceptable to you or not. Things have to be done swiftly. We're ready to resume firing. Unless you surrender, we will have to carry out our night attack as scheduled."

"Cannot the Japanese Army remain in its present position?" asked Percival. "We can resume negotiations again tomorrow at 5:30 A.M."

"What?!" said Yamashita. Gesturing toward Percival with an open hand he angrily said, "I want hostilities to cease tonight, and I want to remind you that the question is strictly a matter of this."

"We shall discontinue firing by [8:30] P.M.," responded Percival in a barely audible tone. "Had we better remain in our present positions tonight?"

Yamashita repeated that his troops should remain in their positions, then said, "I approve of the cessation of hostilities at [8:30] P.M. All British troops should disarm, save 1,000 men we shall permit to carry arms to maintain order. You have agreed to the terms but not yet made yourself clear as to whether you have agreed to unconditional surrender or not?" Percival nodded.

Yamashita at this point told Sugita, who was standing next to him, that he would not accept a nod of the head. Sugita tried to explain to Wild, sitting on Percival's left, what his commander wanted, which led to a lengthy discourse between the two men. Yamashita looked at his watch, then, pointing his finger at Sugita said, "There's no need for all this talk. It is a simple question and I want a simple answer." Turning to Percival, he growled, "If you've accepted our terms, we want to hear 'yes' or 'no' from you. Surrender or fight!"

"Yes, I agree," said Percival, then added that he had a request to make. "Will the Japanese Army protect the women and children and British civilians?"

"We shall see to it," said Yamashita.

"This evening, there will be great confusion in the city," said Percival. "If, by any chance, the Japanese Army should make a triumphal entry into the fortress, it will be impossible to guarantee that unforeseen happenings will not occur. Please wait until tomorrow morning."

"Yes. That will be so," replied Yamashita as he slid a piece of paper over to Percival. "Please sign this truce document."

It was 7:50 P.M., February 15, 1942, and it was over.[42]

No one in the British surrender party, including Percival, was given a copy of the surrender document nor a list of the terms they had agreed to. In signing, although it probably never crossed his mind at that time, Percival had not only surrendered Singapore but part of the British Empire as well—something not done since General Cornwallis surrendered to George Washington at Yorktown in 1781.

By the time Percival got back to Fort Canning it was close to 8:30 P.M. Since the sound of guns could still be heard and shells were landing in the city, the emotionally drained British commander decided to wait until the shooting stopped before notifying Wavell of the surrender.

At that same moment, Mr. Harold Miller, a newspaper reporter with the *Straits Times*, was standing on a fifth floor balcony of the Cathay Building with a British officer. Watching what he called "the pulverizing of Singapore," he said that out on their right:

> Tank Road [was] being methodically broken up by Japanese shells. It was a fascinating spectacle but for the fact that we were witnessing the last agonies of a great city. Dust and earth rose in volumes, and branches snapped from trees. Shells whined over Cathay and whistled into terrific explosions opposite us. From behind us someone asked, "Did that one get Fort Canning?" and

the officer yelled back, "Yes, but not G.H.Q.!" The clatter of AA guns heralded the reappearance of Japanese bombers.... We heard the rumble of explosions. Clouds of dust and debris flew into the air and tongues of flame leaped skyward. It was the Jap Air Force's final curtain call. Then the shelling suddenly ceased. An uncanny silence fell over Singapore.[43]

Businessman Charles Martine also remembered the silence. "It was eerie to a degree," he said. "When you'd been running helter-skelter with explosions and noise all around you, the silence was sudden and dramatic and eerie."[44]

The gunfire silenced, Percival solemnly wrote out the following message to Wavell: "Owing to our losses from enemy action, water, petrol, food, and ammunition practically finished. Unable, therefore, to continue the fight any longer. All ranks have done their best and are grateful for your help."[45]

It was the last message from Singapore.

The next day, Churchill, in a radio broadcast heard throughout the Empire, made the announcement many had anticipated. In his familiar dramatic tone, he said, "I speak to you all under the shadow of a far-reaching military defeat. It is a British and Imperial defeat. Singapore has fallen. All the Malay peninsula has been overrun. This is one of those moments when [the British Empire] can draw from the heart of misfortune the vital impulse of victory."[46]

Meanwhile, many of the men involved in his "Imperial defeat" had hopes of escaping. Some had already made plans. General Ivan Simson, as an example, on Saturday asked Percival for permission to escape so he could, as he said, "carry on the fight." Percival granted the request.

At the same time he arranged for Australian government representative V.G. Bowdon to leave with an escape party that same night. Despite having to fight their way through a large threatening gang of soldiers who were also looking for a way out, the original group of 10, which had grown to 38 by the time they shoved off, made it.

In the meantime, Simson, who was supposed to be one of the original 10 escapees, before leaving drove to Fort Canning to say goodbye to Percival. To his dismay he found the British commander had changed his mind. Without looking up from his desk, he said, "Officers should stay and look after their units."

Flabbergasted by his reasoning, Simson replied that he had no units since being assigned as acting director-general of Civil Defense a month earlier. "I have no ties of any sort to prevent me from going."

"I'm sorry, Simson," said Percival, turning back to the paperwork he had been working on when he came in.[47]

Another man who had been contemplating escape was Gordon Bennett. After the surrender was acknowledged on the afternoon of the fifteenth, he drove to his headquarters at Tanglin Barracks, a mile behind the front lines.

"On my return," he wrote in his diary later, "I called together my unit commanders and appraised them of the situation. I ordered that new clothing and boots be issued to those men who needed them ... and ample rations be issued to all. I then gave detailed instructions allocating assembly points for all units, and laid down where arms were to be dumped, etc."

He then drove to the front. "Passing through unit lines," he said, "I found the men still full of fight. The few to whom I suggested the probability of surrender took it badly. Some of these tall, manly men wept at the idea. It was a sad parting."

On the way back to headquarters, he spotted a group of Indian soldiers moving away from the front, believing apparently that it was all over. Stopping at a nearby signal unit, he phoned Fort Canning to see what was going on. "I learned that the final message had still not come through," he said, "so gave the order for my men to stand fast and to fight on until ordered to cease."

While on the phone the British officer in charge of the Indians entered the tent. Bennett asked him why his men were retiring. "He replied that General Bennett of the Australians had ordered him to do so. He was taken aback when I told him I was General Bennett and that no such order had been given. I firmly urged him to collect his men and re-establish his position."[48]

Back at Tanglin Barracks headquarters, he said he told his senior staff of his intention to escape "so that I could get back to Australia and tell the detailed story, passing on the lessons we had learned during the last few weeks." Unknown to them, however, he had no plans to confer with Percival about his decision. Although three other generals, Brigadiers Paris and Coats of the 12th and 15th Indian Brigades respectively, and Ian Stewart of the Argyll and Southerland Highlanders, made good their escapes, none received the treatment the Australian commander did.

When Bennett, who had successfully commanded the A.I.F. throughout the bitter retreat down the Malay Peninsula and against the main Japanese drive towards Singapore city, safely reached Melbourne, he said his "reception by the Australian General Staff was cold and hostile."

"After a few minutes conversation with General Sturdee, Chief of the General Staff, I was told that my escape was ill-advised and that I should have stayed with my troops until the end."

Bennett was never again asked to serve as a commander in the field. In January 1946, a Court of Inquiry, initiated by a letter from Percival to the Australian Army Board, declared that he was a soldier whose commanding officer had agreed to surrender him, and was therefore not justified in relinquishing his command and leaving Singapore.

Unlike Hong Kong, there would be no grand parade through the streets of Singapore. Yamashita, when asked by one of his staff if he was to prepare for one, the Japanese commander replied, "No. The war isn't finished. We have lost 3,300 men in the campaign. What have the survivors done to deserve it? We must first honor our dead. Then we'll prepare for future campaigns."

Despite Yamashita's reluctance, the capture of the island was celebrated in Tokyo as the greatest land victory in Japanese history. The next morning, *Asahi Shimbun*, the country's leading newspaper, headlined its story of the fall of the island: General Situation of Pacific War Decided. The accompanying story went on to say, in part, that "to seize Singapore Island in as little as eight days was only possible with our Imperial Army. Japan is the sun that shines for world peace.... Those ... who resist shall have no alternative but to go to ruin. Both the United States and Britain should contemplate the 3,000 years of scorching Japanese history."[49]

Two months later with the capture of Corregidor and the fall of the Philippines and the Dutch East Indies, at the time it looked to many like the Pacific war had been decided.

The surrender of the thousands of soldiers was perhaps the least of the problems with which the Japanese were immediately faced. Although the shooting had stopped, the city, with its civilian population of near one million, showed little change when Japanese troops entered early Monday morning. Fires were still raging. Looting was still rampant, and the situations in the hospitals were perhaps worse.

"The first thing in the city to strike the eye was the waves of men in khaki uniforms," wrote Colonel Tsugi. "Many still carried their rifles.... Groups of them were squatting on the road, smoking, talking and shouting in rather loud voices. Strangely enough, however, there was no sign of hostility in their faces. Rather an expression of resignation as shown by the losers in a sporting contest."[50]

For the Japanese, of immediate concern was getting the city's major utilities up and running. To do this, before marching the entire European population off to the Changi prison for the balance of the war, they kept key British municipal workers on the job while forcing hundreds of others to clean up the city.

As for the estimated 35,000 English, 15,000 Australian, 65,000 Indian, and 15,000 Malay soldiers, most were transported to POW camps all across what the Japanese referred to as their Southern Resources Area — Burma, Thailand, Malaya, and the Dutch East Indies. There they were herded into crude camps and forced to endure inhuman treatment, starvation, torture, and unimagined hard labor, leading to deaths by the thousands.

Of the thousands of Chinese in Singapore, the Japanese decided to initiate what they called the Yen his-shan treatment, the name meaning the murder of a few as a threat to the majority to stay in line. Although not close in number to those massacred in Nanking in 1937, when it was over, between 5,000 and 7,000 Singapore Chinese were publicly butchered by Imperial Army soldiers.[51]

Although the Japanese claimed that all of the fixed gun batteries on the island had been demolished, they captured close to 500 undamaged mortars, artillery, anti-tank and anti-aircraft guns. Percival, initially criticized for not ordering them destroyed, was later exonerated. By the time Wavell amended his order to be prepared to fight it out in the city on February 14 and because of the uncertainties of the surrender situation, it was too late.

Of the casualties of those involved in the 8-day battle, the Japanese claimed 5,092, of which 1,714 were killed. On the British side, outside of the capture of an estimated 130,000 men, because of the surrender an exact number could never be established.

In conclusion, not that it would have made any difference in the long run, Percival, in prison with Ivan Simson, one day told him that he had been wrong in his estimation of where the major Japanese attack would come. "He was the only one of all the senior [officers] to admit that his decision on defense had been wrong," wrote Simson later, and that in his opinion, "his admission went a very long way [toward atoning for] his ... error." Yamashita, on the other hand, after the war said that low on ammunition and physically exhausted, he felt that if they had to fight in the city "we would be beaten," and that his strategy in Singapore was "a bluff, a bluff that worked."

Chapter Notes

Chapter One

1. John F. Kinney, *Wake Island Pilot*; hereafter, Kinney. Duane Schultz, *Wake Island*; hereafter, Schultz *Wake*.
2. Schultz *Wake*.
3. W. Scott Cunningham, *Wake Island Command*; hereafter, Cunningham.
4. Robert Cressman, *A Magnificent Fight*; hereafter, Cressman. Duane Schultz, *Hero of Bataan*; hereafter, Schultz *Hero*.
5. Cressman. Schultz *Hero*.
6. James P. S. Devereux, *The Story of Wake Island*; hereafter, Devereux.
7. Cunningham.
8. Ibid.
9. Schultz *Wake*.
10. Ibid.
11. James B. Darden, *Guests of the Emperor*; hereafter, Darden.
12. John Toland, *But Not in Shame*; hereafter, Toland.
13. Gregory Urwin, *The Defense of Wake Island*; hereafter, Urwin.
14. Arthur A. Poindexter, *Our Last Hurrah on Wake Island*; hereafter, Poindexter.
15. Cressman.
16. Poindexter.
17. Ibid.
18. Smith, S. E., *The United States Marine Corps in World War II*; hereafter, Smith.
19. Cressman.
20. Poindexter.
21. Cressman.
22. Schultz *Wake*.
23. Interview with Robert Hanna; hereafter, Hanna.
24. Schultz *Wake*.
25. Hanna.
26. Urwin.
27. Ralph Holewiniski, paper on experiences on Wake Island, night of December 23, 1941; hereafter, Holewiniski.
28. Schultz *Wake*.
29. Darden.
30. Urwin.
31. Ibid.
32. Hanna.
33. Holewiniski.
34. Hanna.
35. Devereux.
36. Ibid. Schultz *Wake*.
37. Cunningham.
38. Schultz *Wake*.
39. Cunningham. Urwin.
40. Ibid.
41. Devereux.
42. Urwin.
43. Devereux.
44. Cunningham.
45. Urwin.
46. Devereux.
47. Ibid.
48. Kinney.
49. Devereux.
50. Kinney.
51. Devereux.
52. Cunningham.
53. Holewiniski.
54. Robert D. Heinl, *The Defense of Wake*.
55. Poindexter.
56. Devereux.
57. Cressman. Darden. Devereux.
58. Darden.
59. Devereux.
60. Ibid.
61. Cressman.

Chapter Two

1. Louis Morton, *The Fall of the Philippines*; hereafter, Morton.
2. Japanese Plans of Maneuvers in the Final Battle of Bataan.
3. Morton.
4. Bataan diary of Col. Richard C. Mallonee; hereafter, Mallonee.
5. Archille C. Tisdelle, "Diary of Major A. C. Tisdelle"; hereafter, Tisdelle.
6. W. H. Waterous, "Reminiscences of Dr. W. H. Waterous Pertinent to World War II in the Philippines"; hereafter, Waterous.
7. Jonathan M. Wainwright, *Gen. Wainwright's Story*; hereafter, Wainwright.
8. Alfred A. Weinsein, *Barbed-Wire Surgeon*; hereafter, Weinstein.
9. Juanita Redmond, *I Served on Bataan*; hereafter, Redmond.
10. William E. Chandler, "The 26th Cavalry — Battles to Glory"; hereafter, Chandler.
11. Ibid.
12. Wainwright.
13. Morton.
14. Wainwright.
15. Donald Knox, *Death March*; hereafter, Knox.
16. Chris Schaefer, *Bataan Diary*.
17. Chandler.
18. John E. Olson, *Anywhere, Anytime*.
19. Carlos P. Romulo, *I Saw the Fall of the Philippines*; hereafter, Romulo. Wainwright.
20. Redmond.
21. Dorothy Cave, *Beyond Courage*.
22. Edgar D. Whitcomb, *Escape from Corregidor*; hereafter, Whitcomb.
23. Col. Richard C. Mallonee, *Diary of 21st Field Artillery Reg., Philippine Army*.
24. Romulo.
25. Morton.
26. Romulo.
27. Ibid.
28. Weinstein.
29. Whitcomb.
30. Calvin E. Chunn, *Of Rice and Men*; hereafter, Chunn.
31. Tisdelle.
32. Cmdr. E. L. Sackett, "History of the *USS Canopus*"; hereafter, Sackett.
33. Chunn.
34. Wainwright.
35. Chunn.
36. Lt. Comdr. John Morrill, *South from Corregidor*; hereafter, Morrill.
37. Robert W. Levering, *Horror Trek*.
38. Andy Miller, *19th Air Base Squadron*.
39. Tisdelle.
40. Salvador P. Lopez,

When Bataan Fell; hereafter, Lopez.
  41. Tisdelle.
  42. Romulo.
  43. Chandler.
  44. Samuel E. Moody, *Reprieve from Hell*.
  45. Knox.
  46. Ernest B. Miller, *Bataan Uncensored*.
  47. Morton. Waterous.
  48. Waterous.
  49. Brig. Gen. W. E. Brougher, *South to Bataan*.
  50. Henry G. Lee, *Nothing but Praise*.
  51. Reynaldo Perez, "Escape."
  52. Lt. Col. Edward Dyess, *The Dyess Story*.

Chapter Three

  1. James H. Belote and William M. Belote, *Corregidor*; hereafter, Belote.
  2. Brig. Gen. George F. Moore, *General Moore's Diary*; hereafter, Moore.
  3. Interview with Robert Farner.
  4. Moore.
  5. Morton.
  6. Steve Mellnik, *Philippine Diary 1938–1945*; hereafter, Mellnik.
  7. Moore.
  8. Redmond.
  9. Wainwright.
  10. Moore.
  11. Morton.
  12. Redmond. Wainwright.
  13. Duane Messimer, *In the Hands of Fate*.
  14. Wainwright.
  15. Schultz *Hero*.
  16. Moore.
  17. Frank O. Hough, Verle E. Ludwig, Henri L. Shaw, Jr., *History of U.S. Marine Corps Operations in World War II, Vol. I*; hereafter, Hough.
  18. Moore.
  19. Schultz *Hero*.
  20. Wainwright.
  21. Belote.
  22. Hough.
  23. Ibid.
  24. Ibid.
  25. The papers of Lt. Col. E. L. Barr, Captain Paul Cornwall, Lt. Charles Kasler, memories of May 5–6, 1942.
  26. Ibid.
  27. J. Michael Miller, *From Shanghai to Corregidor*.
  28. Smith.
  29. Belote.
  30. Smith.
  31. Schultz *Hero*.
  32. Ibid. Wainwright.
  33. Belote.
  34. Morton.
  35. Hough.
  36. Morton.
  37. Ibid.
  38. J. Michael Miller, *From Shanghai*.
  39. Toland.
  40. Belote.
  41. Smith.
  42. Ibid.
  43. Belote.
  44. Eric Morris, *Corregidor*.
  45. Wainwright.
  46. Schultz *Hero*.
  47. Smith. Hough.
  48. Schultz *Hero*. Wainwright.
  49. Diary of Col. Paul D. Bunker, Seaward Defense Commander, Corregidor.
  50. Mellnik.
  51. Schultz *Hero*.
  52. Ibid.
  53. Wainwright's Papers, Vol. I and II; hereafter, Wainwright's Papers. Wainwright.
  54. Ibid.
  55. Smith.
  56. Whitcomb.
  57. Wainwright's Papers.
  58. Ibid.
  59. Joseph Harrington, *Yankee Samurai*.
  60. Belote.
  61. Mellnik.
  62. Melvin McCoy and S. M. Mellnik, *Ten Escape from Tojo*.
  63. Elizabeth Norman, *We Band of Angels*.
  64. Ibid.
  65. Hough.
  66. Toland. Wainwright.
  67. Wainwright's Papers.
  68. Ibid.
  69. Belote.
  70. Morrill.
  71. Wainwright's Papers.
  72. Ibid.
  73. Toland.

Chapter Four

  1. Winston S. Churchill, *The Grand Alliance*. Hereafter, Churchill.
  2. Ted Ferguson, *Desperate Siege*; hereafter, Ferguson. Maj. Gen. S. Woodburn Kirby, *The War Against Japan, Vol. I*; hereafter, Kirby.
  3. Ferguson.
  4. Churchill.
  5. Ferguson.
  6. Kirby.
  7. Ibid.
  8. Ferguson.
  9. Ibid.
  10. Ibid.
  11. Robert B. Edgerton, *Warriors of the Rising Sun*; hereafter, Edgerton. Ferguson.
  12. Kirby.
  13. Ibid.
  14. Ferguson
  15. Ibid.
  16. Ibid.
  17. Churchill.
  18. Edgerton. Ferguson.
  19. Edgerton.
  20. Toland.
  21. Ferguson.
  22. Churchill.

Chapter Five

  1. Noel Barber, *The Sinister Twilight*; hereafter, Barber.
  2. Kenneth Attwill, *Fortress*; hereafter, Attwill.
  3. Frank Legg, *The Gordon Bennett Story*; hereafter, Legg.
  4. Barber.
  5. Col. Masanobu Tsugi, *Japan's Greatest Victory*; hereafter, Tsugi *Japan's*.
  6. Col. Masanobu Tsugi, *Singapore: The Japanese Version*; hereafter, Tsugi *Singapore*.
  7. Barber.
  8. Tsugi *Japan's*.
  9. Tsugi *Singapore*.
  10. Legg.
  11. Attwill.
  12. Churchill.
  13. Barber.
  14. Arthur G. Donahue, *The Last Flight from Singapore*; hereafter, Donahue.
  15. Barber.
  16. Legg.
  17. Attwill.
  18. Legg.
  19. Tsugi *Japan's*.
  20. Legg.
  21. Ibid.
  22. Donahue.
  23. Toland.
  24. Ibid.
  25. Attwill.
  26. Barber
  27. Legg.
  28. Attwill. Barber.
  29. Tsugi *Singapore*.
  30. Churchill.
  31. Tsugi *Singapore*.
  32. Barber.
  33. Legg.
  34. Tsigu *Singapore*.
  35. Churchill.
  36. Legg.
  37. Tsugi *Japan's*.
  38. Ibid.
  39. Attwill.
  40. Toland.
  41. Tsigu *Singapore*.
  42. Attwill. Toland.
  43. Attwill.
  44. Ibid.
  45. Barber.
  46. Churchill.
  47. Barber.
  48. Legg.
  49. Tsugi *Singapore*.
  50. Tsugi *Japan's*.
  51. David Bergamini, *Japan's Imperial Conspiracy*.

Bibliography

Astor, Gerald. *Crisis in the Pacific.* New York: Dell, 1996.

Attwill, Kenneth. *Fortress: The Story of the Siege and Fall of Singapore.* New York: Doubleday, 1960.

Barber, Noel. *The Sinister Twilight.* Boston: Houghton Mifflin, 1968.

Belote, James H., and William M. Belote. *Corregidor: The Saga of a Fortress.* New York: Harper and Row, 1967.

Bergamini, David. *Japan's Imperial Conspiracy.* New York: Morrow, 1971.

Blair, Clay J. *Silent Victory.* New York: Lippincott, 1975.

Brougher, Brig. Gen. W.E. *South to Bataan, North to Mukden.* Athens: University of Georgia Press, 1971.

Brown, Cecil. *Suez to Singapore.* New York: Random House, 1942.

Caffrey, Kate. *Out in the Midday Sun: Singapore 1941–1945.* New York: Stein & Day, 1973.

Churchill, Winston S. *The Grand Alliance.* Houghton Mifflin, 1950.

———. *The Hinge of Fate.* Boston: Houghton Mifflin, 1950.

Cohen, Stan. *Enemy on Island. Issue in Doubt: The Capture of Wake Island, December 1941.* Missoula, MT: Pictorial Histories, 1983.

Collier, Basil. *The War in the Far East.* New York: Morrow, 1969.

Cressman, Robert. *A Magnificent Fight.* Annapolis: Naval Institute Press, 1995.

Cunningham, W. Scott, with Lydel Sims. *Wake Island Command.* Boston: Little, Brown, 1961.

Darden, James B. III. *Guests of the Emperor: The Story of Dick Darden.* Clinton, NC: Greenhouse Press, 1990.

Devereux, James P. S. *The Story of Wake Island.* New York: Lippincott, 1947.

Donahue, Arthur G. *The Last Flight from Singapore.* New York: Macmillan, 1952.

Dyess, Lt. Col. William E. *The Dyess Story.* New York: Putnam, 1944.

Edgerton, Robert G. *Warriors of the Rising Sun.* New York: Norton, 1997.

Falk, Stanley L. *Seventy Days to Singapore.* New York: Putnam & Sons, 1975.

Ferguson, Ted. *Desperate Siege: The Battle for Hong Kong.* New York: Doubleday, 1980.

Greenfell, Russell, Capt. *Main Fleet to Singapore.* New York: Macmillan, 1952.

Harrington, Joseph D. *Yankee Samurai.* Detroit: Pettigrew Enterprises, 1979.

Heinl, Robert D. *The Defense of Wake.* Washington, DC: U.S. Government Printing Office, 1946.

Hough, Frank O., Verle E. Ludwig, and Henri L. Shaw Jr. *History of U.S. Marine Corps Operations in World War II.* Vol. 1. Washington, DC: U.S. Government Printing Office, 1958.

Hoyt, Edwin P. *Japan's War.* New York: McGraw-Hill, 1986.

Karig, Cmdr. Walter, and Lt. Welbourn Kelley. *Battle Report: Pearl Harbor to the Coral Sea.* New York: Farrar and Rinehart, 1944.

Kinney, John F., and James M. McCraffrey. *Wake Island Pilot: A World War II Memoir.* Washington, DC: Brassey's, 1995.

Kirby, Maj. Gen. S. Woodburn. *The War Against Japan.* Vol. 1. *The Loss of Singapore.* London: Her Majesty's Stationery Office, 1957.

Knox, Donald. *Death March: The Survivors of Bataan.* New York: Harvest Books, 1981.

Leasor, James. *Singapore: The Battle That Changed the World.* New York: Doubleday, 1968.

Lee, Henry G. *Nothing But Praise.* Hollywood, CA: Murray and Gee, 1948.

Leek, Jerome. B. *Corregidor G.I.* Culver City, CA: Highland Press, 1948.

Legg, Frank. *The Gordon Bennett Story.* Sydney: Angus & Robertson, 1965.

Levering, Robert W. *Horror Trek.* Dayton, OH: Horstman Printing, 1948.

McCoy, Melvin, and S.M. Mellnik. *Ten Escape from Tojo.* New York: Farrar & Reinhart, 1944.

Mellnik, Steve. *Philippine Diary, 1939–1945.* New York: Van Nostrand Reinhold, 1969.

Messimer, Dwight R. *In the Hands of Fate: The Story of Patrol Wing Ten.* Annapolis: Naval Institute Press, 1985.

Miller, Ernest B. *Bataan Uncensored.* Long Prairie, MN: Hart Publications, 1949.

Miller, J. Michael. *From Shanghai to Corregidor:*

Marines in the Defense of the Philippines. Washington, DC: Marine Corps Historical Center, 1997.

Moody, Samuel E. *Reprieve from Hell.* New York: Pageant Press, 1961.

Morrill, Lt. Cmdr. John, and Pete Martin. *South from Corregidor.* New York: Simon and Schuster, 1943.

Morton, Louis. *The Fall of the Philippines.* Washington, DC: U.S. Army, 1953.

Norman, Elizabeth M. *We Band of Angels.* New York: Random House, 1999.

Olson, John E. *Anywhere, Anytime: History of the Fifty-Seventh Infantry (PS).* San Antonio, TX: Olson, 1982.

Peña, Col. Ambrosio P. *Bataan's Own.* Manila: Munoz Press, 1967.

_____. *The Story of the First Regular Division.* Manila: Bureau of Printing, 1953.

Redmond, Juanita. *I Served on Bataan.* Philadelphia: Lippincott, 1943.

Romulo, Carlos P. *I Saw the Fall of the Philippines.* New York: Doubleday, Doran, 1942.

Schaefer, Chris. *Bataan Diary: An American Family in World War II, 1941–1945.* Houston: Riverview Publishing, 2004.

Schultz, Duane. *Hero of Bataan: The Story of General Jonathan M. Wainwright.* New York: St. Martin's Press, 1981.

_____. *Wake Island: The Heroic, Gallant Fight.* New York: St. Martin's Press, 1978.

Smith, S. E. *The United States Marine Corps in World War II.* New York: Random House, 1969.

Toland, John. *But Not in Shame.* New York: Random House, 1961.

_____. *The Rising Sun.* New York: Random House, 1970.

Tsugi, Masanobu, Col. *Japan's Greatest Victory, Britain's Worst Defeat: The Capture of Singapore, 1942.* Stroud, Glos., UK: Spellmount, 2007.

_____. *Singapore: The Japanese Version.* New York: St. Martin's Press, 1960.

Tuchman, Barbara W. *Stilwell and the American Experience in China.* New York: Macmillan, 1970.

Urwin, Gregory John. *The Defense of Wake Island: Their Two Wars, 1941–1945.* Ann Arbor, MI: University Microfilms International, 1983.

Wainwright, Gen. Jonathan M. *General Wainwright's Story.* New York: Doubleday, 1946.

Weinstein, Alfred A. *Barbed-Wire Surgeon.* New York: Macmillan, 1948.

Whitcomb, Edgar D. *Escape From Corregidor.* Chicago: Henry Regnery, 1958.

Willmott, H. P. *Empires in the Balance.* Annapolis: Naval Institute Press, 1982.

Winslow, W. G. *The Fleet the Gods Forgot.* Annapolis: Naval Institute Press, 1982.

Articles

Chandler, William E. "The 26th Cavalry: Battles to Glory." *Armored Cavalry Journal,* March–August 1947.

Lopez, Salvador P. "When Bataan Fell." *Voice of the Veteran,* memorial edition, 1971, 2–4.

Miller, Andy. "19th Air Base Squadron." Newsletter No. 20, 1987.

Perez, Reynaldo. "Escape." *The Voice of the Veteran,* memorial edition, 1971, 13–17.

Poindexter, Arthur A. "Our Last Hurrah on Wake Island." *American History Illustrated,* January–February, 1992, 64–67, 73–74.

Tisdelle, Maj. Achille C. "Diary of Major A.C. Tisdelle." *Military Affairs,* Summer 1947, 135–146.

Unpublished Sources

Papers

The Papers of Lt. Col. E. L. Barr, Captain Paul Cornwall, and Lt. Charles Kasler, written in prison camp of their memories of May 5–6, 1942. Copy loaned by Al McGrew.

Holewinski, Ralph. Paper on experiences on Wake Island, night of December 23, 1941. Original loaned by John Hanna.

"Japanese Plan of Maneuver in Final Battle of Bataan." Military History Branch, Armed Forces of the Philippines, 1953.

Sackett, Cmdr. E. L. "History of the *USS Canopus.*" U.S. Naval Institute Proceedings, January 1943.

Wainwright's Papers, Vols. 1 and 2. Quezon City, Philippines: New Day, 1980.

Waterous, Dr. W. H. "Reminiscences of Dr. W. H. Waterous Pertinent to World War II in the Philippines." 1953.

Diaries

Diary of Col. Paul D. Bunker, Seaward Defense commander, Corregidor.

Bataan Diary of Col. Richard C. Mallonee, senior instructor of the Philippine Army's 21st Field Artillery Regiment.

Diary of Brig. Gen. George F. Moore. Quezon City, Philippines: New Day, 1980.

Interviews

Robert Hanna

Robert Farner

Index

ABDA 146, 161
Aberdeen 131, 136, 139
Abraham, Sgt. Abie 85
Adam Road 167, 169
Agricultural Experimental Farm Station 70, 74
AIP (Australian Imperial Forces) 174
Alangan River 65, 57, 59, 61, 63, 69, 78
Alexandra Barracks Hospital 162
Alhambra Theater 159
Anders, Capt. Franklin 60
Appomattox 75
Asahi Shimbun (newspaper) 173
Associated Press 158
Astoria, USS 28
Atwill, Kenneth 150
Australian Army Board 173

Bagac-Orion Line 47
Balang-Mati Island 158
Bandoeng, Java 160
Barnes, Boatswain Mate James 15, 16
Barnes, Pvt. Silas 99
Barnick, Lt. Roland 64, 65, 76
Barninger, Lt. Clarence 21, 26, 30, 31, 32, 42
Barratt, Chaplain James 143
Bataan Death March 86
Bataan Field 62, 63, 64
Bataan, Mt. 77, 83, 85
Battery A 3, 8, 21, 26, 42
Battery B 4, 29, 109
Battery Cheney 91, 95, 96
Battery Connaught 158
Battery Craighill 92, 96, 100, 125
Battery Crockett 109
Battery Crofton 96
Battery D 21, 25, 27, 29
Battery Denver 100, 103, 105, 108, 109, 111, 117
Battery E 21, 26, 29, 30, 31, 32
Battery Erie 91
Battery Geary 87, 93
Battery Globe 197
Battery Gulick 106, 107
Battery Hearn 60, 66
Battery Idaho 100
Battery James 90
Battery Johore 157
Battery L 3, 8, 9, 10, 11, 12

Battery Marshall 103, 109, 110
Battery Maxwell-Keys 103, 109, 110, 119
Battery Monja 96
Battery Morrison 90
Battery Rose 96
Battery Smith 65
Battery Stockade 106
Battery Way 91, 92, 93, 94, 96, 100, 101, 106, 107, 111
Battery Wheeler 93, 113
Battery Wilson 96, 126
Bedell Sgt. Henry 9
Beebe, Maj. Gen. Lewis 46, 47, 65, 67, 68, 74, 93, 94, 98, 99, 112, 113, 114, 118, 123, 124
Beecher, Lt. Col. Curtis 97, 103, 104
Bennett, Maj. Gen. Gordon 147, 148, 149, 150, 151, 152, 153, 154, 155, 157, 158, 159, 160, 161, 162, 164, 164, 166, 172, 173
Bennett, Jack 164
Benny, Jack 48
Berih River 147
Berry, Col. Kearie 82
Bess, Maj. Clarence 52, 54
Biggs, Lt. Col. Lloyd 103
Black, Dr. George 141, 142
Blandy, Sgt. John 20
Blanning, Maj. Don 77
Bluemel, Brig. Gen. Clifford 52, 53, 54, 56, 57, 58, 59, 60, 62, 67, 77, 78
Boeden, V.G. 172
Boelens, Sgt. Leo 64, 76
Borth, Gunner Harold 29
Bottomside 88, 91, 96, 124
Bowen Road Hospital 134
Boxer, Maj. Charles 130, 131, 133
Boxing Day 143
Brady, Sgt. Dewey 101
Brewster Buffalo (fighter) 5, 154
Bromeyer, Capt. James 116
Brooke-Popham, Sir Robert 129
Brougher, Brig. Gen. William 82, 83
Brown, Capt. Ben 63, 64
Brown, Maj. Robt. 117
Brown, Cpl. Robert 8, 28, 29, 32
Browne, Col. Harrison 50
Bryan, PFC Pershing 18
Bryan, Robert 21, 35

Buehler, PFC William 9
Bukit Panjang Village 145, 149, 155
Bukit Timah Road 167, 168, 169
Bukit Timah Village 145, 148, 151, 153, 154, 155, 156, 157, 160, 161, 165, 166, 169
Bunker, Col. Paul 60, 69, 113
Burma 174
Butler, Mt. 135, 136

Caballo Isl. 87, 125, 126
Cabcaben 48
Cabcaben Field 61, 64, 65
Cadillac 74, 119, 123
Callahan 115
Cambridge 131
Cameron Mt. 137, 138, 139
Camp 1 6, 15, 16, 17, 21, 30, 36, 37, 38, 40
Camp 2 3, 42
Canopus, USS 68, 198
Cape D'Agular 135
Carabao Isl. 87
Carrol, Sgt. Hubert 124
Castillo, Silvertre 118
Castillo House 122
Castle, Capt. Noel 97, 103
Cathay Bldg. 160, 169, 171
Cathay Theater 159
Catlow, Sgt. Lloyd 119
Cavalry Pt. 94, 95, 98, 99, 118
Cavite 88, 97
Cebu Isl. 63, 64
Cemetery Ridge 65, 72
Chambers, Capt. Robt. 104
Chandler, Maj. William 54, 58, 59, 70
Changi Prison 174
Cheney Ravine 88
Chinatown (Singapore) 164
Chinese Army 113
Chris-Craft 134
Christmas Day 136, 141
Chronister, Lt. Mason 136, 141
Chunn, Capt. Calvin 109
Churchill, Prime Minister Winston 129, 132, 138, 144, 153
CINPAC 5, 6, 8, 27, 30
Cisneros, Pvt. 102
Clark, Capt. Goland 104, 114, 117
Coats, Brig. Gen. 173
Coghlan, Pvt. William 116

Coleman, Lt. Willam 64, 76
Collier, Col. James 55, 62, 63, 74, 75, 76, 77
Collinson, A.C. 141
Conrad, Maj. Eugene 50, 55, 54
Cornwall, Capt. Paul 101, 102
Cornwallis 170
Coulson, Cpl. John 12, 38
Cox, Sgt. Robert 32
Cricket Club 159
Crosby, Bing 132
Crosland, Lt. "Shorty" 64, 76
Cruz, Pvt. T.J. 141, 142
Cummings, Chaplain William 52, 53, 54
Cunningham, Cmdr. W. Scott 3, 5, 6, 8, 9, 27, 28, 30, 31, 32, 34, 40, 42
Curtis, Lt. Col. Donald 112

Dahlness, Capt. Harold 108, 111
Davidson, Lt. Carl 5, 18
Davison, Maude 92, 94, 122
Deede, Lt. Leroy 92, 93
Defense Council 141
Dempsey, Lt. James 94
Des Voeux, Road 144
Devereux, Maj. James 3, 6, 7, 8, 9, 11, 15, 17, 181, 20, 21, 22, 25, 26, 27, 28, 29, 30, 31, 32, 33, 34, 35, 36, 37, 38, 39, 40, 41, 42
Devil's Peak 133
de Voeux, Edward 134
Dickenson, A.E. 166
Donahue, Flt. Lt. Arthur 154, 159
Donaldson, Lt. Jack 63
Dooley, Capt. Tom 50, 51, 117, 118, 119, 123
Doyle, Col. John 59
Drake, Brig. Gen. Charles 51, 120121
Duckworth, Col. James 79, 80
Dudley, Sgt. William 99
Dutch East Indies 154, 173, 174
Dyess, Capt. Edward 63, 64, 85, 86

East Brigade 135, 143
East Road 57, 59, 60, 61, 62, 65, 66, 70, 77, 118
Edison, Lt. Col. Dwight 113
803rd Aviation Engineers 56, 97, 00, 100, 109
18th Division (British) 147, 149, 151, 153, 154, 158, 160, 162, 166, 169
18th Division (Imperial Japanese Army) 155, 162, 165, 166
8th Division (Australian) 147, 154
Eisenhower, Lt. Col. Dwight 106
11th Division (Philippine Army) 55, 82, 83
El Fraile Isl. 87
Elrod, Capt. Hank 4, 22, 24, 33, 35, 42
Engle, Lt. Dorothy 76

F4F (Grumman fighter) 3
Farner, Pvt. Robert 88

Felix, Maj. Pedro 85
Ferguson, QM Clerk Frank 104, 105, 1109
Ferrell, Sgt. Harold 103, 105
5th Division (Imperial Japanese Army) 149, 155, 166
55th Regiment (Imperial Japanese Army) 162
59th Coast Artillery Regiment 109
57th Inf. Reg. (Philippine Scouts) 50, 54, 56, 57, 58, 59, 60, 80
515th AA Battalion 59, 61, 63, 77
5/7 Rajputs 129
1st Defense Battalion 3
1st Division (Philippine Army) 82, 84
1st Infantry Regiment (Philippine Army) 82, 84
1st Malay Brigade 162, 163
1st Middlesex Battalion 129, 131
Fisher Cpl. Cyrus 17
Fisher, Maj. Henry 52
Fletcher, Adm. Frank Jack 5, 6, 28
Ford Factory 169, 170
Fort Canning (Malaya Command Headquarters) 154, 158, 160, 161, 166, 169, 171, 172, 173
Fort Changi 146, 147
Fort Drum 87, 96, 97, 106, 107, 125, 126
Fort Frank 87, 96, 125
Fort Hughes 87, 92, 97, 100, 117, 125, 126
Fort Mills 87
Fort Stanley 136, 138, 139, 140, 141, 143
Fortress HQ Hong Kong (Battle Box) 131, 132, 134, 135, 136, 137, 138, 140, 141, 143
Fortress Singapore 145, 158
45h Inf. Reg. (Philippine Scouts) 50, 52, 59, 62, 81, 82
41st Division (Philippine Army) 83
44th Indian Brigade 141, 155
Foster, Col Val 125, 126
14th Army (Imperial Japanese Army) 74, 107, 113
14th Naval District 27
4th Division (Imperial Japanese Army) 97
4th Marine Defense Battalion 108, 114
4th Marine Regiment 95
4th Philippine Constabulary Regiment 57
Franklin, Cpl. Edwin 99
Fraser, Colonial Secretary Hugh 167, 169
Fremantle (Australia) 94
Fueler, Lt. Herbert 4
Fuller, Chief Burt 93
Funk, Brig. Gen. Arnold 54, 55, 60, 76

Ganahl, Capt. Joseph 59, 60
Garrity, Lt. Tom 45
Gator, Cpl. Hubert 61, 78

Gay, Paul 21, 25, 35, 36
Geneva Convention 75
Gibbons, Fred 35
Gibbons, George 35
Gillespie, Col. James 80, 81
Godbold, Capt. Bryghte (Dan) 25
Gough, Mt. 139
Government Ravine 95, 104
Gragg, Sgt. Raymond 26, 31
Grant, Cary 159
Grant, Ulysses 75
Graves, Cpl. Leon 25, 26, 27, 29
Greeley, Lt. Robt. 29
Grumman J2F (Duck) 63, 64, 65, 76
Gulick, Capt. John 91, 96, 106, 107
Gun No. 10 12
Guyton, Capt. Benson 101

H-Station (Harbor Defense Command Post) 97, 98, 113, 114, 120, 121
Haba, Col. Hikaro 129
Halstead, Cpl. William (Whitey) 13, 14
Hammas, Gunner John 8, 31, 41, 42
Hanna, Lt. Robert 21, 22, 23, 24, 25, 35, 40, 42
Happy Valley 137, 138
Happy Valley Racetrack 137, 140
Harris, Lt. 111
Haskin, Sgt. John 105
Hassig, Sgt. Edwin 10, 41
Hauck, Sgt. Edwin 109, 116
Hawaii 5, 28
Hayate (Imperial Japanese Navy destroyer) 3
Haynes, Gunnery Sgt. Tex 99
Head, John 126
Heath, Gen. Lewis 153, 158, 161, 167
Heath, Cpl. Norman 134
Hewlett, Frank 48
Hoeffel, Ensign Kenneth 114
Hogaboom, Lt. William 104, 105, 111
Holewinski, Cpl. Ralph 21, 22, 23, 25, 35, 36
Holland Village 158
Homma, Gen. Masaharu 47, 48, 66, 74, 107, 113, 114, 117, 118, 119, 122, 123, 124, 125, 127, 128
Hong Kong 47, 92, 129, 130, 131, 132, 133, 134, 136, 140, 141, 142, 144, 173
Honolulu 114, 115
Hook, Lt. Willa 53
Hooker Pt. 98
Hornos Point 94
Hospital No. 1 49, 52, 61, 62, 66, 68, 79, 80, 81
Hospital No. 2 53, 58, 61, 66, 70, 76, 80, 81
Howard, Col. Samuel 95, 96, 97, 98, 104, 106, 108, 109, 112
Hurricane (fighter) 154
Hurt, Maj. Marshall 66, 67, 68, 69, 70, 74, 75, 76, 77, 78

Index

Imperial Guards Division (Imperial Japanese Army) 152, 153
Imperial Japanese Army 125, 127, 145
Ind, Capt. Allison 48
Indo-China 47
Infantry Point 95, 99
Irwin Col. Constant 59
Irwin, Col. John 57, 61
Isidoro, Lt. Francisco 74
Ito, Staff Officer 149
Ito Battalion 165

Jalandoni, Col. Rafael 58
James, Lt. David 164
James Ravine 91, 94, 95, 96, 97, 113
Jardine's Lookout 137
Java 146, 153, 160, 161
Jenkins, Lt. Robt. 91, 95
Johnson, Lt. Col. Howard 60
Johnson, Cpl. John 12, 14
Johnson, Cpl. Joseph 99
Jones, Brig. Gen. Albert 46, 48, 55, 62, 67, 68, 81, 83
Jurong Line 151, 152, 153, 154, 155
Jurong River 151
Jurong Road 155, 156

Kahn, Dr. Mason 32, 33, 41
Kajioka, Adm. Sadamichi 42
Kalakika, Lt. Col. Theodore 120, 121
Kalang Field 154
Kawai, Capt. 143
Keator, Lt. Randy 63
Keene, Cmdr. Campbell 31, 40
Kessler, Lt. Woodrow 8, 15, 29, 30, 31, 32
Key, Brig. Gen. B.W. 161
KGEI 48
Kimmel. Adm. Husband 56
Kindley Field 88, 89, 97, 100, 110, 114, 116, 117
King, Capt. Ben 126
King, Maj. Gen. Edward P. 47, 49, 50, 54, 55, 56, 59, 60, 61, 62, 63, 66, 67, 68, 69, 70, 73, 74, 75, 76, 77, 86
King, Lt. William 64
Kinney, Lt. John 5, 33, 34, 42
Kirkpatrick, Col. Lewis 126
Kliewer, Lt. David 20, 21, 22, 23, 30, 36
Kobayashi, Col. 152, 153
Kopacz, Cpl. Joseph 103
Kowloon 130, 132, 133
Kranji River 147, 151, 152
Kranji-Woodlands Line 151, 154, 155
Kranji-Woodlands Road 147, 151, 151
Kuku Point 6, 8, 10, 12
Kuliniski, Sgt. Walter 111, 112
KZRH (radio) 50, 127

Lamao Barrio 67, 69, 74, 77, 78, 98
Lamao River 60, 63, 67, 68, 69, 70, 77

Lanao, Lake 93
Lawrence, Lt. Ray 98, 99, 100, 119
Lawrence, Maj. William 118, 123
Lawson, Col. John K. 129, 131, 135
Lay, Brig. Gen. W.O. 153
Lee, Lt. Henry G. 48, 83
Lee, Gen. Robert E. 75
Leek, Sgt. Jerome 65
Lehtola, Eric 21, 25, 35
Leighton Hill 136, 137, 139, 140
Levering, Cpl. Robt. 65, 72
Lewis, Pvt. 163
Lewis, Lt. Wally 26, 31, 32
Limay barrio 60, 83
Little Baguio 49, 63, 65, 67, 68, 70, 74, 76, 78, 80, 81
Lloyd, Ensign James 108
Lohman, PFC Ben 116
London 141, 145, 158, 163
London Daily News (newspaper) 133
London Times (newspaper) 133
Lopez, Maj. Salvador 74
Lough, Brig. Gen. Max 83
Loyd, Col. Frank 58
Lund, Capt. "Ozzie" 63
Luzon, USS 92, 126
Ly Mun Fort 131, 132, 134
Ly Mun Passage 132, 134
Ly Mun Peninsula 134
Lynn, Vera 132

MacArthur, Gen. Douglas 43, 45, 46, 55, 59, 60, 61, 62, 63, 66, 70, 86
MacRitchie Reservoir 163
Malaya 47, 93, 94, 115, 122, 127, 128, 145, 147, 149, 153, 157, 159, 161, 162, 165, 174
Malinta Hill 88, 89, 90, 118, 121, 124
Malinta Tunnel 45, 61, 68, 73, 76, 88, 89, 90, 91, 95, 98, 100, 101, 102, 103, 104, 108, 109, 111, 113, 114, 116, 117, 118, 119, 120, 121, 122, 124, 125, 127
Malleck, Sgt. Donald 32, 33, 34, 35, 37, 38
Mallon, Pv. Ernie 73
Mallonee, Col. Richard 45, 49, 61
Maltby, Gen. C.M. 129, 130, 131, 132, 133, 134, 135, 136, 137, 138, 139, 140, 141, 143
Mamala River 54, 55, 56, 57, 63
Mandi Village 154, 155
Manila Bay 43, 73, 87, 115, 117, 122, 124, 127
Manners, Maj. Charles 140
Manning, Lt. Alan 97, 114
Marine Fighter Squadron 211 (VMF 211) 3
Mariveles 45, 47, 49, 59, 61, 62, 63, 65, 66, 70, 72, 76, 78, 81, 82
Mariveles Field 73, 85, 86
Mariveles Harbor 68
Mariveles Mountain 57
Marshall, Gen. George C. 46, 55, 66, 93, 196, 115, 128
Marshall, Ken 169

Marshall Islands 6
Martine, Charles 172
Massello, Capt. Bill 91, 92, 101, 107, 111, 112
Maxwell, Brig. Gen D.S. 152, 153
McAllister, Lt. John 8, 9, 10, 11, 12, 13, 14, 38, 39, 40
McAnally, Cpl. Winford 26, 27, 29
McCoy, Cmdr. Melvin 115, 121, 122
McDaniel, Lt. Larry 64
McDaniel, Yates 158, 159, 160
McHewan, Cpl. 163
McKinstry, Gunner Clarence 9, 10, 12, 13, 14, 15, 38, 39, 40
Mead, Maj. Everett 50
Mealor, Capt. Gladys 94
Medal of Honor 24, 35, 99, 128, 135
Melbourne 73
Mellnick, Maj. Steven 89, 114, 121, 122
Mercantile Bank 164
Mercurio, Sgt. John 99
Middleside 88, 116
Miller, Pvt. Andy 53
Miller, Col. Ernest B. 45, 50, 52, 79
Miller, Capt. Fred 112
Miller, Harold 171
Mindanao, USS 93
Mindanao Island 45, 60, 92, 93, 94, 122, 124, 126, 127
Minneapolis, USS 5
Mitchell (patrol boat) 76
Mobile Battery 97, 99, 100, 104, 110
Mobile Reserve 15, 17, 18, 36
Monkey Point 100, 116
Moody, Sgt. Sam 78
Moore, Maj. Gen. George F. 46, 59, 87, 88, 90, 91, 92, 93, 94, 96, 97, 98, 106, 107, 109, 112, 113, 114, 117, 119, 120, 121, 125
Moore, Capt. Joe 64
Morrill, Lt. Cmdr. John 72, 125, 126
Morrison Hill 88, 90, 124
Moses, Maj. Charles 155, 156

NAFI Canteen 76
Nagano, Maj. Kameichiro 70, 74
Nakamura, Lt. 122, 123, 127
Nakayama, Col. Motoo 74, 75, 114, 117, 118, 123, 124, 125
Nanking, Rape of 120, 174
Nara, Lt. Gen Akira 83, 84
Navy Tunnel 89, 112, 117, 121
Neches, USS 5
Nelson, Capt. 61
Nesbit, Jose 92
New Channel 10
New Territories 129, 130, 133, 136
Newbiggin, Brig. Gen. A.G. 167, 168, 169, 170
Nicholson, Mt. 135, 136, 137
Niimi, Adm. Masaichi 133, 144
Nimitz, Adm. Chester 6

Index

91st Coast Artillery Reg. (Philippine Scouts) 91, 97, 99
92nd Coast Artillery Reg. (Philippine Scouts) 97, 103
North Africa 147
North Channel 49, 61, 73, 97, 98, 107, 122
North Dakota 76
North Dock 68, 76, 91, 118
North Point 91, 94, 97, 98, 100, 106, 107, 125, 130, 131, 133, 134, 136, 137, 140
North Shore 91, 97, 100, 103, 105, 107, 111, 114, 124
North Shore (Hong Kong) 133, 136, 140
North Shore Road 102
Nowlin, PFC Jesse 32

Oahu, USS 92
Olongapo 62
194th Tank Battalion 45, 50, 51, 78
Operation Matador 145
Ordnance Point 102
Orion, Mt. 51
Osborn, Sgt. Maj John 135
Otter, Lt. Bethel 108

P-35 (fighter) 63, 64
P-40 (fighter) 43, 63, 64
Pacific Fleet 5
Pan-Am Hotel 29
Panay Isl. 65, 76
Pandan-Holland Road 158
Pantigan River 55, 82, 84, 85
Parade Ground 113
Paris, Brig. Gen. 173
Parker, Brig. Gen. Richard 50, 54, 57, 60, 83
Parker, Mt. 134, 136
Parkinson, Capt. 163
Patrol Craft 32 35
Patrol Craft 33 20, 21
Patterson, Maj. 134
Peacock Point 3, 6, 18, 21, 26, 31, 32, 42
Peacock Triangle 26
Peakites 131
Peale Island 4, 8, 15, 21, 25, 27, 29, 30, 31, 38, 41
Pearce, Thomas 134
Pearl Harbor 5, 6, 8, 27, 28, 130
Pena, Lt. Ambrosio 51
Percival, Lt. Gen. Arthur 146, 147, 148, 149, 151, 153, 154, 157, 158, 161, 162, 163, 164, 166, 167, 168, 169 170, 171, 172, 173, 174
Perez, Lt. Reynaldo 83, 84, 85
Perkins, Lt. Robert 102, 103
Philadelphia Story (movie) 159
Philippine Army 43, 49, 50, 51, 57, 73, 74, 82, 83, 85, 90, 96, 97, 104
Philippine Division 43, 48, 50, 51, 59, 81, 83
Philippine Scouts 43, 44, 57, 83, 96, 97, 98, 116, 119
Pickett, Pvt. "Hezzie" 26
Pickup, Capt. Lewis 97, 103, 104

Pilar-Bagac Road 84
Plan Pontiac 112, 116
Platt, Capt. Wesley 7, 8, 9, 11, 12, 13, 14, 22, 28, 39, 40
Poindexter, Lt. Arthur 15, 16, 17, 18, 22, 36, 37, 38, 39, 40
Pollock, Lt. Tom 92, 93
Potter, Maj. George 25, 26, 27, 29, 30, 31, 32
Prison Road 140, 141
Prohibition 143
Provincial Air Corps Regiment 57, 78, 78
Provisional Tank Group 44
Pugh, Lt. Col. Johnny 94, 106, 117, 118, 123, 124, 125
Pulford, Air Vice Marshall C.W.H. 160, 161
Pulu Ubin Island 151
Putnam, Maj. Paul 4, 18, 20, 22, 23, 24, 25, 35, 40
Pye, Vice Adm. William 6, 27, 28

Quail, USS 126
Quarantine Dock 47, 62, 68, 76
Quarantine Station 47, 70
Queen Victoria 144
Queen Victoria Street 144
Quezon, Pres. Manuel 61
Quinlen, Capt. Clifton 79

Radio Intercept Tunnel 100, 116
Raffles Hotel 159
Ramsey Ravine 95
Rasor, PFC James 17
Ray, PFC Sanford 10, 11, 12
Read, Forest 13
Red Cross 50, 53, 79, 80, 141, 162, 163
Redmond, Lt. Juanita 53, 61, 62, 90, 92, 93
Reed, Cpl. Alvey 12
Reformatory Road 155, 157
Repulse Bay 131, 136, 137
Repulse Bay Hotel 139, 140, 141
Reyes, Lt. Norman 74, 76
RJ (road junction) 21 103
RJ (road junction) 43 100
Robb, Lt. Stewart 64, 76
Robinson's Department Store 159
Rogers, Lt. 163
Roi-Namur Island 6
Romulo, Col. Carlos 60, 61, 62, 64, 65, 66, 76
Roosevelt, Pres. Franklin D. 45, 46, 106, 115
Rose, Col.l H.B. 136, 137
Royal Air Force (RAF) 136, 137, 154
Royal Engineers 147, 164
Royal Navy 137, 146
Royal Navy Base 146
Royal Rifles 129, 131, 137, 138, 139
Rush, Sgt. Davis 17, 18
Rutledge, Raymond 16

Saalman, St. Otis 108, 110
Sackett, Cmdr. Earl 68
Sai Wan Hill 134

St. Andrews Cathedral 164
St. Stevens College 139, 141
Sakai, Lt. Gen. Takashi 133, 144
Sakakida, Sgt. Richard 113, 118
Salt Lake City 124
Samat, Mt. 48, 15, 51
San Francisco 48
San Francisco, USS 5, 34
San Jose barrio 89, 124
Santo Tomas University 93
San Vicente River 51
San Vicente River Line 51
Saratoga, USS 28, 56
Sato, Col. Gempachi 98, 99, 100, 103, 107, 109, 110, 113, 116, 124, 125
Schultz, John 13
Schultz, Maj. Paul 78
Schwartz, Col. Jack 80, 81
II Corps 48, 50, 51, 54, 55, 56, 57, 58, 59, 60, 62, 63, 67, 70, 77, 78, 81, 118
2nd Engineer Battalion (Philippine Army) 58
2nd Royal Scott 129, 131
Sekeguchi, Maj. Hisashi 80
7th Tank Regiment (Imperial Japanese Army) 97
71st Division 85
Shanghai 92
Shanghai Marines 116
Sharp, Brig. Gen. William F. 122, 123, 124, 127, 128
Shields, Andrew 140
Signal Hill 77, 83
Simson, Brig. Gen. Ivan 147, 149, 160, 161, 166, 172, 174
Singapopre City 153, 160, 164, 169, 173
Singapore General Hospital 164
Singapore Island 129, 144, 145, 147, 153, 154, 157, 158, 159, 160 161, 162, 163, 165, 166, 169, 171, 172, 173, 174
Singapore River 164
65th Brigade (Imperial Japanese Army) 82, 83, 84
61st Infantry Regiment (Imperial Japanese Army) 97
67th Infantry Regiment (Imperial Japanese Army) 53
Skelton, Pvt. Sidney 142
Sloman, PFC Wiley 14, 40
Smiley, Capt. 103
Smith, "Chuck" 13
Snellings, QM Clerk Herman 105
Sorenson, John P. 23, 24
Soryu (Imperial Japanese Navy aircraft carrier) 29
South China Morning Post (newspaper) 141
South Dock 73, 118
South Shore 97, 100
South Shore Road 103, 116, 117
Southerland Highlanders 173
Southern Resources Area 174
Spearfish, USS 94
Special Naval Landing Forces (SNLF) 11, 24

Index

Spielman, PFC Robert 122
Stanley Mound 139
Stanley Peninsula 131135, 141, 143
Stanley Prison 139
Stanley Village 139
Stevens, PFC Robert 38
Stevens Road 169
Steward, Cpl. Alvin 107
Steward, Evan 137
Stewart, Brig. Gen. Ian 173
Stewart, Lt. Col. Leslie 140, 141
Stoker, Sgt. Bill 143
Stokes Mortar 43, 105
Straits of Johore 145, 146, 148, 151, 159
Straits Times (newspaper) 158, 159, 162, 171
Strobing, Cpl. Irving 114, 115
Sturdee, Gen 173
Subic Bay 62
Sugita, Lt. Col. Ichiji 157, 166, 168, 169, 170, 171
Sumatra 156
Sutherland, Lt. Gen. Richard 45, 46, 93, 94
Sutton, Pvt. 163
Sweeney, Sgt. Thomas 105

Tada, Col. Tokashi 130, 133
Takano, Ensign Toyoji 10, 13, 15
Tangier, USS 5, 6
Tanglin Barracks 162, 172, 173
Tank Road 171
Task Force 14 5, 6
Tatsuta (Imperial Japanese Navy cruiser) 8
Taylor, Brig. Gen. H.B. 148, 149, 150, 151, 153, 158
Teeters, Dan 31
Tengah Airfield 150, 157, 158
Tenryu (Imperial Japanese Navy cruiser) 8
Thailand 145, 174
Therin, Capt. Frank 42
38th Division (Imperial Japanese Army) 130
31st Division (Philippine Army) 57
31st Infantry Regiment 43, 45, 50, 51, 52, 54, 56, 57, 58, 59, 70, 78, 81, 83
Thomas, Gov. Shenton 158, 159, 161, 163
Thorne, Capt. Hank 63, 64
Thracian, HMS (Royal Navy destroyer) 132
Tipperary (song) 143
Tisdale, Maj. Achille 49, 67, 74, 75
Toki Point 4, 8, 15, 29
Tokyo 47, 64, 128, 133, 165, 166, 173
Topside 88, 91, 95, 107, 116, 119, 122, 124, 126

Torrance, Brig. Gen. K.A. 169, 170
Torres, Lt. Vincente 58
Trail 2 54, 57
Trails 6–8 51
Trail 7 83
Trail 8 82, 83, 84
Trail 9 82
Trail 20 55, 59, 77, 78
Trail 29 83
Trail 46 54
Traywick, Lt. Col. Jesse 69, 127
Trego, Sgt. Carroll 20
Triton, USS 9, 27
Tsugi, Col. Masanobu 148, 151, 153, 158, 162, 163, 164, 165, 168, 170, 174
25th Army (Imperial Japanese Army) 148, 149, 151, 162
21st Field Artillery (Philippine Army) 45, 49
22nd AIF Brigade 147, 148, 149, 150, 151, 152, 155, 157, 158, 162
27nd AIF Brigade 147, 151, 153, 154
26th Cavalry (Philippine Scouts) 43, 54, 56, 57, 58, 59, 77
2/14 Punjabis 129, 131
201st Engineers (Philippine Army) 52
200th AA Battalion 59, 61, 63, 77, 78
230th Inf. Reg. (Imperial Japanese Army) 136
228th Inf. Regiment (Imperial Japanese Army) 133
229th Inf. Reg. (Imperial Japanese Army) 133

Union Jack 161, 167, 170
Uno, Kazumaro 124
Uramura, Lt. 117, 118, 123
USAFFE (U.S. Armed Forces Far East) 46
USFIP (U.S. Forces in Philippines) 47, 48

Valov, John 16
Victoria 131, 132, 133, 135, 136, 137, 139, 140, 141, 143, 144
Victoria Cross 135
Victoria Harbor 129, 130
Victoria Peak 131
Visayan Islands 122, 127
Voice of Freedom 60, 74, 76, 112, 113, 114
Volunteer Defense Force ("Old Boys") 129, 134, 135, 137

Wachi, Gen. Takeji 47
Wade, Sgt Q.T. 15, 16, 17, 18
Wainwright, Gen. Jonathan M. 43, 45, 46, 47, 48, 50, 51, 54, 55, 56, 59, 60, 62, 63, 64, 67, 68, 69, 70, 74, 75, 81, 87, 89, 90, 91, 92, 93, 94, 95, 96, 98, 106, 112, 114, 115, 117, 118, 119, 120, 121, 122, 123, 124, 125, 126, 127, 128
Wake Island 3, 4, 5, 6, 7, 9, 11, 13, 15, 17, 19, 21, 23, 24, 25, 26, 27, 28, 31, 32, 35, 36, 37, 38, 39, 40, 42
Wall, Pvt. James 45
Wallis, Brig. Gen. Charles 131, 132, 135, 139
War Council 43
War Plan Orange-Three (WPO-3) 43, 44
Washington, George 171
Water Tank Hill 100, 101, 103, 104, 114, 117
Waterous, Col. W.L. 80, 81
Wavell, Gen. Sir Archibald 146, 147, 153, 154, 155, 161, 163, 167, 171, 172, 174
Weinstein, Dr. Alfred 52, 53, 61, 66, 79
West Brigade HQ 135, 136, 137
West Point 113, 120
West Road 70, 72, 83
West Sector 136
Weston, Lt. 162
Whitcomb, Lt. Edgar 45, 48, 61, 66, 116, 117
Whitney, Capt. John 141, 142
Wild, Capt. Cyril 167, 168, 169, 170, 171
Wilkes Channel 7, 17, 38
Wilkes Island 3, 6, 7, 8, 9, 10, 11, 12, 14, 15, 17, 30, 38, 39, 40, 41
Williams, Col. Everett 66, 67, 68, 69, 70, 75
Williams, Maj. Francis 108, 109, 111, 112, 114
Williams, Maude 89
Wilson Park Ridge 101, 102
Winnipeg Grenadiers (Canadian) 129, 131
Wohlfield, Capt. Mark 57, 78
Wong Nei Chong Gap 131, 135, 137, 138
Woodlands Road 147, 151, 153, 154, 155
Woodleigh 163
WTJ (radio station) 114

Yamashita, Gen. Tomoyoki 149, 153, 157, 161, 167, 168, 169, 170, 171, 173, 174
Yorktown 170
Young, Gov. Sir Mark 130, 131, 132, 133, 141
Yubari (Imperial Japanese Navy cruiser) 3

www.ingramcontent.com/pod-product-compliance
Ingram Content Group UK Ltd.
Pitfield, Milton Keynes, MK11 3LW, UK
UKHW050523150426
5217IPUK00026B/1771